MW00775376

# HESSIANS

# HESSIANS

## MERCENARIES, REBELS, AND THE
## WAR FOR BRITISH NORTH AMERICA

Brady J. Crytzer

WESTHOLME
Yardley

Westholme Publishing, LLC
904 Edgewood Road
Yardley, Pennsylvania 19067
Visit our Web site at www.westholmepublishing.com

First Printing May 2015
10 9 8 7 6 5 4 3 2 1
ISBN: 978-1-59416-224-4
Also available as an eBook.

Printed in the United States of America.

For Carter Joseph

# CONTENTS

## List of Maps

# PREFACE

*"How often was he thrown into complete dismay by some rushing blast,
howling among the trees, in the idea that it was the Galloping Hessian
on one of his nightly scourings!"*—"The Legend of Sleepy Hollow"

S ET LESS THAN A DECADE AFTER THE AMERICAN REVOLUTION, "THE
Legend of Sleepy Hollow" is considered an American classic.
Although the haunting tale of the schoolmaster Ichabod Crane supposedly occurred in the year 1790 in New York's Hudson Valley,
Washington Irving wrote in 1820, in London. Irving described his
home state of New York, a land that had seen some of the most horrifying and costly fighting of the revolution. He wanted his ghostly
story to be a testament to the enchanting countryside of his youth,
a land of history and secrecy—perfect for a spine-chilling yarn. He
had his setting, but he still needed his ghost.

His post-Revolutionary bogeyman would be no British Redcoat;
that would be far too easy. He likewise could not be a Tory partisan,
as the familiarity between opponents was what made the Patriot-
Loyalist struggle in New York so terrible in the minds of most
Americans. Along those same lines, in 1790 the Indian warrior was
still too present a threat to be paranormal. Irving needed an out-
sider, an individual universally despised in the American states and
equally misunderstood. He did not have to search very hard for this
sorrowful specter, for deep in the American psyche was a figure that
already fit the mold of the dreaded Headless Horseman. After nearly four decades, the Hessian soldier who fought on behalf of the
British remained fixed as the great adversary of liberty.

"The Legend of Sleepy Hollow" was a success on both sides of the Atlantic, and American and British readers alike identified with the sorrows of Ichabod Crane. But what in the story made it resonate so? If the Galloping Hessian had been a Sauntering Scot, would it have held the same grip over the popular imagination of the age? Probably not. Irving's choice to cast the Hessian as the shadowy apparition drew on a time-honored tradition. Irving did not need to convince a nineteenth-century New Yorker or Pennsylvanian to cast aspersions on the Hessian, for they had been doing this for several generations. From their arrival on American soil, the Hessians were defined in Patriot newspapers as "ugly devils," dogs, murderers, and rapists.[1]

These are ugly terms, but another vilifying word—"mercenary"—has adhered to the Hessians and overshadowed their story. Nearly all history textbooks frame their discussion of the more than thirty thousand German soldiers who fought and died in the American Revolution with one word, so loaded with anger and emotion that it has plagued historians from the day Thomas Jefferson wrote it into the Declaration of Independence. The label has been used throughout history, and the term still accurately describes many fighting forces today. But as controversial as this word remains, it would have been even more liberally applied in the age of the American Revolution.

In many respects the Patriot movement in the American revolutionary era was the single greatest political campaign in modern history. Like all great crusades it required support in the hearts and minds of the people to be successful, and that often meant turning very ordinary events into something glorious or despotic to persuade those who were on the fence. These campaigns of misinformation permeated both sides of the American Revolution, and they were equally effective in their own way. To the average American in the eighteenth century, the German auxiliaries that the British Empire procured to suppress the colonial revolt were the very definition of the term "mercenary." They were viewed as calloused soldiers of fortune guided not by principles or patriotism, but only by war profiteering. Conversely, the Germans' worldview had shaped their opinions of the American revolutionaries. Rather than seeing George Washington's Continental Army as freedom fighters or defenders of liberty, the Germans saw them as opportunistic usurpers who threatened the modern social order.

This book follows three individuals who were in the theater of the Revolutionary War for various reasons: an officer, the wife of an officer, and a military chaplain. Captain Johann Ewald was a dedicated student of war from Hesse-Cassel serving in a force that was frozen in a perpetual deadlock against George Washington's Continental Army. Baroness Frederika von Riedesel from Brunswick-Wolfenbüttel followed her husband into the wilds of Canada in General John Burgoyne's ill-fated Saratoga campaign. The curious and insightful chaplain Philip Waldeck journeyed through the Caribbean and the American South. The trio's firsthand accounts offer a vital outside perspective on colonial America and the American Revolution. Their commentaries on all aspects of provincial life from slavery to religion to basic perceptions of self-governance further our understanding of the deeply complex subject of British North America.

THE THIRTY THOUSAND GERMANS WHO SERVED DURING THE AMERICAN Revolution came from six separate states, but as more than half came from the polities of Hesse-Casse and Hesse-Hanau they were all generally called "Hessians." By the end of the war that moniker no longer described mere birth in Hessian territory, for it was quickly transformed into a loaded, derogatory term applied to all of the armies that were effectively "rented" by the Crown to battle the American colonists. Although they were also Brunswickers, Waldeckers, Anhalters, and Anspachers, I have chosen to name this book "Hessians" because of the deep and pervasive history of that loaded term.

War by its very nature is a political venture, as is the language that describes the participants. To the American revolutionaries their German enemies were mercenaries, whereas the Germans viewed themselves as "auxiliaries" to the British effort; to them the revolutionaries were rebels. As these chapters reflect the perspective of the Germans in a strange land, the terms "mercenaries" and "rebels" will be used. In the end this book is a story of conflicting politics between the conservative Old World and the enlightened New.

# PROLOGUE

### *London, Fall 1775–Spring 1776*

T HE NEWS IN ENGLAND WAS GRIM. SINCE 1770 WHEN A SMALL party of soldiers opened fire on an unruly group of civilians, the New England colonies in North America were becoming increasingly problematic. Two years earlier a band of miscreants destroyed a fortune's worth of British East India Company property by publicly dumping chests of tea into Boston Harbor, and distrust and disorder seemed to grow with each passing day. For their part the king and his administrators had taken what they believed to be practicable steps to resolve the matter of American unrest by implementing policies designed to both punish and subdue the agitators along the Atlantic seaboard. But in what was becoming an ominous trend they too seemed to only exacerbate the existing fault lines between the colonists and their sovereign. Before anything else George III was a monarch, and like all great kings he sought to set the agenda rather than simply react to events as they developed. While he did not understand the complex nature of the stirring American rebellion itself, he did appreciate what was at stake. In 1775, however, the dispute between the North American colonies and their imperial masters was not a matter of separation. In fact it was not even a matter of war, but merely perceived as a troublesome flare-up of sedition that so often plagued empires of the eighteenth century. George III and his advisors knew that a firm hand was essential in suppressing such sedition and zero tolerance became their official stance. A year earlier the king wrote to chancellor of the exchequer and future prime minister Frederick North, 2nd Earl of Guilford, that "The dye is now cast. The colonies must either submit or triumph. I do not wish to come to severer measures, but we must not retreat; by coolness and an unremitted pursuit of the measures that I have adopted I trust they will come to submit."[1]

But developments from across the Atlantic did not indicate submission or triumph. In April 1775 American rebels and British regulars exchanged fire at Lexington Green and Concord in the countryside of Massachusetts. While the tensions that so deeply troubled the king and his advisors had seemingly begun over the rights of taxation and the cause of royal authority, the struggle was becoming an open and violent insurrection in the British Empire's most profitable colonies. From the imperial standpoint small uprisings had proven to be an infectious ordeal, and if proper inoculation did not occur they could easily spread. Already in the colonial capital of Philadelphia representatives of thirteen of Britain's most vital possessions were meeting under the pretenses of being a Continental Congress of sovereign bodies, and while the idea was absurd to many in Parliament, circumstances in the Western Hemisphere were quickly spinning out of London's control.

The conflict had already led to blows in Massachusetts, and few believed that if the damage was not mitigated that it would ever stop with that now famous pair of battles in April 1775. As unthinkable as a full-scale military action to subdue the colonies seemed, it was becoming more of a possibility with each passing week. Aside from the obvious challenges of utilizing British forces against British peoples, imperial policy makers faced a logistical nightmare when calculating the strength of forces needed for such a dire circumstance. After winning the Seven Years' War and crushing their greatest rival, France, the British could now lay claim to the largest imperial domain in the history of the Western world. Stretching across five continents, the possessions of King George were a point of great pride among the British people themselves, but a terrible burden on the public treasury. After the Treaty of Paris the imperial debt skyrocketed, and Indian uprisings in North America in its immediate aftermath had proven that London had not yet developed a strategy for effectively governing such a vast dominion as the one that it gained in 1763.

One of the most glaring problems faced was that administrators lacked the military strength to match the grand imperial presence that they so boastfully portrayed. George III had approximately forty-five thousand troops on hand in 1775, and they were thinly spread from the American colonies and Caribbean to India and the Philippines. Prior to the Seven Years' War troop levels seemed to suffice given the amount of territory that London controlled, but following the immense postwar land acquisition that relatively strong army had been reduced to a veritable skeleton crew. The situation in the American colonies was deteriorating rapidly, and troop levels would need to be increased if London's brain trust was going to suppress the oncoming revolt before it became unmanageable. But how would these new soldiers be procured? What would be the cost? With the imperial debt so vastly engorged there was no fiscally responsible way to do it, and there was little popular support for a conscript draft. The American rebellion was still in its infancy, but already it was proving costly to King George and his advisors.[2]

In the eighteenth century Europe was in an almost constant state of war. From the year beginning the century to 1775 there had been upward of forty armed conflicts on the continent between major powers, and countless other rebellions, uprisings, and insurrections. The era was also one of great change, as the Enlightenment caused a great ripple effect throughout the geopolitical structure of the Old World. Because of the tumult and uncertainty brought on by the century of violence, Europe often found itself divided into fluctuating strategic alliances and tenuous neutrality. Fortunately for British policy makers, throughout all of the unrest there were always those seeking out opportunistic arrangements. In the summer of 1775 Whitehall was still stunned by the news of the battles of Lexington and Concord, and with a growing sense of urgency they began to send out feelers to their traditional allies also recovering from the sting of rebellion.

In 1775 the empire of Russia was fully engaged in suppressing a two-year peasant uprising in its southernmost provinces known as Pugachev's Rebellion. With this common strand between them, British ambassador Colonel Gunning traveled to Moscow to meet with Russian prime minister Nikita Panin. Their discussions centered on the potential for a strategic alliance and by all accounts the proceedings were promising. As a representative of the Crown, Gunning offered a robust sum of money to the Russians in exchange for twenty thousand soldiers to travel to North America and crush the American rebellion. While Panin was generally positive regarding the transaction, Empress Catherine the Great flatly refused. As an enlightened monarch she was the embodiment of the modern liberal rulers of Europe. She claimed in a letter to London that

Russia had only begun to enjoy peace, and to sell her own weary soldiers to the highest bidder was an indignity unworthy of her seat.
Dejected, the king's cabinet next sent an envoy to their traditional
ally of Holland, but again their offer was rejected. As an added
affront, Baron von der Capellan, a respected Dutch statesman,
admonished the administration, claiming that as a fellow republic
the Dutch would never aid any military aggression toward peoples
seeking freedom.[3]

After being rebuffed very assertively by some of the most powerful states in Europe, Great Britain still faced a dramatic troop short-
age. The rebellion in New England was growing more and more
hostile by the day, and dampening spirits further still were recent
reports from former commander-in-chief and current
Massachusetts military governor Thomas Gage. In his estimation
the colony would be embroiled in full-scale war if left unattended,
and he added that his paltry eight thousand men were simply not
enough to handle the unruly colonists. While Gage knew that it was
unfeasible, he wrote that at least twenty-five thousand soldiers
would be needed given the circumstances. Desperate and determined, the unyielding advisors to King George pointed their efforts
in an entirely different direction. As a member of the Hanover line,
the king of England focused his new attentions on the German
lands of his ancient familial heritage in hopes of finding a solution.
This decision would embolden the American separatists more than
ever.

In the eighteenth century the Holy Roman Empire was Europe
writ small. As a collection of over three hundred and fifty separate
political entities all united historically under one imperial domain,
it was a varied and diverse population of peoples representing all
walks of life. Each small polity had its own ruler, army, and power
structure yet all officially aligned themselves as part of a larger
German world. At its height in the Middle Ages the Holy Roman
Empire extended its borders into modern France, Belgium, the
Netherlands, Switzerland, and Italy, but by the eighteenth century
its borders had shrunk to cover only modern Germany and small
territories of its immediate neighbors. Like most European powers
the empire participated in small engagements throughout the century with limited results until finally being drawn headlong into the
Seven Years' War. At its core the war pitted Great Britain and
France against one another to determine the fate of empire
throughout most of the world, and the other powers of Europe

chose sides accordingly. Throughout the conflict Frederick the Great swore to defend King George's interests on the continent, and because he did so with such gusto the British were able to focus most of their energies overseas with a special emphasis on their North American provinces. At the close of the conflict Britain tallied its single greatest victory over its ancient French enemy and, because of their alliance, Prussia's stock rose as well. The close of the Seven Years' War saw a great reshuffling of Europe's imperial hierarchy, and with each great power attempting to reestablish itself within the new geopolitical order. The 1763 Peace of Paris established the northern kingdom of Prussia as the supreme German state in the region and its ruler Frederick the Great proved to be a magnetic and respected enlightened politician. To the south Prussia was challenged for regional superiority only by the long-standing European power broker of Austria.

As Prussia and Austria gained prominence in central Europe in the wake of the postwar reorganization, the smaller polities began to do whatever was necessary to maintain relevance in an ever changing world. For those left out of the Austro-Prussian sphere of influence, there were few ways to remain competitive in the international arena. There were few natural resources to sell on the open market and because of their tiny territorial possessions, few found realistic opportunities to expand their wealth. While they lacked the commodities typically associated with increased revenue through wider economic pursuits, it seemed the only true domestic product that many of the smaller states of the Holy Roman Empire had to offer were the people themselves. With a large population held in subjugation due to an adherence to a dying feudal system, many regional German rulers began exploring new ways to turn their otherwise shrinking revenue streams into hefty channels of profit. Their means of doing so became known as *Soldatenhandel*, or the soldier trade. Typically speaking, the small states of the German empire, like Hesse-Cassel, bolstered their army's numbers through either conscription or hiring mercenaries themselves, but few ever considered actually renting their armies to outside powers. When it was discovered that there was a market for such an unusual practice as *Soldatenhandel*, the kings and lords of the German countryside began to dramatically increase their draft totals. By 1776 in the simplest terms the otherwise insignificant German states made themselves relevant to the great powers of Europe by offering their own citizens to the highest bidder.[4]

Although the soldier trade was practiced by several of the more hardened conservative states in the German empire, it was not without its critics. Frederick the Great of Prussia was utterly appalled by the practice. In a June 1776 letter to the philosopher Voltaire, the German king wrote: "Had the Landgrave come out of my school he would not have sold his subjects to the English as one sells cattle to be dragged to the shambles. This is an unbecoming trait in the character of a prince who sets himself up as a teacher of rulers. Such conduct is caused by nothing but dirty selfishness. I pity the poor Hessians who end their lives unhappily and uselessly in America."[5] He of course was not alone; all throughout Germany and Europe the new educated elite of the Enlightenment saw "the skin trade" as the worst of many bad institutions that had managed to remain in practice despite the considerable societal advancements made otherwise. Whatever the moralistic arguments put forth by its critics, the fact remained that *Soldatenhandel* would not have existed without wealthy customers consuming the product, and they were many in number. Public opinion it seemed was not enough to overcome the basic reality that renting an army was simply less expensive than maintaining one.

For the high-ranking administration of the British Empire, consulting the willing states of the Holy Roman Empire was never out of the realm of possibility due to the royal family's own German heritage. Earlier in 1775 they had enlisted Hanoverian soldiers to stand guard at the colony of Gibraltar so their regular forces could be sent to America in response to the rebel invasion of Canada. Even more revealing was the fact that even before Russia and Holland refused to send troops, a handful of covetous German princes had already reached out to London expressing their soldiers' availability. For George III's cabinet, though, there were some distinct drawbacks to pursuing the employment of German soldiers in the New World, but not ethics. There was a fear among British officials that given North America's robust German population many of the enlisted soldiers would likely desert their regiments to live as free men; after all, the alternative was returning to Germany under their feudal lord. But given the circumstances and the obvious logistical challenges that still plagued them, royal advisors elected to open the channels of communication to any willing German princes and actively seek the services of their armies.

In the fall of 1775 British agents furtively moved into the boundaries of the Holy Roman Empire; for the right price they believed that all of their troubles, including the American rebellion, would simply melt away.

THE DISCUSSIONS OF THE FALL MONTHS IN 1775 WERE MANY, BUT ONLY a handful produced results that were suitable for both parties. If there was a typical pattern to be found amongst the negotiations it was simply that Britain wanted to acquire a large number of troops with as little delay as possible. For the German princes, however, their only concern was the amount of money that they could gain for their services. With the Second Continental Congress already in session in the American colonies, the Court of St. James was feeling the pressure of time passing, and their primary agents in the Holy Roman Empire were producing mixed results. There was no short-age of German rulers offering contracts for the service of their armies, in fact there were probably far too many; for London, how-ever, the entire search was quickly becoming a matter of quality over quantity. In one instance the Elector of Bavaria Maximilian III enthusiastically approached British officials regarding a potential arrangement, but his army was in such poor condition and so badly equipped that it was simply not worth the money to purchase them. In another case Karl Eugen, the Duke of Württemberg, offered very favorable terms to the British, but the determined Prussian Frederick the Great forbid the rented force from moving through his lands, unsettling the entire negotiation.[6]

But for all of the diplomatic pitfalls that the British operatives fell into, on the whole they found overwhelming success. By January 1776 the British Empire had drafted agreements with five separate German princes including the regional powerhouse of Hesse-Cassel and its sister state of Hesse-Hanau. Along with these treaties there were also signed agreements with Brunswick-Wolfenbüttel, Anspach-Beyreuth, and the Principality of Waldeck. Later in 1777 the empire would ultimately settle terms with the relatively minor state of Anhalt-Zerbst, bringing their final treaty count to six sepa-rate German entities. Although these states would all furnish armies to sail to America and fight George Washington's Continental Army, like all things in the Holy Roman Empire not all were equal in their contribution. The Landgrave of Hesse-Cassel Frederick II supplied the single largest armed force, 16,992 men, for a total sum of £2,959,800. The Duke of Brunswick provided 5,723 souls for

£750,000, and Hesse-Hanau lent 2,422 men for £343,000. Margrave Karl Alexander of Anspach-Bayreuth sent 2,353 men, and signing over the least amount of soldiers were Prince Frederick of Waldeck at 1,225 and Prince Frederick Augustus of Anhalt-Zerbst at 1,160 for £109,120.[7]

The treaties originally signed with the six individual German princes differed from each other in specifics, but all effectively offered the same general terms. The armies were "rented" for a term of six, seven, or eight years and the agreed-upon subsidy would go directly to the landgrave, duke, or margrave who ratified the treaty. The individual soldiers forced to serve in North America would receive none of those funds, but would be paid by the British Empire at roughly the same rate that they would pay their own regular soldiers. While the treaties were agreed upon in principle there were still small line items to be negotiated. One such point of contention was that some of the German princes demanded that London pay the soldiers' salaries to the princes directly; British administrators balked at this assertion as they were almost certain that the dishonest German rulers would simply pocket the money for themselves. Another issue was the inevitable matter of wartime casualties, in which the British offered to reimburse the states for each man lost. Perhaps the most startling development, though, came from the inclusion of a contracted casualty reimbursement; for every man killed or wounded their prince would be additionally compensated in turn. The German soldier traveled to the New World knowing that he was, quite literally, worth more dead than alive.

By the winter of 1776 the British Empire had contracted nearly eighteen thousand German soldiers to travel to North America and suppress the growing revolt that was stirring in the Atlantic colonies. Of those men over half were provided by Hesse-Cassel, therefore the term "Hessian" would be generically applied to all German auxiliaries employed in the New World. For the unlucky soldier commanded by his feudal lord to travel across the sea and battle the American rebels there was little hope; they were doomed to fight a rebellion for which they stood to gain nothing. Even worse, their services in the field would pay them only a small amount more than the measly salary that they already received, while their indignant rulers had already profited immensely. By 1776 the soldier trade had been long dead in other parts of the world, but it existed as a positive revenue stream for the German states that still employed it.

Although the activities of the British agents operating in the Holy Roman Empire were no secret, there was a fear among some British politicians that the entire matter would be viewed negatively on the world stage. Leading the charge against the ratification of the proposed treaties with the six German rulers was David Hartley, the leader of the leftist Whig Party. Hartley and his liberal colleagues understood that they lacked the votes to stop the controversial hiring of these German soldiers on merit and that the corresponding argument would fall flat in the House of Commons. Rather than arguing against the measure on ethical grounds alone, Hartley organized a practical opposition based on what he considered to be the best interests of the Crown; it was not necessarily a lost cause, but judging by the Parliamentary makeup even he knew that it was unlikely to succeed. On February 14, 1776, Parliament reconvened after a winter break with a relatively long list of bills drafted for consideration, and although it was not at the top of the agenda the ratification of the German treaties was the most anticipated vote of all.[8]

Despite the heated debate surrounding the treaties they were not brought to the House of Commons until February 29, and it was done so with a sense of inevitability by their Conservative sponsors. Lord North was a respected politician and an emerging face of right-leaning British politics, and when introducing the measures he presented his arguments in the form of fiscal responsibility. North explained that the use of foreign soldiers was far less expensive than raising new domestic regiments of their own, and, stressing the bloated imperial debt, he believed there was simply no better option. He continued by claiming that upon further study of the treaties he felt that the price of these armies had actually been much lower than initially anticipated; he was only making the proverbial pot sweeter for his colleagues who were still undecided. In an attempt to sway his peace-loving Whig opponents, Lord North included an intriguing point that the German auxiliaries' reputation for excellence and discipline would be enough to force the American rebels to abandon their cause: the best way to avoid war was to eliminate it preemptively with overwhelming force. When some of his colleagues expressed concerns about using foreign armies to suppress fellow citizens, Lord North retorted that he "always imagined that a civil war called most urgently for speedy and effectual suppression. Such wars were no novelties in this country. Were not the Irish our fellow-subjects in 1690? Were not the

Scotch so in 1715 and 1745? And did any person ever assign it as a reason that those rebellions should not be crushed, because the Rebels were our fellow-subjects?"[9] It was an uninspired speech given by a frustratingly parsimonious man, and while it enraged his liberal opponents it clearly explained the Tory argument.[10]

The partisan parade of Conservative speakers continued throughout the day, and all of them held firm to the agreed upon script: practical fiscal responsibility. Expert witnesses one after another were brought into the House of Commons to give testimony that clearly supported the right wing of the chamber. In one case a former payroll clerk named Gordon testified that he examined the treaties thoroughly and could only conclude that in each instance the Crown was receiving the more prosperous deal. At the conclusion of each demonstration the liberal opposition would harrumph and jeer the obviously partisan showing that they were forced to bear witness to until it was their turn to have the floor. The tension in the House of Commons was thick as usual, and Lord George Germain delivered a speech pointing out that the British Empire had regularly used foreign armies to supplement their own in previous wars; he sardonically noted that many of his Whig colleagues now opposed had affirmed those earlier votes.[11]

After the Tory representatives concluded their efforts the liberal Whigs took to the floor. Lord John Cavendish delivered a speech in which he believed the entire affair to be detrimental to the respectability of the Crown. The Whig leader David Hartley next addressed the House of Commons by offering a scathing critique of the diplomacy used to acquire these treaties. He claimed that the German rulers were notable scoundrels and that before the treaty was expired they would unexpectedly demand military protection or additional money from the Crown. On that same theme of dishonest partners, Lord Irnham humorously compared the German rulers to Don Quixote's companion Sancho Panza, who declared that if he were king he would sell his entire country's population in exchange for cash.[12]

Despite the noted figures who voiced their opinions, by far the most poignant moment of the political opposition to the purchase and application of these armies came though from one Alderman Bull. In a passionate speech he placed the responsibility on his colleagues themselves and forced them to consider what type of empire Great Britain was to be. He declared:

The war that you are now waging is an unjust one; it is founded in oppression, and its end will be distress and disgrace. Let not the historian be obliged to say that the Russian and the German slave was hired to subdue the sons of Englishmen and of freedom; and that, in the reign of a Prince of the House of Brunswick, every infamous attempt was made to extinguish that spirit which brought his ancestors to the throne, and, in spite of treachery and rebellion, seated them firmly upon it. I shall not now trouble the House any further than to declare my abhorrence of all the measures which have been adopted against America, measures equally inimical to the principles of commerce, to the spirit of the Constitution, and to the honour, faith, and true dignity of the British nation.[13]

For all of the passions embodied by the liberal Whig element of Parliament, they could never produce a cohesive defense of why the drastic measure should not be passed that did not base itself on strictly moral grounds. They skirted the issue of morality for fear of the political consequences of perceived "softness" on rebellion; it was a cardinal sin in an imperial world. Instead of appealing to the better angels of the legislative body they focused their efforts on raising practical concerns of governance, a field held in virtual monopoly by their Conservative opposition. As typical in a highly politicized environment such as Whitehall in the eighteenth century, the votes were largely in place before the matter was even discussed, and most of the arguments were done solely for posterity's sake. The debate was certainly fiery and the positions were entirely hardened, but in spite of the controversy the House of Commons approved the measure by a final tally of 242-88. One week later on March 5, 1776, the House of Lords voted 100-32 in favor as well. The matter was closed.

THREE MONTHS LATER IN THE SWELTERING JUNE HEAT OF PHILADELPHIA, Thomas Jefferson was completing what would become the first draft of the Declaration of Independence. Days earlier on June 11, 1776, the Continental Congress appointed a "Committee of Five" to oversee the completion of a great document designed to officially announce that the thirteen Atlantic colonies were separating from their imperial masters and forming their own nation. It was a heavy task, and the men selected to represent the new republic were among its most distinguished: John Adams of Massachusetts, Benjamin Franklin of Pennsylvania, Robert Livingston of New York, Roger Sherman of Connecticut, and Thomas Jefferson of Virginia. Their initial meetings remain lost to history, but their decision to elect the quiet and erudite Virginian to write this document is not in doubt.

Some days later Thomas Jefferson was working feverishly in a small boardinghouse in the colonial capital to meet the standards set by his peers. As he worked his way through the document he systematically listed the perceived injuries, injustices, and insults that so offended the American colonies. He added a host of complaints regarding the overreach of the British Empire including issues of representation, taxation, tenure of office, Indian insurrection, and judicial procedure. Then as his twenty-fifth grievance he added one more fateful line: "He is at this time transporting large Armies of foreign Mercenaries to compleat the works of death, desolation, and tyranny, already begun with circumstances of Cruelty & Perfidy scarcely paralleled in the most barbarous ages, and totally unworthy of the Head of a civilized nation."

Jefferson selected his words with care; he penned that phrase with a particular political motive. Just weeks earlier word had come of Parliament's fateful decision to employ German auxiliaries against the American colonies, and although these troops had not yet left Europe, Jefferson wanted to define their presence long before they ever arrived. It was a rare chance to control a narrative and enlist the support of countless people across North America. The astute Jefferson jumped at the chance and elected to call the foreign troops "Mercenaries." Though he did not know it at the time, his inclusion of the hired Hessian troops as a grievance in the nation's founding document would play a critical role in redefining a colonial rebellion as the American Revolution.

The decision to employ the armies of Europe to suppress the rebels of North America appeared as a ready solution to a worsening situation, but it would be far more costly than any ledger could tally. By the end of the American Revolution there would be over thirty thousand foreign soldiers marching through forests and streets of the New World, and their presence would redefine the conflict.

# I

## Johann Ewald

*Captain, Field-Jäger Corps
Hessen-Cassel*

1776–1781

# New York

*October–December 1776*

New York was a cruel welcome to the New World. Captain Johann Ewald had been on the continent for just over twenty-four hours, and the condition of this place spoke volumes as to the state of the rebellion in the American colonies. From his own estimation the city had over three thousand homes, most of them well built and sturdy, but by his arrival on October 18, 1776, the streets and neighborhoods had fallen into disrepair. He had not known what to expect after his months-long voyage at sea, and as his vessel traversed the bay and ultimately the mouth of the Hudson River he and his men were prepared for anything; what they found was a country at war.

Since July 1776 a massive British force under the command of General William Howe had sailed to New York as part of a grand strategy to destroy the American rebellion while still in its infancy. Howe had already been expelled unceremoniously from his occupation of Boston that spring, and while his evacuation was humiliating, he took solace in the fact that his army had nearly every conceivable advantage in a war that Parliament knew was just beginning. Howe's army landed at Staten Island with ease, and moved to Long Island soon after. Sailing with nearly four hundred ships, it was the largest armada to ever touch the shores of a foreign enemy in British history. The general offered terms of peace to the insurgent General George Washington throughout the summer, but the overtures fell on deaf ears. By August, Howe had amassed an impressive force of almost thirty thousand troops under his command, a number larger than the population of the continent's grandest city of Philadelphia. It had now become clear that capturing all of New York and its countryside was part of his larger plan of attack.[1]

On August 27, in what would become the largest battle of the war, Howe routed Washington and his Continental Army at the Battle of Long Island. Although the rebels tried to entrench their position at Brooklyn Heights, the sheer size of the British force forced them to flee to Manhattan Island itself. By September Howe had ordered twelve thousand men to pursue and Washington's army was pushed as far north as Harlem; despite the fact that the Americans had built a small fort in Lower Manhattan dubbed "Fort Washington," it seemed that Howe had his enemy reeling. The end of the American rebellion was only a matter of time.

When Captain Ewald and his fellow Hessians landed that October he entered a New York that was in the midst of a military occupation. He wrote that he saw over a thousand homes abandoned in the wake of the British arrival, and General Howe's army plundered the vacant houses and burned many to the ground. It was a country torn apart by war.[2]

BORN IN 1744 IN THE CITY OF CASSEL, JOHANN EWALD WAS RAISED IN the capital city of a kingdom deeply connected to its medieval heritage. As the heart of the Landgraviate of Hesse-Cassel, the small but populous corner of the Holy Roman Empire was an eclectic city governed by tradition and the firm hand of its ruler Frederick II. Despite his accomplished military service record in 1776 he came from modest stock; his father was a bookkeeper and his mother was the daughter of simple city merchant. He was close to his parents, but they died when he was still a child and his grandparents raised him into his teens. Even from the age of fourteen the young Johann was obsessed with war, and he idolized the military officers that defended his city. At the age of sixteen he enrolled in the Hessian army and saw action almost immediately in the Seven Years' War, and for the remainder of his life he was thoroughly fascinated by the martial arts. As a younger officer he steadily climbed the ranks until gaining entry into the Collegium Carolinum; he published his first book in 1774. Because of his diligence he was awarded a captain's commission that same year, and when Frederick II contracted his army to serve alongside the British in the New World in 1776, the thirty-two-year-old Johann jumped at the opportunity.

Ewald and his men had a difficult road ahead of them after landing at New York. After a sea voyage that had cost them dozens of lives from terrible maladies such as scurvy and dysentery, however, they were all thankful to finally be on land. For the next week the Hessians remained in camp to recover from their crossing, and though there was plenty to eat they could not partake in the feasting. Over their months-long voyage their bodies had gone into a survival mode or sorts, and the limited sustenance of salted pork and stale crackers had fixed them in such a state that to dine on fresh meat and vegetables sent their bodies into a twisted, writhing pain. It was no matter to Captain Ewald, who led a soldier's life; this was the type of idle time that he loathed more than any pains of digestion.

While the captain was new to his surroundings, his understanding of the overall mission strengthened his resolve. Since pushing the Continentals out of New York itself, General Howe developed a strategy to destroy Washington's army through cunning rather than brute force. Howe understood that the Americans would be pressing northward, and rather than chasing down Washington's wily force, the British commander opted to flank his opponent in a surprise assault. This maneuver entailed sailing his men, with nine thousand Hessians in tow, up the East River and landing at a point dubbed "New Rochelle" several miles farther north than the Continental Army had yet marched. With Washington's focus on the British forces posted to his south, Howe hoped to sweep in from both sides and crush the unsuspecting Rebels.

Encamped at New Rochelle, approximately twenty-two miles north of Lower Manhattan, Ewald received orders to move his men on October 23. At the outset of their march, Ewald had the privilege of parading his men before General Howe himself, which was a memorable experience for the captain in this harsh new place. It was then also that Captain Ewald was informed that he would be the lead force during the maneuver to push the Continental Army out of New York and into the cold throngs of New Jersey once and for all. This was a position that Ewald relished, not because he was a glutton for such pain but because of the reputation of his men. He was at the helm of the 2nd Jäger Company, a designation that did not come lightly. Unlike the redcoats that surrounded him in the British army, Ewald's Jägers wore a brilliant green trimmed with red. It was so unusual that their British allies and even the German immigrants they encountered referred to them as *grünröcke*, or Green Coats. This made for an unusual sight when his men appeared, for even his fellow Hessian infantrymen wore a distinct royal blue. The Jägers were a different sort, and their appearance was a testament to their unique abilities. As skirmishers, Ewald's rangers had the unique privilege of serving at the vanguard of the army; that is, being the first into any combat zone, and generally the last out. If William Howe was going to march anywhere in October 1776, he would rely on the Jäger Corps to lead the charge.

The word *jäger* itself was not necessarily a specialized military term, for in Ewald's native German tongue it means "hunter." It was, however, entirely appropriate for the skill set that his unit possessed. Johann Ewald represented a specialized force in this strange New World, his was only one of two companies provided by his home of Hesse-Cassel in the fall of 1776. As a primary engagement force the Jägers would need to be crack shots, first-rate marksmen in an age where careful aim was considered to be a wasteful venture. Unlike most infantrymen who relied on volley fire in the general direction of an enemy to do damage, the Jäger Corps was selected for their ability to hit singular targets at long range. The musket utilized by most infantrymen was a careless, sloppy weapon with an effective range of less than fifty yards; the rifle used by the Jäger Corps, however, had a range of nearly twice that. Unlike the smooth-bore musket of the day, the Jäger rifle was heavier, slower to load, and required much more careful skill in aiming. Its hexagonal barrel allowed for an expert marksman to excel, and its firing range made placement behind cover a meaningful alternative to simply standing in formation.

The weapon did have its drawbacks. The most notable was that its dramatically shorter, rifled barrel allowed no room for the placement of a standard bayonet. Because of this, the Jäger Corps would often carry *blankwaffen*, or short swords, to fend off enemies in close quarters. Finished off with a tricorn hat, the Jägers' appearance was stunning and unique.

After traveling for some hours at the head of the large British column, Ewald was roused from his cold, droning march by the crackling of muskets. Immediately to his left, a party of American rangers opened fire on his company. It was a surreal scene for the Hessians. Thousands of miles from their ancestral homelands, on the other side of the world, they were engaged with an enemy in the forests of North America for the first time. Captain Ewald quickly surveyed his position and determined that there was no high ground or strategic advantage available; he would have to fight. Believing that reinforcements were coming, Ewald denied any calls for retreat but likewise restrained himself from advancing as his 2nd Company faced the enemy alone. He ordered his Jägers to form a circle, at his estimation covering an acre, and continued to engage the rebels. Minutes later, his Hessian commanding officer Colonel Carl von Donop shouted at him to retreat. Ewald retorted that to do so would guarantee a catastrophic loss of men. Donop shouted back that despite the captain's wishes, America would not be conquered in a single day.³ As the firefight continued, a British battalion of light infantry with two cannons appeared and unleashed several devastating volleys into the wilderness at their American foes, and it was this reinforcement that allowed Ewald's Jägers to escape the melee.

Donop was constantly tracking Ewald's movements, and though he was a harsh officer, he was no common grunt. Donop stood as a testament to the decrepit, almost medieval social system that defined life in Hesse-Cassel. Born into nobility and bearing the distinguished title of "von" indicating landed gentry, Donop was adjutant to the Landgraf Frederick II himself. At the age of 44, Donop had high hopes of climbing the sociopolitical ladder in Hesse-Cassel, and his service in America was a critical step in completing that process. Born into a superior family lineage, he could aim for advancement and social mobility, a privilege that the vast majority of his countrymen would never enjoy.

All told, Captain Ewald tallied six dead, eleven wounded, and two captured. This exchange of fire, however, was no battle; it was merely a skirmish. The dead would have no monument, the wounded no locale to which to attach their injuries. The British soldiers who rushed forward to cover the Hessians slunk back to the safety they emerged from, and in the line of duty Ewald ordered his men in only one direction . . . forward.

Such was the life of a Jäger. In the two days since their initial shootout with the Patriot militia, the Hessians of Ewald's Jäger Company were adjusting to the realities of early winter in New York. The roads of the region were narrow, and following these snaking paths through the emerging countryside gave a soldier little warning as to the position of one's enemy. On more than one occasion the Hessians had literally stumbled across the still smoldering remnants of an enemy's campfire from only hours earlier. From his vantage point Ewald was the eyes and ears of Howe's army, and when the Americans were discovered it was often at the expense of the men under his command.

The encounter from earlier in the week was a very small one by most measures; however, it reduced Ewald's manpower by nearly 20 percent. With only eighty men under his command, the captain would need to be very selective of when and how he planned on engaging his enemy. As the march came to a halt, orders were given to establish camp. Using a local farmstead as their base, the British established themselves on an advantageous piece of ground called Ward's Plantation. With their primary headquarters selected and the Bronx River providing protection in front, it was decided that their far flanks should be covered by the Hessian Jägers. Colonel Donop would take the right flank while Captain Ewald was ordered to secure the left.

Ewald found his first true respite in almost a week from this position, a small piece of farmland that he deemed to be most suitable. In many ways this farm epitomized the simple life of an American farmer in the eighteenth century, and Ewald quickly became enamored with his quaint new position. Located atop a small knoll, the captain established a defensive perimeter on either side of the farm. With his duties done for the day, Ewald strolled the grounds until he came upon a simple apple orchard surrounded by a rudimentary wall of fieldstone. In the midst of the most terrible conflict the region had ever seen, Ewald sat against the trunk of one of the abandoned trees and let his mind wander.

In Germany Ewald had always taken a special interest in partisan warfare. The notion of a civil body disregarding its common enemies to attack itself had always intrigued him; the fact that the hand-built farm and picked-over orchard was now a military encampment fueled his interests even more. That evening he gloried in the challenges that his present conflict faced, and he did his best to recall the treatises on insurgent combat that he had analyzed so intently during his studies back home. Indeed, many men claimed to relish the experience of combat, but Ewald was perhaps one of the few that truly did.

In the strictest sense, General Howe's present campaign was a textbook example of counter-insurgency doctrine. By taking command of New York, the general was giving British forces a strong base of operations to defeat the Patriot rebellion. As a coastal city New York would be an essential port for reinforcement and supplies, and because it was a major population center Howe could convince the residents of the area that supporting the rebel movement was a dangerous and deadly proposition. The more cities that the British could occupy, the more likely it was that the rebellion would crumble, so it was only sensible that Philadelphia would be next on the commander's list. Once New York and its countryside was secure, the beginning of the end was sure to be in sight.

The following morning just before sunrise, a local farmer approached the Hessian picket. He requested an audience with the

commanding officer and Ewald obliged. The man was from a nearby village offering information on the movement of Washington's
army. He was by the standards of the day a Loyalist, and his volunteerism was certainly expected. As Howe and the British army tight-
ened their grip on the region, more and more individuals would
begin to defect or align themselves with the imperial authorities.
From Ewald's perspective things were falling into place. The farmer
stated that the Americans were using a nearby plantation to store
supplies and munitions. With a small payment the informant left
the camp to melt away into the countryside, and Ewald set his Jägers
into motion. Along with twenty Royal Dragoons, the Hessians
made their way to the rebel position.

The fighting that occurred at the site was intense, but the situation was never out of hand. In Ewald's estimation nearly every
American that did not flee was either struck down or taken captive.
With the cache now secure, the Jägers loaded the contraband into
wagons and sent them directly back to General Howe himself; the
remainder of the supplies were destroyed. It was certainly a nasty
business, but rarely thankless. Ewald wrote soon after that the general personally offered his gratitude for his action, a sentiment
which he treasured greatly.[4] The time for pleasantries, however, was
coming to an end as Howe's mighty force prepared to engage
General Washington's rebels on the hills of White Plains.

LEADING UP TO THE LAST BATTLE OF OCTOBER 1776, A COMPLEX SERIES
of maneuvers dramatically highlights the style of warfare in the
American Revolution. Unlike a conventional war in which both
armies are striving for a similar goal, the objectives of insurgent
warfare are very different and often lead to unsatisfactory conclu-
sions. From William Howe's perspective, a head-on collision with
the Americans was exactly what he needed to be effective. By elim-
inating General Washington's ragtag militia, he would have effectively ended the American rebellion. His primary mission therefore
was not to merely take a hill or command a position, but it was to
engage and eliminate the Continental Army itself. From the
American perspective, however, it was very different war.

Washington could ill afford to engage Howe in too many pitched
battles as his army was shrinking from lack of enlistments and an
even greater lack of morale. Should he confront the British and

Hessians in anything that resembled a massive engagement, he could only achieve a pyrrhic victory at best. Howe could always receive reinforcements, yet the Continental Army could not. Earlier in the month, Washington had received word from his scouts that Howe's army had indeed landed north of their current encampment at Fort Washington, in New York. With this unexpected development, the American commander ordered his men to race northward with hopes that the British march toward his present position was slow enough that he could avoid a general confrontation until it could be fought on his own terms. His gamble, though risky, was a success. Howe's men had landed at New Rochelle, but their progress was so inept that the bulk of Washington's force slipped by them before they achieved their intended objective. It was during this slow and burdensome maneuver that Captain Ewald's aforementioned combat experiences near their farm encampment took place. There was so little care afforded to standing pat in fact that Washington even went so far as to abandon 1,200 of his own men in the confines of Fort Washington in order to prepare a stronger position farther north; by the end of October the meager fort was actually behind enemy lines and surrounded. Therefore, with scouts of his own alerting him as to Howe's positioning and movements, Washington established himself on a well-defended series of ridges in the vicinity of White Plains, New York. Deciding that it would be the most capable place for a stout defense, Washington used the home of a local man named Elijah Miller as his headquarters. By October 23 the Americans had begun constructing entrenchments in two lines, and in only a short time they had created a protective barrier more than three miles long.

It was not perfect, but the American rebels had little expectation of perfection during the desperate final months of 1776. The formation at White Plains best utilized the land available to them, and their basic needs were satisfied. To the east was the formidable Hudson River, and to their backs the Croton. Should they need a route of retreat, a northern evacuation was Washington's clearest option, and at that point there was nothing to suggest that he wouldn't use it. Perhaps the most intriguing portion of the Americans' design was the placement of several hundred militiamen on high ground to his right called Chatterton's Hill. At an elevation of just under two hundred feet and three quarters of a mile long, Chatterton's Hill commanded a valuable sight over the Bronx River. The hillside was covered in dense forest and it made for a perfect natural obstacle to whatever attack would approach. It was merely a stopgap measure, however, for even if Washington were able to defeat Howe on the field, it gained him little ground. The British still occupied New York, and the best that Washington could hope for was to minimize his losses in the coming engagement.[5]

By the morning of October 24 Howe had sent almost 7,500 men in pursuit of the rebels; they marched in two columns toward their destination. The force on the left was led by General Leopold Philip de Heister, a Hessian officer who had been in New York nearly as long as Howe himself. It was not uncommon for a German auxiliary to assume such a significant role in major campaigns and critical maneuvers during the time period. In many instances, as was the case on October 28, German soldiers made up almost half of all the forces under Howe's command. On the opposite side was the British General Henry Clinton—an experienced and savvy veteran with a penchant for questioning orders and challenging his commanding officer. By the morning of the battle, Clinton and Howe were so at odds that they barely spoke. Both of these large columns were a diverse mixture of imperial forces, and each was lead by the Jägers.

Captain Ewald and his 2nd Company were at the front of General Clinton's command, and as in most cases they would absorb the first actions of the battle. At the outset of the fighting, Colonel Johann Rall at the head of the left column achieved a great deal of success early by forcing a large number of American rebels to retreat from the right flank; after continuing their march, Rall set his sights on Chatterton's Hill. At this same time, Ewald looked on frustrated as his commander, General Clinton, declined to engage the enemy under the pretense that an assault at that moment would not be a timely one. Ewald complained that despite his great respect for General Clinton's status and service, his reluctance to engage the enemy in a timely fashion frustrated him immensely.[6]

From atop Chatterton's Hill the Americans poured fire into Rall's Hessians, and although the attack was spirited it was repeatedly pushed back. Holding this hillside was critical for the overall integrity of Washington's army, and when Rall's men were stymied the entire British force behind them was brought to a halt.

It was during this great stalemate at midday that General Howe devised a new plan of attack, now with the benefit of surveying his enemies' position. He would send Rall's Hessians again to attack the American right flank, and press Colonel Donop's Hessians directly into the muck-bottomed American center. Because of its proximity to the Bronx River, the middle of the battlefield was a thick, boggy patch of unkind terrain that was a less-than-ideal lane of attack. As Donop was Captain Ewald's commanding officer, his 2nd Jäger Company would lead the charge through the treacherous swamp. By early evening the great assault came and produced spectacular results. Rall's charge broke the right flank of Washington's army and forced a chaotic retreat. The fighting in the American center became even more ferocious. Ewald recalled that two Jäger companies had to charge headlong into a barrage of cannon and musket fire, and after passing through the storm stumbled on a group of rebel riflemen posted deep in a ravine. The Germans engaged the Patriots, but the militia soon broke away.[7]

With the collapse of the American right flank, a disciplined retreat began. From the left a Patriot regiment continued fire to cover Washington's escape and disabled any pursuit by Howe's men. As planned, the Continentals began their hasty retreat toward the Croton River. The fighting and skirmishing would continue throughout the day, and it was likely that despite the battle's perceived end there was little rest for the Jägers and American Rangers, who skirmished for several more hours. Now on their way north, Washington's army appeared to have escaped Howe's grasp yet again. The numbers vary regarding the bloody aftermath, but some estimate that as many as 200 Americans and 260 British and Hessian soldiers had died in the day's fighting. Ewald wrote that the devastation in his mind appeared to be equal and he counted over a thousand dead.[8]

Following the conclusion of the battle, as both armies returned to a state of encamped readiness, General Howe considered all options. To allow Washington to recover would be a mistake, but to allow his army to escape would be a disaster. Two days would pass, and both sides prepared for what seemed to likely be a second round of fighting at White Plains. With escape still on his mind, Washington had sunk back closer to the Croton River just north of his previous position, but rather than fully retreating across the waterway to safety, the American general opted to reform his lines to avoid being overrun by his much larger enemy in pursuit. Howe, on the other hand, had utilized the gains of the previous battle to place himself in a position to be victorious for the first time in over a month. Now in command of the previously abandoned Chatterton's Hill, Howe was pleased to receive reinforcements in the form of another group of Germans. These men were not just

Hessians, but also a small contingent of Waldeckers. Howe's army proved that though they spoke the same language and shared the same cultural heritage, the Germans were anything but a unified group.

With his new reinforcements in place on October 30, Howe planned to strike Washington's recoiling line the following day; those plans, however, soon fell to pieces. Throughout the night and early morning hours, a torrential storm tore through the two armies' positions. The Germans and British hunkered down in the wind and rain, and the next day found a shocking surprise: the Continental Army was gone. On October 31 George Washington used the terrible storm to his advantage. He maneuvered his exhausted army northward, away from Howe to a new camp at North Castle, New York. Conventional wisdom dictated that an army of that size should never attempt a movement such as Washington's during inclement weather; however, convention was not a luxury that the Americans enjoyed.

The situation to which Howe bore witness was one of great fortune for the Americans, but also opportunity for the Crown. The rebels had the advantage of being in the New York region for months prior to the British, and as a result they had installed a number of "contingencies" to maintain their communications in the case of a British assault. Using his knowledge of the area, and his understanding of the importance of these Patriot installations, Howe quickly turned his attention to gaining an upper hand over Washington's army.

Although Washington had moved out of Howe's reach, immediately to his south was the Patriot fortification of Fort Washington, garrisoned only by 1,300 men. Howe believed that by moving on the tiny position he could possibly draw the flighty Washington back into Manhattan to engage him yet again. To capture Fort Washington would deal a tremendous blow to the rebel cause as it was the last remaining vestige of Patriot control on the island deemed essential to stopping the insurgency. Taking the fort, Howe believed, would be an easy victory and perhaps just the venture to finally bring Washington into his midst.

Fort Washington was by most standards a modest fortification in its day. It sat on the eastern bank of the Hudson River with a commanding view of the critical water passage. On the opposite bank sat its sister outpost, Fort Lee. The combination of Fort Washington in New York and Fort Lee in New Jersey would effectively cut off

the Hudson as a means of travel toward Albany or the Loyalist
stronghold of the Mohawk River valley for any of the hundreds of
British warships further south. Now, though, considering the disastrous events of the last three months, Fort Washington and its tri-
fling garrison was little more than a proverbial sitting duck.[9]

On November 4, Howe gave the order to move his army southward to begin his assault. For the men under his command, it was a
time of great contemplation; first among them was Captain Ewald.
As he led his Jägers southward, his theoretical fascination with civil
war turned practical. His men, again the lead element of Howe's
large force, were able to have more personal interactions with the
residents of the countryside than their counterparts toward the rear.
Upon their approach to the small village of Dobbs Ferry, Ewald
came across a number of notable Loyalist dwellings along the main
road. Rather than homes with families cowering inside, these villages were now smoldering piles of ashes left in the wake of
Washington's rebels. For Ewald, despite a lifetime of military service, the emotion of the scene overwhelmed him. In a moment of
weakness he recalled that he was so enraged that he swore to hunt
down the partisans and personally punish them for burning the
homes to the ground. It was an unrealistic promise, but Ewald was
finding it more and more difficult to remain detached from the terrible human drama playing out before him.

Still encamped at Dobbs Ferry, Ewald and his Hessians watched
the general's larger plans begin to unfold. While stationed, the captain took note of a British frigate that arrived shortly after to unload
supplies for the coming attack. Although it did fall under fire from
the Forts Lee and Washington as it sailed up the Hudson, the ship
survived the onslaught through what Ewald could describe only as
a flaw in Fort Washington's design. In his estimation the ground on
which it sat was simply too high, and the balls passed harmlessly
overhead. In the face of this new challenge, Ewald was relieved to
see that their intended target could not complete its intended duty;
it certainly would not withstand a coordinated assault.

Howe's plan for capturing Fort Washington was a complex series
of maneuvers in which four separate commanders would attack the
post from three different directions. Like most maneuvers of its
kind, timing would be its most precious asset. From the north, the
commanding general of Hessian forces Wilhelm von Knyphausen
led the charge. From the south and east the British Lt. General
Hugh Percy and General Lord Charles Cornwallis would attack,

respectively. A fourth regiment, the 42nd Highlanders (also known as the Black Watch), would land just south of the fort on the eastern side as a diversionary tactic.

On November 14 Colonel Donop called upon Ewald's 2nd Jäger Company to provide useful intelligence regarding the situation and station of Fort Washington in the final days before the assault would begin. He took two of his finest German scouts and kept a detailed record of the entire landscape before; it would prove to be invaluable to his commander.[10] What Ewald saw was that the position of Fort Washington would serve Howe's plan well, but the situation within had changed. A day earlier General Washington had arrived at Fort Lee directly across the river, and with the addition of some reinforcements Fort Washington's garrison had swelled to approximately three thousand men. It was no matter, however; the overall strategy would remain unchanged. Captain Ewald signaled to his young scouts to return to camp quietly to relay the information that he had found.

At dawn on November 16 the full might of General William Howe's artillery unleashed its fury on the tiny Fort Washington. From the northern side Hessian cannons bombarded an American battery, and from the Hudson the British frigate *Pearl* blasted away at the Patriot earthwork entrenchments that protected the position. The British navy had rarely been used effectively against the American rebels, and the *Pearl*'s guns were only but a small taste of what His Majesty could deliver; to the south Lt. General Percy fired on the fort itself. As the morning wore on the tide began to rise, and General Knyphausen led a force of four thousand Hessians toward the American position. After some brief fighting with a group of Pennsylvania volunteers, the Patriot line collapsed toward the safety of the fort. On the opposite side of the field Lt. General Percy was patiently waiting with his three thousand men for the great feint of the 42nd Highlanders to take place. When the Black Watch finally reached shore, the Americans had no choice but to take precious reinforcements out of Fort Washington to face this newly landed enemy.

Now supported by the storming Highlanders, Percy's attack from the south forced the Americans into the fort; they were surrounded. Across the Hudson River from New Jersey, George Washington could only look on as his vital last stand on Manhattan Island collapsed. He penned a letter to the fort's commandant, Colonel Robert Magaw, to hold out until nightfall with the hopes of using the cover of darkness to escape yet again. But for Magaw there was no time. The Hessian Colonel Johann Rall was given the honor of petitioning the defeated Americans to surrender, and there was no choice by to accept. General Washington would later write, "the loss of such a number of Officers and Men, many of whom have been trained with more than common attention, will, I fear, be severely felt. But when that of the Arms and Accoutrements is added, much more so."[11] At the end of the fighting Howe's men suffered 84 killed and 374 wounded. General Washington's losses tallied to 59 killed, 96 wounded, and a staggering 2,838 taken prisoner. By 3:00 P.M. the surrender of Fort Washington was announced and an hour later the flag of Great Britain flew overhead. The captured trophy was renamed Fort Knyphausen. The Hessians had their day.

ON THE MORNING OF DECEMBER 1, CAPTAIN JOHANN EWALD WAS struggling to keep his composure. Howe's army had pursued the American army deep into New Jersey and had established a camp along the Raritan River. The weather had been steadily foul and his British superiors bogged down their army with what Ewald considered to be ragged indecision. Two weeks earlier his Jägers were riding a wave of self-confidence at the fall of Fort Washington, and four days after that their resolve was only strengthened when Fort Lee fell to the British. The rebels had been shaken and their ranks had fled desperately into the countryside to escape, but even retreat did not spare American losses. During the weeks prior, when more than two thousand men from the Continental Army saw their enlistments expire, they simply walked off.

Of course for the Jägers there was rarely an engagement that they did not take fire. As the tip of Howe's spear, they fought the enemy on a regular basis in small bursts. They fought in the mornings, they fought at dusk. Their action almost never received reinforcement or much attention from either Howe or Washington. As skirmishers they were expected to weather such storms.

On that particular day, despite the fact that Howe's army had dug entrenchments on the left bank of the Raritan, Ewald and his Jägers were engaged in a firefight to claim one of the few bridges that crossed the river. The Patriot Rangers militia had taken command of a small homestead on the opposite side, and the Jägers had exchanged shots throughout the day. There was cannon fire from both forces, but the bulk of the fighting was highlighted with the small arms fire of Captain Ewald and his men. The bursts of rifles continued well into the night, and it became increasingly clear that there was unlikely to be a winner in an engagement such as this one. As usual the Americans used to cover of darkness to slink away from the action and before morning their enemies had simply abandoned the fight. Among the dead from the day's fighting was a Captain Weitershausen; Captain Ewald penned that he had lost one of his dearest friends.[12]

The following morning the Jägers simply crossed the bridge that they had previously fought so hard to capture, and raided the local plantations for supplies; each wagon load was sent back into the camp to supply Howe's army. While his men were loading the confiscated goods, New Jersey Loyalists filed into his company with new information about Washington's movements and the state of his Continental Army. Ewald described his opponents as wretched and weak, and he believed that with the right decisions made by his own superiors they could be dispersed in a matter of days. It was estimated by the loyal informers that Washington's entire force was now less than eight thousand men. In his studies of partisan warfare it appeared to the captain that Howe was in a position to deliver the final blow, but much to the chagrin of Ewald and his Jägers their orders were to stand firm, not pursue. Five days had passed and the men were filled with rage and anxiety over what they believed to be a missed opportunity.[13]

Ewald agreed. As a trained soldier in a foreign land he would never voice his concerns, but his journal entry spoke volumes and revealed a great deal about the state of the war in the winter of 1776: Ewald believed that the campaign that year had been nothing but one ill-advised folly after another, and his only conclusion was that the British command hoped to end the rebellion with as little bloodshed as possible. That was becoming more unlikely by the day.[14]

## New Jersey
*April–December 1777*

Immediately following the capture of Fort Washington and Fort Lee, December of the previous year appeared to be a promising one for the British forces of William Howe. New York had been cleared of Patriot support and the region again belonged to the Crown.

When he consolidated his grasp on the region, Howe began to put in motion a larger strategy to quickly end the rebellion by extending his control to the entire Northeast. The general ordered six thousand men under the commands of the insubordinate Henry Clinton and Hugh Percy to capture Newport, Rhode Island, for a potential strike on New England. He next sent Charles Cornwallis into New Jersey with the sole duty of finding and crushing George Washington's Continental Army.

By mid-December Howe had declared success from his headquarters: Clinton and Percy took Newport with relative ease, and Cornwallis reported that Washington's rebels had fled unceremoniously across the Delaware River into the safe wintry confines of Pennsylvania. As the cold season fell, like all commanders of his day Howe next set his sights on establishing a sound encampment that would house his men and keep the ground that he had struggled so hard to obtain. Like a chain beginning in Perth Amboy just west of Staten Island, the British and Hessians took seasonal quarters throughout New Jersey. In the days that followed, Loyalists began to appear more openly throughout the state, and they filled Howe's coffers with new useful intelligence regarding the condition and placement of the enemy.

Colonel Donop was a savvy officer, and he found that winter quarters were a time when the great vice of idleness could wreak havoc on a fighting force. By December 14 the small city of Trenton was fully under Hessian control, and commanding officer Donop placed Johann Rall in charge of the town and its people. There was a distinct level of distrust between the two men, mainly because Rall had a difficult time keeping control of the soldiers beneath him. The Hessians were the product of a distinct Old World, and their experiences dictated their perspectives. Like the British and Americans they had a sense of honor, but unlike their counterparts their honor was derived from one's ability to serve their king, not necessarily defense of an individual sense of respect. It was a matter of fulfilling one's duty at any cost. There was no valuing an individual life over the whole, so completing an assigned task was essential even if extremely dangerous, even life-threatening. Rall had apparently not proven that he fully subscribed to this harsh martial virtue as of yet, as one of Rall's men claimed, "his love of life was too great, and firm decisions often eluded him."[15]

For all of his perceived faults, history has vindicated Rall by some small measure. Throughout his two-week command at Trenton he regularly held council with a variety of local Loyalist informants who kept him abreast of Washington's movements in Pennsylvania. He did petition superiors for reinforcements upon hearing rumor of a potential Patriot assault against his small camp, but those requests were denied.

For Colonel Donop, though, encampment was just the beginning; winter was a time of rest, but it was certainly no offseason. As the southernmost links in Howe's winter quarters in New Jersey, Trenton and Bordentown were deemed as the most susceptible to rebel raids that winter. Donop was well aware of this, and to be sure there had already been a number of tiny skirmishes between the Hessians and whatever remnants of Washington's army remained in the state. The colonel took great care to locate these insurgents, and a series of particularly useful Loyalist spies kept him abreast of exactly when and where these irregulars were stationed; one such report indicated that there were as many as 800 rebels in one location. After conferencing with other local commanders, Thomas Stirling of the Black Watch even told Donop that he believed they could easily match their opponents.[16]

On the morning of December 23, Colonel Donop led more than three thousand Hessians and Scots toward Mount Holly; at the vanguard was Captain Johann Ewald and his Jägers. Trenton, now twenty miles to his back, was seemingly secure, and Donop could place his full attention on the militia in front of him. Ewald's Jägers were the first to engage, and the Americans seemed to lack spirit before the much larger force. The fighting was intense, but by midday the militia gave ground in a slow, methodical manner. Ewald wrote the Jägers and Scots pursued the enemy for several miles but to no avail.[17] The day was theirs, and because there were no pressing duties for them elsewhere Donop unleashed his men on the village of Mount Holly to celebrate. The Germans and Scots caroused for hours in the abandoned town, and by the end of the celebration not a single barrel of whiskey or cask of wine remained. Ewald, who despised disorder, vented in his journal that the entire garrison was drunk by that evening and controlling them in a dignified way was virtually impossible.[18]

For the next two days Colonel Donop instructed his men to remain in the town and patrol the nearby roads in support of their camps to the north. On December 25, Captain Ewald received a piece of intelligence, that a high-profile colonel in the local militia named Thomas Reynolds and two of his fellow officers were prepar-

ing for a secret rendezvous with their wives in a nearby home outside
of the village. With great excitement Ewald petitioned Donop to
surprise his foe, and with his commander's approval the captain
marched with eight Jägers and twenty Scots to do exactly that.

Ewald and his men quietly surrounded the homestead and the
captain proceeded to knock on the door. Answered with a call of
"come in!" he politely entered and greeted the rebel leaders and
their wives. There, around the table, was Colonel Reynolds and his
cohorts enjoying hot tea in the midst of a cold New Jersey winter.
Noticing that he was covered in snow but not that he was a Hessian,
Reynolds asked the shivering stranger to join them; Ewald declined.
At that moment one of the women attempted to quietly leave the
room when she was shoved back by a waiting Scot who entered
through a side door. The party broke off into a panic, swords drawn,
until more soldiers stormed the chamber and Ewald stated that the
next person to move would be, in his words, "cut down."

With the enemy in his hands Ewald gave his word that if all rules
were followed no one would be hurt. With his prisoners in tow,
Captain Ewald and his command of Jägers and Highlanders
returned to the recently captured Mount Holly in a spirited mood.
That merriment, however, was to be short-lived.

The next afternoon a messenger rushed into the village in full
alarm with news that Washington and the rebels had crossed the
Delaware River into New Jersey, slunk furtively through the night
despite the terrible defeats he had been handed only weeks earlier,
and captured the entire encampment at Trenton. In all, 22 Germans
had been killed, 83 wounded, and a staggering 896 had been captured. Colonel Johann Rall himself had been struck with a musket
ball while in retreat and later died. It stood as Washington's great
triumph of the early war, and one that he desperately needed.
Although he was shocked and enraged by the news, Ewald had no
idea that the battle at Mount Holly that he had just fought was actually a coordinated diversion by Washington to draw Donop and his
men away from Trenton, making it a vulnerable target. In the entire
attack the Americans only lost two men, both to exposure in the
frozen night. Ewald was incensed, yet resolved to have his
revenge.[19]

The victory at Trenton had a profound impact on the American
army at the time, but it alone would win no revolution. Aware the
Howe was unlikely to allow this victory to go unpunished,
Washington positioned his men for a counterattack outside of

Trenton at Assunpink Creek. Although his men were hopeful following their previous success, it was quickly revealed the Charles Cornwallis was marching toward their position with a force of five thousand Jägers, Scots, and British Regulars. Mostly men of the Hessian camp of Princeton, Cornwallis's small army was determined to hit the Americans at midday and potentially finish them by nightfall. Even as they marched heartily, rebel militia posts between the British and Washington greatly slowed the progress of Cornwallis's force, and soon morning turned to afternoon, and afternoon to nightfall. By the time that the British had reached Assunpink Creek it was already dusk.

Ewald, who was serving in the vanguard of the force, took great pride in his ability to draw a significant portion of the fire off of the primary columns of the army and onto his own men. His Jägers succeeded throughout the dark and confusing battle by occupying not only Washington's infantry, but some cavalry and artillery as well. His Jägers had positioned themselves in a small series of homes in order to better distract their foes, and therefore empower the men behind them. Ewald claimed proudly that they held the position until nightfall.[20]

Cornwallis initiated his attack on January 2, 1777, despite the lateness of the hour, and after three separate unsuccessful attempts to uproot the Americans the general decided to halt the offensive until the next morning. This was a moment of controversy within Cornwallis's camp; his quartermaster William Erskine pleaded, "If Washington is the General I take him to be, his army will not be found there in the morning."[21] Unknown to Cornwallis at the time, Washington was planning an escape of exactly that sort. By the time that the sun rose on January 3, the British were dismayed to find that the American rebels had entirely abandoned the field of battle during the night. George Washington had escaped yet again. This time, although a retreat of that nature was anticipated, the commander's next maneuver was completely unexpected. In the early morning hours of January 3 the Americans stormed into the British camp at Princeton to their north and delivered yet another devastating attack on Howe's army. Ewald recalls that on the morning of the third they learned that Washington had abruptly abandoned his position, and when they were surprised to hear cannon fire to their rear they rushed to Princeton. The captain claimed that when they arrived they only found the corpses of their countrymen strewn about the ground.[22]

For the second time in a week Washington's once-beaten army delivered two crushing blows to Howe's massive force in New Jersey. By January 6 the obstinate Washington had established a winter camp at Morristown, and the dejected Howe abandoned nearly every previously held encampment in the state with the exception of New Brunswick and Perth Amboy. The first two weeks of January had been disastrous for the imperial cause, but the year 1777 was just beginning and Philadelphia remained well within reach.

By THE BEGINNING OF 1777 THERE WAS ALREADY A CLEAR PATTERN TO wintering in North America. The armies of Great Britain and the rebels of George Washington focused more on surviving the elements than fending off enemy attacks. But with each passing week the cold monotony of winter grew warmer and with the coming thaw combat operations would soon begin anew. By late March Captain Ewald and his Jägers stood ready to begin their march. Spring had come in New Jersey, and the roads that had been impassable for the past several months were now hardening. Whether or not Howe's entire army could have them was at that point uncertain, but Ewald's Jägers had already earned a great reputation among the British as one of its primary strike forces. The slow drum of winter encampment was the worst time of the fighting year for Ewald, and though it was still a month before the actual combat season the Hessian captain had already had his fill of idleness.

It was April 1777 and his target was a small outpost called Bound Brook, recently occupied as the forward operating post of George Washington's Continental Army; the main force had chosen Morristown, further west, as its primary camp. Ewald had been anxious to deliver a blow to the rebels ever since their craven victories over his fellow Hessians at Trenton and Princeton four months earlier. Bound Brook would be a small measure of revenge for Ewald, but it would be sweetened by the fact that victory, should it find them, would be his. Two months earlier, in February, the captain had the privilege to be personally called on by General Lord Charles Cornwallis himself to devise a strategic assault on the Patriot position at Bound Brook. Ewald was a soldier, but he was as much a student of the art of war as anyone else on the continent.

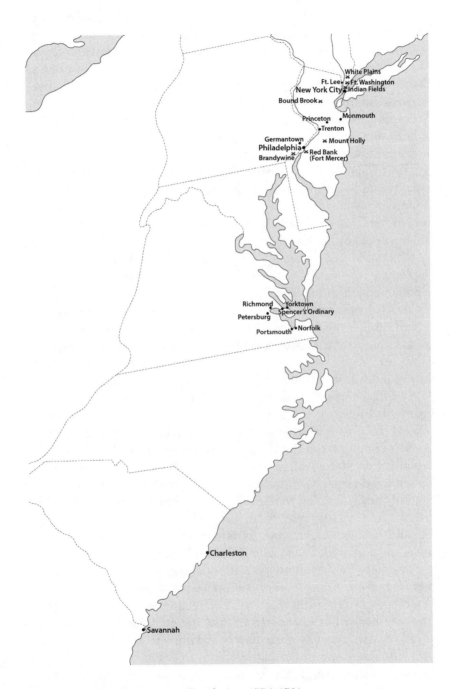

Johann Ewald in the American Revolution, 1776–1781.

Ewald's plan for striking the base was a multipronged attack aimed at cutting off his target by storming it from two sides. The approach was fundamentally sound, but it involved a river crossing that was impossible until the spring thaw allowed the Raritan River to rise. He would sit in camp at New Brunswick with the rest of his British associates until April. Although Ewald was anxious to avenge the losses of Trenton and Princeton, Cornwallis was equally restless. According to European conventions of war, fighting occurred in the spring, summer, and fall, while winter was a mutual season of rest and encampment. Washington, however, took advantage of this respite to plague the western wing of Howe's army with guerilla assaults and pestering raids. In the mind of Cornwallis, to capture Bound Brook was to silence the rebels until the fighting season began; for Ewald it finally meant peace for his Jägers as they took the brunt of the skirmishing.

When the attack finally came on April 12, Lord Cornwallis implemented Ewald's plan and moved four thousand British and German troops across the Raritan River. The right flank, in which Ewald's Jägers served as the vanguard, would march on Bound Brook directly. Along the way it would detach two light infantry companies to sever the road that connected the operating base to Washington's camp in Morristown. From the center Colonel Donop and Cornwallis himself would strike and deliver the final blow.

Ewald's perceived attack fell to pieces after the assault began, mostly because of the Hessian captain himself. His maneuver toward the post was designed to be a feint so as to strengthen the assaults coming from the center; however, his Jägers' zeal to fight actually pressed the Americans all the way to the artillery bastion of Bound Brook itself. Cornwallis and Donop's advances were successful, but they had failed to cut off the road blocking the Americans' retreat. The victory was total; the rebel commandant Benjamin Lincoln fled so quickly that he left behind all of his belongings, including correspondence from General Washington himself.

Although Ewald's strategy had collapsed, the overall objective was achieved. The Jägers plundered the site and startled Washington sufficiently that the American general began to question whether or not Howe had actually initiated the fighting season ahead of schedule. The great flaw of the implementation of Ewald's plan, though, came in the battle's aftermath. Once the British and Hessian forces returned to their base across the Raritan, Washington's men simply retook the now spoiled position and began to rebuild anew. That was of no consequence to Ewald; his first major assault in North America was a success, and he had avenged the loss of his countrymen.

THE SPRING THAW SIGNALED THE BEGINNING OF A NEW CAMPAIGN season, and with the victory at Bound Brook behind them the Jägers prepared for their next great attempt to secure the North American continent from the hands of Washington's rebels. Ewald, along with fifteen thousand others, was in the midst of a momentous sailing from their previous base at New York to an amphibious landing through the Chesapeake Bay. Their intended target was Philadelphia, and once that city was captured their commanders believed that both the Continental Congress and American rebellion would collapse once and for all. It was now August, and 1777 would potentially stand as the single greatest victory the British Empire had accomplished yet.

Their plan was one of the greatest strategic undertakings of the eighteenth century and entailed assaults from both the north and south to bring the American Revolution to its knees. General Howe believed that Philadelphia was the most critical component to stamping out any insurgency, but it was only part of a much larger puzzle. Throughout the early months of 1777 policy makers and military strategists in London determined that the rebellion was merely a regional phenomenon, and by securing the most belligerent regions the whole of the war would come to an end. From Quebec, strategists would send the affluent and hopeful General John Burgoyne with eight thousand soldiers southward through the Lake Champlain and Lake George corridor, down the Hudson River to New York which would sever the seditious New England colonies from the rest of their more tame compatriots. After capturing Philadelphia, plans dictated that General Howe would meet Burgoyne's charging force in support. It was a massive campaign that would require many pieces to fall into place, but each goal was well organized and obtainable. Howe's late start to his season was due to the logistics of organizing such a titanic venture through transatlantic communication and the time needed to construct the necessary sailing crafts.

On August 25 Howe's army completed their journey through the Chesapeake Bay and landed at the head of the Elk River in

Maryland, positioning themselves less than fifty miles from Philadelphia. Marching in impressive fashion, Howe's forces made steady progress toward their intended destination, and the rebel militia did little to slow their progress. In preparation to stifle the attack, Washington positioned his men on the eastern bank of the Brandywine Creek in Pennsylvania, hoping to initiate a great battle to protect Philadelphia from the invading army. From Howe's vantage point the odds were greatly in his favor, and rather than engaging the Americans in a location they had chosen, he wanted to implement a flanking maneuver that would reset the combat on his terms.

Brandywine Creek was typical of many small waterways that ran through colonial America; it was only passable by a number of small fords, and protecting these crossings would be essential for victory. While Washington's army controlled the fords immediately before them, Howe divided his army to pass much farther north of the Americans on September 11. By the time that Howe had crossed the creek, Washington had already engaged the British. A Hessian attack at the center led by General Knyphausen forced the rebels to withdraw from the field; had the attack been better coordinated, Washington might not have had any escape route. Ewald's Jägers traded furious fire throughout the battle, and the observant captain remained critical of his British superiors despite the victory. He believed that in his soul Clinton was a good general, but his inability to execute plans properly virtually guaranteed more costly mistakes would occur in the future.[23]

The Americans suffered nearly a thousand casualties at Brandywine, whereas Howe lost fewer than five hundred. On September 16, Washington crossed the Schuylkill River in an effort to protect the capital city only to recross it immediately after to attempt to fight Howe again. The American general sent forward an advanced guard under the command of General Anthony Wayne. In response, Howe ordered Colonel Donop and Ewald's Jägers ahead to meet them. The fighting that would occur thirty miles west of Philadelphia was nasty, short, and unproductive because of the howling wind and driving rain. Though Washington ultimately decided to disengage because of the terrible weather, it did not spare Ewald's men hours of fighting in the treacherous conditions. Their weapons were rendered useless by the rain, and Ewald ordered his men to charge the enemy with their swords drawn. Armed only with their bayonets and overmatched by the German blades, the rebels quickly escaped the field. Still, Ewald's Jäger company alone suffered fifteen casualties, and Colonel Donop himself was nearly taken captive. The skirmish known as "the Battle of the Clouds" ended as a confused and abortive stalemate.[24]

Ten days later General Howe regained his momentum and marched into the city of Philadelphia on September 26. Only a week earlier British forces overran a position at Paoli Tavern, and the capital city soon fell to the Crown. The seditious Continental Congress fled the city days before its anticipated sacking, and the political and spiritual heart of the Revolution now fell under control of the Great Britain. New York and Philadelphia once again were under the control of the Union Jack, and the colonies' rebellion was one step closer to being reined in by the forces of King George III. Unlike previous wars, however, this military occupation of an opposing capital did not signal much of an end to anything. The traditional military axiom is that when a capital city falls, the end of the war is all but secure. In this instance, the rebellion lived not in one central location, but in the strength and sustainability of Washington's army. Losing the city was a major blow, but it rendered little damage to the Continental Army itself.

Ewald recalls first marching into Philadelphia, where he witnessed cultivated fields and a vibrant German community, but his former countrymen were clearly on the side of the rebels and had nothing but venom to offer his Jägers. This should have come as no surprise to Ewald or any German soldier at the time. Since the moment of the announcement that they would be brought into service, the American political machine took every effort to cast them, and the British, as scoundrels. Describing the Germans as "mercenaries" and the British as "cowardly," print publications made the epithet *der Hess* a term of slander among German Americans for the next hundred years. Ewald, while marching into the heart of Philadelphia with his men, described an encounter with a Palatinate German woman. Thirsty from their march, the captain begged her for a glass of water, and though she obliged she rhetorically asked him what her family had done to deserve being targeted as an enemy by the British army. Ewald accepted the water but coldly ignored her sarcasm.[25]

Howe's great triumph should have played well for the empire in the effort to quash the Patriot cause, but as was the case in most rebellions it was the countryside—not the cities—that held the true heart of the revolution. While it was advantageous, taking

Philadelphia was not enough for the British to claim true victory. The Continental Congress had simply relocated itself to nearby Lancaster, and Washington positioned his men around the occupied city in preparation for a retaliatory assault. With the Jägers marching through the streets and keeping the city of roughly twenty thousand inhabitants under constant patrol, Howe decided to divide his forces to best deal with the pressing rebel response. Leaving only a fraction of his men in the capital city, the general established his primary camp of nine thousand troops five miles north of Philadelphia at Germantown.

In the meantime, the occupation of the American capital again brought waves of reinvigorated Loyalists out of hiding. For days after the initial occupation settlers and farmers from the Pennsylvania countryside brought wagonloads of goods and produce into the city to sell to Howe's army. Although Philadelphia was occupied by an invading force, war had a remarkable way of proving itself to be the greatest economic stimulus of all.

On October 3 Captain Ewald was approached by a Professor William Smith, a notable clergyman and the first provost of the Academy and College of Philadelphia (later the University of Pennsylvania). Smith pulled the captain aside to relay the message that he was indeed a supporter of Washington, but that the fair and equitable treatment offered by the Germans had earned his friendship forever. He quickly added that Washington's army had moved toward a new position, and slipped away into the busy streets of the city.[26]

Ewald rushed to his superiors with his new information, which readily reached William Howe himself. Assuredly, by the next morning it was at Germantown that Washington and his rebel army saw the weakest point in Howe's divided force. While he hoped to mimic his previous assaults on Trenton and Princeton, Howe's men were fighting from a very different position than in the previous year.

The camp at Germantown was nearly four miles across, and by 2 A.M. on October 4 Washington had positioned himself only two miles from Howe's pickets. By 5 A.M. they were within a half mile. When the attack came, Washington's men surged forward in four columns; at the right-center of the attack an American column led by John Sullivan broke the British line. The fog was thick that morning and the loss of visibility in the chaos of battle was disastrous. Following Sullivan's breakthrough, many of his men began to run low on ammunition and were forced to retreat, largely due to a heroic stand by a British Colonel Thomas Musgrave at a local mansion called Chew's House; in their flight they smashed directly into more American reinforcements attempting to capitalize on their breakthrough. After shooting at each other in a confused and blind display of friendly fire, both rebel forces retreated.[27]

With Sullivan's column off the field of battle, the troops that were defending the British left went to support those fighting elsewhere. Nathanael Greene's column fell soon after, and Washington's army was forced to flee. After the battle, Ewald proclaimed that Musgrave was a shining example of how bravery, discipline, and loyalty could produce superior results.[28]

Despite Washington's repulse at Germantown, Howe was in no condition to remain a divided unit. As he had learned the previous year in New Jersey, dividing an army and extending deeply into an enemy territory was a foolhardy and costly position. Two weeks after the battle ended, Howe abandoned his position at Germantown and pulled his men back into the city of Philadelphia itself; with the winter season approaching, and considering Washington's penchant for creative tactical maneuvers, Howe wanted to take no chances. Compounding matters for the general was the news that on October 7, General Burgoyne's entire army had been defeated and captured by the rebel leader Horatio Gates at Saratoga, and the grand push to sever New England via the Hudson River had been a failure.

There can be no question that Howe retained the upper hand in the fall of 1777, but his success at wintering in Philadelphia and continuing his occupation was wholly dependent on his ability to supply the army around him. In this way, Washington and his rebels remained a thorn in his side. Like the Patriot army had done on the Hudson with Forts Lee and Washington, the Americans had cleverly commanded two posts on opposing sides of the Delaware River just south of the capital city. Fort Mifflin and Fort Mercer, in Pennsylvania and New Jersey, respectively, sealed off British ship travel on the Delaware River from the Atlantic Ocean; as a result Howe and his tired army were effectively cut off from receiving both supplies and manpower.

It was a difficult reality for Howe, but not one that he had failed to foresee. One week after the Battle of Germantown, the general ordered a small artillery battery to be constructed for an assault on Fort Mifflin. It was a strong position, but not one that could ultimately disable the post; a steady bombardment of Fort Mifflin would serve as a diversion for a larger attack on its more valuable partner. Timing was of the essence, and the sooner that the rebel posts collapsed the sooner Howe's army could fully take control of Philadelphia. For this job there was no room for error, and Howe called upon 1,200 Hessians for the difficult yet necessary assault.

Commanding the Hessians for the great attack on Fort Mercer at Red Bank would be Colonel Carl von Donop. Still bitter from the previous battles in New Jersey, Donop was hopeful that by securing the rebel post he would avenge his previous losses and continue to build on his already respected family legacy in Hesse-Cassel. His attack would require fording the Delaware River, but a crossing too close to Fort Mercer would give away his position. On the morning of October 22, Donop crossed the river at Cooper's Ferry, today's Gloucester City, New Jersey, and marched his men four miles south to their destination. This attack was in many ways the first opportunity that Donop had to assert his abilities in the Hessian ranks; previously General Knyphausen and the late Colonel Rall had garnered most of the attention. Though this maneuver could appear trivial along the banks of a river that was thousands of miles from his German home, the successful completion of his mission would elevate his status in the eyes of his Landgraf Frederick II and promise untold amounts of political capital upon his return. He stated plainly to his men just moments before the assault that, "either this fort will be called Fort Donop, or I shall have fallen."[29]

Donop prepared his attack by dividing his 1,200 Hessians into two columns, one to attack from the south, and the other from the north and east. His overall assault would be supported by British naval vessels from the river, and with a garrison of only 400 rebels to speak of it seemed that Fort Mercer would fall by sundown. Before the attack, Donop sent a message to the men inside reading, "The King of England commands his rebellious subjects to lay down their arms, and they are warned that if they wait until the battle, no quarter would be given on either side."[30]

From within the commandant retorted with his own message claiming that no quarter would be given on either side, and that no capitulation was in order. The battle for Fort Mercer, it seemed, was set to begin. It may seem unusual that Donop and the Hessians would take such care to attack a post in the name of a king in which they had no national obligation; but when the Hessians battled the American rebels, they were fighting to support not just the British monarch, but the ideal of monarchy in its entirety. From their vantage point their tradition lifted the best among them to steward the masses below. To support an American rebellion was to question all royal authority, and ultimately condone disorder and civil unrest and undermine duty, honor, and obligation. The American Revolution was not just a battle of men, but of two fundamentally different worldviews.

With his previous experience of reconnoitering of Fort Washington a year earlier, Ewald was summoned by Donop to provide vital intelligence on the target now ahead of him. He took a small contingent of his Jägers along, and moved to within rifle shot of Fort Mercer. Ewald noted that the fort contained a breastwork twelve feet high dressed with assault stakes, and returned to Donop's headquarters with his findings. In response to this news, Ewald was dismayed to discover that few of his commanders thought much of the Americans' defenses. They sneered at the post and continued with their personal conversations. Upon leaving the tent Ewald was pulled aside by Captain George Krug to whom he expressed his concerns that the matter was being treated far too lightly; Ewald stressed that such hubris was bound to be dangerous.[31]

The Battle of Red Bank began in earnest. Hessian artillery blasted Fort Mercer, and the troops attacking the southern face of the post rushed forth. Led by a Colonel von Linsing, his Hessians charged the fort's walls where they were met with sudden and then steady cannon fire. His men were cut down by the rebel gunners, and musket volleys turned their lines into a total retreat. At the northern side of Fort Mercer Colonel Friedrich Ludwig von Minnigerode's grenadiers were able to climb over the walls of the fort. As they poured into Fort Mercer it was discovered that the portion they scaled was actually an abandoned wing of the site, and awaiting them on the other side were fallen trees with sharpened points. With no tools in hand the momentarily undisciplined Hessians began to tear at the hastily built wall with their bare hands and were soon blanketed with musket fire from above. The attack on Fort Mercer was a complete disaster, and Ewald blamed its failure on the arrogance of his superiors.[32]

As the Hessians ran, the Americans did not pursue, believing that the retreat was merely a feint to draw them out. Because of that decision the dead and wounded were left in place, the injured suffering throughout the night. In the midst of the chaos, along the defensive ditch that surrounded Fort Mercer, Colonel Carl von Donop lay abandoned, slowly dying of a grievous wound to his right leg when a piece of metal tore through his thigh. Hours later he was found, barely alive, beneath a pile of dead Hessians, and while being carried from the battlefield the colonel rambled about his failings as an officer. He wept for the dead, and panicked over the fearful retribution of the Landgraf when news of his defeat reached Hesse-Cassel. Then, following three agonizing days in the commandeered home of a local Quaker, Carl Emil Kurt von Donop died. His last words epitomized his German tradition, and provided his conquerors with one last message in defiance of their revolution: "It is finishing a noble career early; but I die the victim of my ambition, and of the avarice of my sovereign."[33]

Ewald was emotionally torn by the loss, and wrote that never in his life had he ever left a battle in such a state of sorrow and despair. He added that he had lost his greatest friend in the world, and Donop's legacy would not be forgotten. Whatever fighting would arise in the days to come would be done in his name.[34]

IN THE WINTRY MONTHS OF 1777 DECISIONS HAD TO BE MADE, AND with the failed attempt to capture Fort Mercer, Howe was pressed into further action. On November 10, Howe unleashed a days-long artillery bombardment on Pennsylvania's Fort Mifflin that was supported by six British vessels. Facing near-impossible odds and having suffered 250 casualties in a garrison of only 400, the commandant abandoned the rebel base. By November 16 the fort was left empty, and the British flew the Union Jack over the post after landing there unopposed. With the left bank of the Delaware River contained, a force of five thousand under the command of General Cornwallis landed in New Jersey to attack Fort Mercer a second time. By the time that his army arrived, it too had been simply deserted.

In one final push to draw the British out of his capital city, Washington established himself at White Marsh, sixteen miles north of the center of Philadelphia. On December 5, sensing his final opportunity to eliminate the rebels before winter encampment, Howe pressed a half-hearted attack. Though the two armies skirmished for three days, the British commander believed that his enemy was simply too well entrenched to do the necessary damage in the time that remained. Howe called his army back to Philadelphia to signal the official end of the campaign season. Seeing the British fall back into the city, Washington led his troops to a long, hard January at Valley Forge.

Ewald knew that the longer the American rebellion lasted, the worse the imperial force fared. Insurgencies had to be stopped quickly, for the longer they survived the more credibility was gained by the rebel force, and lost by the superior. The campaign of 1777 was a time of great change in Philadelphia, and the loss of Colonel Donop was only the beginning. Charles Cornwallis, leader of the great cavalier wing of Howe's army and the man who personally empowered the Jäger Corps more than any other British officer, was recalled to England shortly after encampment began. Before he sailed, Captain Ewald received a letter from the departing general:

> Sir,
> I cannot leave this country without desiring you to accept my best thanks for your good services during the two Campaigns in which I have had the honour to command the Hessian Chasseurs. If the war should continue, I hope we shall again serve together. If we should be separated, I shall ever remember the distinguished merit and Ability's of Captain Ewald.
> I am Sir—
> with great esteem & regard
> your most obed t. & most
> humble Servant
> Cornwallis[35]

The campaign season, known as the Philadelphia Campaign, had come to an end for 1777. For Ewald, it signaled the end of a hard year of constant fighting with little more to show for it than a captured rebel capital and a still determined rebel army. From New York to New Jersey to Pennsylvania, Ewald had engaged in combat of all types, and as a true lover of the game it had been the experience of a lifetime. In characteristic fashion, the captain ended his journal entry with a brief, workmanlike statement that only scarcely revealed the man behind the uniform in one fleeting glimpse. He offered that in all the marching, skirmishing, and fighting, he had taken for granted the simple joy of being recognized for one's achievements in Cornwallis's letter. It was the sweetest moment he had experienced in months.

PHILADELPHIA

*January–August 1778*

The month of January 1778 was the slowest Johann Ewald had ever experienced. After nearly two years at war the Hessian captain had decided that daily regimentation and constant vigilance were far more rewarding than the terrible grind that was winter in North America. His men sat in idleness while the city of Philadelphia slowly but surely grew accustomed to occupation. Ewald wrote that winter supplies had begun to trickle steadily into the city from residents anxious to restart their stalled livelihoods; the soldiers themselves were happy to oblige. Unlike the experience of Hessians fighting in prior decades, as servicemen under the command of Great Britain, they were all entitled to pay equal that of a British citizen of the same rank; in Ewald's estimation he had never seen an army so rich as the one in which he fought now. It may have seemed so, for on a daily basis each soldier received twelve ounces of salted pork or beef, along with more than a pound of wheat flour—and that was just courtesy of the empire. Because of the increasing capital now flowing into occupied Philadelphia, soldiers were also able to purchase whatever else they may have desired with their imperial stipend. The captain wrote that it was not uncommon to see fanciful balls, public concerts, and gambling halls filled with soldiers.[36]

Winter complacency had set in for Ewald, and, never one to find satisfaction in such inactivity, he began to take on a number of other small projects. One of them was the particularly fascinating case of Reverend Dr. Caspar Dietrich Weyberg, the pastor of the First Reformed Church of Philadelphia. Like Ewald, Weyberg was of the Reformed faith; unlike the captain, however, the pastor's political leanings had taken him down a very different path. Earlier in the occupation, Weyberg was arrested and jailed by Howe's men for delivering fiery sermons supporting an especially radical form of resistance to imperial authority. He remained locked away, and Ewald took it upon himself to petition for the man's release.

Although Weyberg did advocate the rebel cause, Ewald gave him a pass due to his old age and complete lack of participation in any actual partisan fighting. While the captain did feel some connection because of their shared religious and cultural German heritage, his real concern was for the incarcerated man's family. His plight had become something of a pet project for Ewald, and was likely more motivated by boredom than altruism. Even so, the captain was able to use his political capital to free the man on January 10. After being released, the repentant Weyberg promised the captain that his days of preaching were over.[37]

The city of Philadelphia was begging to revert to some state of normality by 1778, and while Ewald busied himself with a number of trivial diversions in the meantime, major changes were already being set in motion. Although he did not know it at the time, those changes, some visible and some not, had consequences that would change the war entirely.

AT THE CONCLUSION OF 1777, WHICH SOME HAD ALREADY BEGUN TO call "The Year of the Hangman," the American Revolution took a dramatic and momentous turn. Following the Battle of Saratoga in October, the fledgling American rebellion not only achieved its greatest victory to date, but also had earned the respect of Britain's only true imperial rival. By 1778 the empire of France had seen enough from Washington's Continental Army that it decided to fully support the revolutionary cause by pouring money into the American colonies and lending the use of its great royal navy. Washington's sufferings were never from a lack of spirit, but nearly always from a lack of funds; after Horatio Gates defeated John Burgoyne three months earlier, that problem was soon to disappear. France had entered the war on the side of the Americans, and by every standard saved the struggling rebellion that had so often teetered on the brink of ruination.

While the particulars were still coming together with the new American-Franco alliance, one of the great shakeups came not from overseas, but from within the British army itself. After the tumultuous events of October, General William Howe had tendered his resignation under the grievances that he was never properly supported by the Crown and the reason for his failings was simply a lack of manpower. To submit such a document was not uncommon, as resignations became customary following a defeat, but in April 1778 royal authorities responded by officially relieving him of his post. In his place they promoted his great political rival Sir Henry Clinton.

What had begun as a sectional rebellion in North America had grown into a major geopolitical shift thanks in part to the inability of the king's commanders to snuff out the revolution in its infant stages. While the capture and occupation of New York and Philadelphia had been major benchmarks of Howe's tenure on the continent, Washington's penchant for escape had allowed a supposedly containable problem to spread. The loss at Saratoga and the entry of France had helped to legitimize the rebel cause. Now, with Washington's army rejuvenated at Valley Forge, the British would have to not only deal with his rebels but also focus their military efforts elsewhere. As the Americans had no navy to speak of initially, they could not pose any meaningful threat to Britain's island holdings around the world; the arrival of France, however, suddenly had George III fighting a defensive war, on land and on the seas.

Ewald wrote extensively of the monumental day when it was announced that General Howe would be replaced, for it also signaled the return of a figure who had been absent from the continent for over six months and whose fortunes had been so entwined with his own since 1776. On the same ship that declared the removal of the general, it was also proclaimed that Charles Cornwallis would return to North America.[38]

The occupation of Philadelphia was not entirely restful for Ewald, and the regular tasks of a modern military still needed to be performed. Part of the captain's routine was to patrol the roads leading into the city from the surrounding countryside, and while this was mostly uneventful, there were flares of intensity. In one such instance, Ewald came upon a small party of rebels transporting supplies to Valley Forge; after a sharp exchange, all but one of them escaped. The captive Patriot informed Ewald that help was on the way, and that he was simply the lead element of a much larger column. When he advised the Jägers to free him or suffer the wrath of this oncoming unit, Ewald was so sure that the man was bluffing that he stood firm in place until 9 P.M., a period of more than five hours.[39]

Philadelphia in the spring of 1778 was a closed environment, and like all situations under such scrutiny it did not take much kindling to fuel the fires of rumor and scandal. Ewald recalls one particular story that left a vivid image in his mind. Calling it the story of the "zealous patriot" in his journals, the Hessian captain told the story of a local farmer whom he described as a true friend of the king. Living on the east bank of the Delaware River at Gloucester Point, the Loyalist had a brother serving as a captain in the ranks of the Continental Army at Valley Forge. Under orders from the general himself, the Patriot brother led a party to burn the supplies of loyal tenants living around the occupied city. Out of sheer spite, Ewald continues, the Patriot brother made it a point to destroy his own brother's crops. It was at that moment with his harvest devastated that the rebel sibling declared that if his brother did not immediately sever ties to the British, he would turn his name over to the rebel command and request the most severe punishment be dealt out to him.[40]

Ewald attests that he spoke to the man personally, and while this is the only mention of this action from 1778, there is little doubt of its authenticity. Many have described the American Revolution as a civil war, pitting neighbor versus neighbor and brother versus brother. In some regards this is true, but that label can be misleading and should only be used with care. This was no civil war to define the future of a country, but a war of ideologies. While in the traditional sense the winner of a civil war *redefines* the direction of a nation, this was a struggle to *create* a new one. In that sense the American Revolution was no coup d'état, but a separatist movement. The Loyalist Americans were only struggling to protect their homelands in the strictest sense; in reality they were battling to defend their imperial worldview.

From the perspective of the Hessians, a people that still lived under a system marred by the dying breaths of feudalism in Central Europe, this American land was the most liberal place they had ever seen. They perceived no tyrannical oppression in British North America, so by their standards the rebellion they battled was the stuff of politics, not legitimate grievance. It was a world that they could only dream of in Europe, and despite the realization of that goal the Americans were still demanding more. For most Hessians this only hardened their faith in an autocratic system, for without the singular rule of an unquestioned sovereign the unruly masses would tear their own country apart; the American rebels were proof of that. One Hessian wrote:

> This land is now a stage for the cruellest [sic] scenes. Here there is one neighbor against the other, children against their father. Whoever thinks or speaks differently from the Congress in those provinces in which it is obeyed soon becomes looked on as an enemy, is given over to the hangman, or must take flight, either into our lines or back into the wilderness. But for the tyranny of the Congress party, no people in the world could have lived better than these.[41]

While the British officers made their quarters in the heart of metropolitan Philadelphia, Johann Ewald had no such luxury, nor did he expect it. As his men typically marched at the vanguard of the army for the previous two years, it was only natural that they would establish themselves on the very outskirts of the American capital. On a typical night his Jägers would keep a vigilant guard throughout the night, and he himself would lodge in a nearby home commandeered at the start of the occupation. It was a fairly routine schedule for Ewald, and as a soldier he took comfort in that; if there was to be any unusual or anomalous behavior, however, he was certain to take note of it. One such evening in late April saw the usual sentry duty take hold late until the evening, when the still of the night was broken by the sound of a violin. Upon hearing the strange music being played, Ewald leapt to his window to shout at his men. The music, which he described as barely intelligible compared to the finest German composers, was out of place to say the least. On further inspection the captain found the mystery musician. Standing before him and strumming intently on his instrument was a black man, unquestionably a slave. He explained to the captain that his mistress was in labor, and he was simply spreading the joy that the family was feeling at the time. It was a sign that amid the conflict, the city was still going about its business. As the young man sauntered off with fiddle in hand it was the last bit of excitement that the Jägers would see on that night's duty.[42]

At times it is easy to fall into the perception that America and Britain were only distant cousins, yet the traditions shared by the two populaces separated by the enormity of the Atlantic Ocean were reminders of just how similar they really were. May 2 was a joyous time in the city as British soldiers and Americans alike celebrated the annual festival of St. George, the patron saint of England. The feast had become a day of great merriment in the spring season around the British world, and the atmosphere was so light that even the Hessians joined in the festivities. Although the spirit of the day remained the same, it was nearly impossible for politics to avoid souring the mood. At midday a contingent of obstinate Americans paraded through the streets carrying a board painted with the kneeling likeness of King George; beside him was the image of a much more gallant-looking George Washington. Beneath the provocative display were the words: "My dear King, if you wish to beg for something, bend your knee, then let me speak." Ewald did not take the bait, and he allowed the rabble-rousing party to skip by, but he did make note of the offense. Critical of his opponent's lax regulation, Ewald wrote that he was shocked that General Washington would ever allow such insolence in his ranks.[43]

During the tenuously inactive spring of 1778, Ewald's singular fixation on the art of war began to fade. While earlier he had written commentary on the nature and movements of belligerents in partisan warfare, at this time he wrote increasingly about the state of America and its progress. The American capital was a fascinating place to Ewald, and his studies on combat soon led him to interest in seeing other curiosities of the day. One visit took him to the Academy and College of Philadelphia, where a local professor showed him all the wonders of cutting-edge eighteenth-century technology. Ewald next moved on to the campus library, which contained books from the English tradition that he had never seen before. The main attraction, however, was the recently invented orrery, a mechanical device that demonstrated the orbit of the planets and moons in miniature around the solar system. Created by Dr. David Rittenhouse in 1771, the small device captivated Ewald's imagination. He marveled at the contraption, and wrote in wonder that the secrets of the universe were being revealed more and more each day.[44] The Rittenhouse orrery was one of the most impressive astronomical inventions of its time, and even in the twenty-first century that same device that Ewald marveled over can still be found on the campus of the University of Pennsylvania in Philadelphia.

By May, the American Revolution had changed. On February 6, 1778, a Treaty of Amity and Commerce and a Treaty of Alliance were officially signed between France and the United States of America, bringing Britain's oldest rival into the war. It was a time of great uncertainty for the empire as the largest insurrection in its history had spread into a global conflict. In London, politicians furiously debated the next step in the painful process of confronting the Americans, but they were no longer a singular problem. For the better part of two hundred years the empires of Great Britain and France had shadowed each other's expansion across the globe. From India to Africa to North America, the rival superpowers jockeyed for supremacy, only to settle the matter momentarily fifteen years prior at the end of the Seven Years' War. In that almost decade-long struggle, Britain had been able to conquer and claim from the French teritories of Canada, Gorée, the Senegal River settlements in West Africa, and major trading posts in India. Much more valuable, however, were the Caribbean sugar islands of Martinique,

Saint Lucia, Grenada, Saint Vincent, Dominica, Tobago, and the
Grenadines taken from the French. The Treaty of Paris in 1763
gave Britain sole possession of most of its conquests. The French
grew sour with thoughts of revenge for the next fifteen years; now
with old hostilities reignited, London's enemies were surfacing
again.

In Philadelphia, global affairs were never as distant as they
seemed. On May 10 Sir Henry Clinton officially took the reins of
the British army from William Howe, and the latter would wait ten
days before returning to England in hopes of defending his decisions over the previous two years. By the time Clinton assumed
command, Washington's army had begun to stir at Valley Forge and
emerged as a rejuvenated fighting force in the wake of its new influx
of foreign money and supplies. For Clinton, keeping the capital city
under royal occupation had become a fool's errand. If the Americans
had been in their previous wretched state, Philadelphia would have
been an excellent headquarters for a summer campaign, but the
newly global engagement dictated otherwise.

With the French fully invested in the American Revolution,
Clinton had to face the reality of a powerful enemy with a maritime
presence. First, the highly valuable and supremely wealthy island
colonies of the British Caribbean were now a viable target within
the reach of Louis XVI. In response Clinton would be forced by
Parliament to surrender five thousand soldiers from his command
to be placed in defense of the rich sugar islands. Second, Clinton
now faced more than a rabble of armed patriots; the entry of France
brought the French navy as well. Britain was the uncontested naval
superpower of the world, and France was no threat in that way,
however, the mere presence of an enemy maritime wing drastically
changed the strategy in North America. By standing pat in
Philadelphia, Clinton was effectively leaving the city of New York
exposed to a French invasion from the Atlantic. Even if Clinton had
not given five thousand men over to reinforce the Caribbean, he
probably could not have staved off an attack of that magnitude; the
fact that he was short-staffed only worsened that problem. With
limited manpower on hand, there was simply no way both American
cities could be defended adequately, and Clinton came to one logical conclusion: after more than a year of British occupation,
Philadelphia would have to be abandoned.

The same night that Clinton took command, there was a palpable
buzz in the city. A fresh crop of three hundred Hessian recruits had

arrived with Clinton, and like Ewald two years prior they were taken by the sights and sounds of the New World. Some of them piqued the captain's interest, but he thought most were the lowly dregs of his home country. As night fell, a runner arrived at Ewald's post with a message that General Wilhelm von Knyphausen requested his presence. Ewald made the journey to the general's quarters and was surprised to see five other officers awaiting his arrival.

In that tiny room, Ewald found himself surrounded by some of the most powerful men in the entire Hessian military command in North America. As he stood at attention, the aged General Knyphausen removed a letter from the table and presented it to Ewald. The document was an official recognition from the Landgraf Frederick II himself honoring the service of Ewald's Jägers; it had arrived on the same boat as the reinforcements earlier that day. The coveted honor within was that of the Hessian knighthood *pour la vertu militaire*, and the captain was filled with pride to receive it. Holding his coveted title, Ewald allowed his mind to drift back to Hesse-Cassel, a kingdom aged well beyond its years and continually sliding into decline, and humorously wrote that it took him back to another time when a man would be honored with the greatest of pomp and circumstance; today, however, he only received a modest pair of cuffs.

EVACUATING PHILADELPHIA WAS A HERCULEAN TASK. NOT ONLY WOULD Clinton need to move more than ten thousand soldiers, but he would also have to find a way to transport the supplies and support staff required to sustain an army of that size. It was no small job, and the fact that William Howe had a self-indulgent gala in honor of his service in the midst of it slowed the process greatly. The Mischianza, as it is known, was a day-long celebration including dancing, fireworks, and a great parade to send Howe on his way. In the midst of this adventure in ineptitude General Washington took advantage of the distraction to reconnoiter his enemy's position. Led by the Marquis de Lafayette, this intelligence gathering expedition was soon discovered and pursued; the resulting battle two days later known as Barren Hill saw the young commander narrowly escape. At the conclusion of the encounter Ewald noted that it was the first time that he had personally seen a Frenchman on the field of battle in North America.

By May 22 Ewald and his Jägers were ordered to begin the slow process of breaking down the occupation of Philadelphia before the race to save New York. On the banks of the Delaware River, the captain oversaw the loading of what he described as "heavy equipment" onto transport ships that would be sent southeastward to the Atlantic. All the while, though, Ewald was forced to confront one of the terrible consequences of such a task during a partisan conflict, what would happen to those left behind.

Thousands of Loyalists who had initially fled the city at the start of the revolution and took refuge in the countryside had celebrated the occupation of Philadelphia as it gave them a chance to return to their homes. They vocally announced their support for the Crown despite the threats of their rebellious neighbors; when the army left, however, their fate was left hanging in the balance. The revolution, like many political creations, was driven initially by the vocal minority. By the year 1778, it was very likely that less than 40 percent of Americans actually supported the war, but pressure to choose sides forced the hand of many noncommittal citizens. Early on to take a moderate stance was acceptable, but the proverbial middle was soon eradicated by extremists on both sides. Ewald wrote that he was crushed to see that just by merely associating with the British these people were now declared as enemies and forsaken by their friends and neighbors.[45]

By June, Clinton's army was prepared for the long haul back to New York, and after he consolidated his men in New Jersey the trek began in earnest. At the front of his column was General Knyphausen and four thousand Hessians, with Clinton and the remaining six thousand filling in behind. By the time that his army and supply train were fully extended Clinton's column stretched for twelve miles, and tensions ran high, as Washington's army had also started to move. Since the winter season had ended, the Patriot army experienced a rebirth and swelled to thirteen thousand five hundred men; considering the protracted nature of Clinton's troops, an encounter with a rebel force of that size could spell disaster for the new commander. If Washington were to attack, Clinton calculated, he would do so when the British were attempting to cross the Raritan River at their most vulnerable point. If the rebels waited until that slow and cumbersome crossing they could also join forces with Horatio Gates marching southward and deliver a killing blow.[46]

Although his original intended march route would have been a much faster and direct path through the state, Henry Clinton feared encountering Washington at the Raritan. Instead he selected a more circuitous route toward Allentown, Pennsylvania, moving north, and while it would add several days to the journey, he believed that he could avoid an engagement at that potentially disastrous river crossing.

At this same time, however, Washington and his rebel command were formulating a plan of their own. With the British Army leaving the capital, the American general and his subordinates found themselves in the midst of a heated debate. Should they engage Clinton as he fled or simply allow him to leave? Philadelphia was theirs once again, but was a general engagement worth the cost? It was agreed that a full-scale battle was certain to go against them, but some offensive endeavor should be undertaken. Earlier that spring the American army had received word that a French fleet under Admiral Charles Hector, Comte d'Estaing, had sailed from Toulon in April 1778. If d'Estaing's arrival was timely, it could potentially crush Clinton's army before it ever reached New York. As the strategizing continued, Washington's plan became to slow the enemy's progress by harassing the British as they fled, specifically targeting the rearguard of Clinton's army led by none other than the recently returned Charles Cornwallis. Since he was the last portion of the extended British line, it was decided that when Cornwallis moved the rest of the army would be far enough ahead that a minor attack could commence. If the engagement could subsist, Washington hoped, then Clinton would be delayed enough for d'Estaing's forces to complete their objective.

On June 28, as Clinton's army plodded its way toward Monmouth Courthouse in New Jersey, Washington's strike was set in motion. Led by Major General Charles Lee, the rebel forces assaulted Cornwallis's rear column with five thousand men. The fighting was intense, and with temperatures skyrocketing toward a hundred degrees men on both sides began keeling over from the heat. Although the attack was unexpected, issues within the American command began to cause its collapse. Orders were given shoddily, and before long Lee's initial engagement broke down into a retreat; then it was a rout. Washington himself was advancing toward Cornwallis when he encountered Lee's fleeing force. After some less than dignified arguing the major general was relieved of duty, and Washington commanded his men forward. At that same time though, Cornwallis's rear guard was in hot pursuit of the retreating Patriots, and what began as a skirmish transformed into a full-scale battle.

The clash that ensued lasted the entire day. All elements of the British command were engaged in the fight including the Black Watch and the highly specialized Coldstream Guards. On the Patriot side American officers stood arm in arm with French commanders to fend off their mutual enemy. It was a massive encounter, pitting eleven thousand Americans against nearly fifteen thousand British, and by the end of the day a thousand were killed or wounded. Washington was far from beaten and pushed his men for a final attack, but the setting sun made such a venture a dangerous proposition. That night, with New York as their primary objective, Clinton and his men pressed their march forward, leaving General Washington and his army far behind them. It had been a tactical victory for the Crown, but the Battle of Monmouth was a pyrrhic one at best. For the first time in the war Washington's army had proven that it could stand toe-to-toe with the enemy; he commanded the battlefield despite the unsatisfying result.

For Captain Johann Ewald, who commanded his Jäger in the most terrible of conditions, the battle was especially taxing. Although it was his duty, the constant skirmishing was beginning to take an emotional toll. The Battle of Monmouth would stand as the single largest one-day battle of the entire American Revolution; it also would be the last major engagement in the American Northeast. Ewald took great care to analyze the battle and concluded the following day that if the Americans had not made early mistakes, they could have very easily won the day.[47]

By July 1, Clinton's army had made its way as far as Sandy Hook, and by July 7 the British had completed their hundred-mile journey from Philadelphia to New York. Within days, d'Estaing's fleet of sixteen ships arrived well behind schedule. Had the French landed in time, they certainly could have made Clinton's journey to New York much more difficult, but because of the uncertainties of maritime travel they were forced to face an enemy that was well fortified and well supplied. The game was afoot in and around Manhattan; with the British navy tightly hugging the coastline, d'Estaing was given two options of attack. The first would be to overwhelm the British fleet itself. While the French had superior naval power at the time, they correctly anticipated that their much larger vessels would be unable to cross the shallow bars near the bay. The second option, however, was much more enticing as the secondary British post at Newport, Rhode Island, was almost fully exposed, and therefore ripe for an attack. In coordination with General Washington, the French commander devised a plot to capture the occupied city to his north. It would come to pass on August 8.

Although supported by rebel forces led by General John Sullivan, the attack on Newport was largely a failure. French troops were landed to aid the attack, but reboarded after it appeared that British numbers were increasing in the area. After taking his ships out to sea to battle the British navy, d'Estaing was suddenly hit by a severe storm that disabled his own, as well as his enemy's fleet. Back in Rhode Island the Patriot commander was infuriated, and sensing that he could not complete his objective quickly, he retreated. The Battle of Newport was a failure, and the Crown retained control of the city. Perhaps the greatest casualty of the venture though was the momentary but deep resentment between American and French commanders.

For Ewald, however, in New York, the situation had become eerily familiar. Just as was the case in 1776, the British had solid control over Manhattan Island, and the rebels under Washington were once again entrenched in the region of White Plains. From a strategic vantage point it was as though the years 1777 and 1778 had never occurred, the primary difference being that Washington's army was much larger and well supplied than he could have ever dreamed of two years prior. It was indeed a terrible stalemate in the late summer of 1778, and it had become clear to both parties that New York would need to stay in British hands for the Crown to stop the American rebellion.

With the British seeking to protect their primary base of operation in North America by consolidating on the island of Manhattan, Washington and his rebels wanted to maintain a strong presence into the fall at White Plains; although they were outnumbered, the Patriots believed that they could track the whereabouts and movements of Clinton's army while keeping the imperial forces bogged down with one swift placement of the French navy. It was this standoff that transformed the New York region into a geopolitical quagmire; the British were unwilling to budge from their position, and the rebels had little interest in taking it.

The stretch of land between the two armies, today the Bronx and Yonkers, was transformed into a veritable no man's land by September. Skirmishing between the light infantry and irregulars of both sides was almost constant in this region that the Jägers grew to call home. Time and again the rebels and rangers would exchange fire, and while the clashes would rarely escalate, there was always the potential for more intense hostilities. One such event was as revealing a moment as Ewald had ever experienced, and its conclusion gave him the fullest taste of North American partisan combat yet.

At midday, a party of American rangers had become embroiled in a firefight with a small number of Clinton's Loyalists, although the opening of the hostilities was minor, it very quickly spread. Occurring on and around the plantation of a local man named Frederick DeVoe, Ewald and his Jägers were called upon in reinforcement of the Loyalist ranger company. The enemy, as the Hessians soon discovered, was a mixed force of rebels and Indian warriors that had allied with the Patriot cause. The native contingent that joined the fighting were allied Mohicans who, because of their strong ties to the village of Stockbridge, Massachusetts, adopted the name of their political center. The "Stockbridges" as they were called had approached General Washington months earlier about supporting the Continental Army and had participated in the Battle of Monmouth only three months prior. The native population of North America was heavily divided throughout the war. In most cases those peoples that were geographically closer to the American states in the east tended to side with the Patriots; those on the frontier allied themselves with the empire.

Ewald's men took to the battlefield with great anxiety, as they had never before battled an Indian enemy. Like the same forces of propaganda that so greatly tarnished their own name, the Hessians had heard numerous stories of the "savages" and their terrible ways of war. It was an advantage that native warriors across the continent often held against their enemies, and they often fought their hardest to convince their opposition that their reputation had preceded them. This engagement, often referenced as "Indian Fields," was unlike the other massive battles of its day. Rather than having two forces moving to play out some grand strategy, this attack consisted of multiple parties firing on each other from cover. It was the Jägers' kind of fight to be sure, and the result was long periods of chaotic exchanges followed by swift and cautious moves to new positions. Men were pulled from their horses and stabbed; others were thrown to the ground and bludgeoned with rifle butts and war clubs.

By the end of the fighting, the Americans had disengaged and the Stockbridge leader named Nimham was dead. The fighting was intensely personal, with most of the dead killed at close range following hand-to-hand combat. Perhaps the most chilling aspect of the battle though was the role that prejudices and misconceptions played in its aftermath, for while the wounded were taken prisoner, no quarter was given to the Stockbridges. Multiple native warriors fought to the last, but in most instances those who surrendered were simply executed on the spot. It was a horrifying moment in a war that was defined by violent politics.

When the battle came to a close, Ewald's natural instincts of curiosity took over, and he began to record the aftermath. He had never seen an Indian before, and now with the piles of dead that remained he was able to describe them in detail, and wrote that he was struck by their fit and muscular bodies. He claimed that they wore clothing and shoes made of deerskin, and adorned their noses and ears with piercings and rings. Their heads were shaven with the exception of a tiny patch of hair, and they were armed with rifles, arrows, and tomahawks. Ewald's Jägers had fought in close quarters before, and after nearly three years of fighting even the most hardened soldier was growing tired of the grinding bore. North America was demanding and settings were familiar, but both the enemy and the stakes were changing in unexpected ways.[48] The rebellion that they had fought so hard to stamp out, it seemed, was becoming a revolution.

## THE HUDSON RIVER VALLEY

*January–September 1779*

Warfare had always been a curious thing for Ewald. He was a man who had dedicated his life to his craft, and his rewards would be measured by the graces of his king an ocean away. Leading men onto the field of battle came naturally to him, and he could navigate potentially life-threatening situations by instinct. War had given him a career, war had placed food on his table, and war had been good to him. At his core was his duty, and it was an undeniable fact of the soldier's life that duty prospered when only when authority was respected and burning questions remained unasked. Yet despite his natural predisposition for the martial arts, Ewald could not help but note the irony of a conflict as unpredictable and unprecedented as this American rebellion. He had been in North America for three years, and his earliest experiences brought him to the burned-out city of New York. With momentum on their side his Jägers had marched all the way to the colonial capital of Philadelphia in what was considered a fatal blow to George Washington's army, and now, a year later, the Hudson River lay before him again. He understood the strategic importance of New York; if he had been in full command the imperial forces would be in this same place, yet to return to virtually the same position as he began was demoralizing.

The winter encampment of 1779 was probably the most industrious respite during his entire service in North America. His men were satisfied: their pockets were filled and spirits were up. As a major port, New York brought constant sustenance from the icy waters of the North Atlantic, and with those plentiful supply vessels also came promising news. In January the encamped British and German forces received word that only a few weeks earlier Lieutenant Colonel Archibald Campbell had successfully captured Savannah. To that point the capture of such a high value target was easily one of the king's greatest victories of the entire conflict, and coupled with the fact that Campbell's forces sustained less than twenty-five casualties made the conquest even sweeter. The decision to move south was a major shift in imperial strategy, and it was not one that Ewald held in the highest regard. In his experience such radical shifts in policy were wholly reactionary, and never an indicator of a confident nation at war.[49]

The push to the South was a product of experience from three years of fighting in a heavily divided North American continent. British policy makers had seen that while the conflict was outwardly a rebellion, the situation on the American mainland had revealed itself to be a civil war. In moving south, the empire hoped to exploit this partisan divide by enlisting the assistance of Loyalist Americans living in the agricultural southern colonies. Stigmatized Loyalists had been a critical source of intelligence in and around New York, and the strategists simply could not resist the much less hostile atmosphere of the South. With the fall of Savannah it seemed their calculations were correct. By February the good news continued to pour into occupied New York. On February 26 Ewald records that the wintering soldiers were thrilled at the news that Major General James Grant had taken possession of the sugar giant of St. Lucia in the Caribbean with a force of four thousand men. The jewel of the Caribbean was considered a key to the economic health of King Louis's empire, and after the French involved themselves in the revolution months earlier the British were happy to engage them in the war that they so anxiously sought. From his earliest experiences with combat Ewald harbored ill will toward the French, the nemesis of his homeland. When Ewald was fourteen, in 1758, his father attempted to dissuade him from service by taking him to view a recently vacated battlefield, and upon seeing the dead the young man recalled, "Oh, how happy are they who died for their country in such a way!" By 1760 the teenaged Ewald was battling France in the global conflict dubbed the Seven Years' War and was serving in the army of the Duke of Brunswick. At the age of seventeen he was wounded in battle attempting to reclaim Cassel from the French, and was promoted to ensign for his gallantry. Now, twenty years later, a blow to his old enemy was a victory for his people regardless of who delivered it.[50]

With the spring thaw under way by late April, Ewald and his Jägers were fully rested and recuperated. They had not suffered the hardships of previous years, and their strategic placement on the Atlantic kept them well-stocked and upbeat; the most traumatic experience was an eight-day bread shortage in which the men had to gather their starchy intake from grits—far from the frigid hardship of Valley Forge. In early May Ewald wrote gleefully that the British navy had achieved one of their most dynamic scores yet as the warship *Galatea* was able to capture the fugitive privateer Gustavus Conyngham and bring him into custody. Conyngham was effectively an American-sponsored pirate responsible for sinking dozens of British ships across the seas of northern Europe in his cutter aptly dubbed *Revenge*. As a man of the ancient order of the Old World, Ewald delighted in seeing such a troublesome and uncivilized criminal brought to justice. With the campaign season of 1779 set to begin the event served to validate exactly what virtues he was fighting so hard to defend.

The setting that defined the opening of hostilities in 1779 was familiar for British commanders. With their own forces of over twenty thousand stationed in and around Manhattan, Sir Henry Clinton remained focused on the most direct line to suppressing the American rebellion: capture Washington's army. For the newly minted commander, though, that task was proving to be a herculean one; approximately forty miles west of Clinton's station in New York sat the wintering encampment of the Continental Army at Middlebrook. Although the scene had similarities with the British and German camps, 1779 was a very different experience for American commanders. Unlike the previous three winters, including the most desperate at Valley Forge, the Patriot rebels were enjoying their new influx of French money, supplies, and manpow-

er. It was in this recent development that Clinton was the most
flummoxed.

At his best estimates, Clinton believed that Washington likely
had over eight thousand men on hand at Middlebrook. This number was still paltry compared to his own strength, but it was substantial enough to give the British general pause. To compound the situation, the Patriots also had firm control over a strategic parcel of
land on an "S" shaped bend of the Hudson called West Point, in the
form of Fort Clinton fifty miles to his north. Now that Washington
had a true army, this was no longer about crushing a band of Patriot
rabble. Still confident, Clinton knew that an assault on a rebel camp
was a much taller task than it had been before. For this reason
Clinton mobilized his forces (including Captain Ewald's Jägers) into
action in an attempt to draw the Continentals into an open environment for a single pitched battle. In the minds of most British commanders in New York all that was necessary to end this drawn-out
rebellion was one major victory over George Washington fought on
their own terms.

When Ewald received his orders to begin to prepare for the campaign season in late May he knew that heavy casualties were to be
expected. The enemy camp was separated from his men by a vast
expanse of uneven terrain, and to take the fight to the rebels would
mean traversing a landscape that was not favorable to a force the
size of Clinton's. All things considered, however, the Jägers had
their fill of the dullness of winter life.[51]

The Jägers were ordered to assemble at Flushing on the northern edge of Long Island where they proceeded to march to today's
College Point; Ewald and his men boarded flatboats and sailed the
short distance to Willets Point. On May 30 the Jägers received their
orders and boarded a waiting fleet of transport vessels alongside
hundreds of their comrades. The transport ships were destined to
move northward up the Hudson River, and it carried no small force.
Along with the Jägers the ships carried most of the army's
grenadiers, Ewald's count of four English regiments, and a collection of light infantry, six thousand souls in all. Ewald wrote of the
scene that over eight hundred men were packed tightly in each vessel, and they were instructed to leave all of their possessions behind
to conserve space. He guessed that not even a slice of bread could
be squeezed in.[52]

If the hasty boarding and lack of supplies was any indication,
their journey was sure to be a short one. In fact their destination was

only thirty-five miles upriver. Since the beginning of the war there had been a strong belief among British officials that the rebellion was a *regional* phenomenon. Therefore, if the afflicted region could be quarantined from the remainder of the colonies the revolution could be stopped cold. It was this understanding that gave birth to the failed Saratoga campaign two years earlier, and this principle still guided Clinton's thinking. The objective of the previously failure had been to control the Hudson River and therefore sever the agitators in the New England colonies from their American brethren; though the movement had spread to all thirteen colonies Clinton still saw merit in commanding that vital waterway. From his vantage point to the south, Clinton saw the Americans beginning to entrench themselves along the river at key points. If his forces were able to take control of these critical positions, the shared sentiment among his command was that the Hudson would finally come under British control.

Along the river's east and west banks all the way north Clinton identified a series of locations that if taken over would disrupt Washington's plans. North of the British encampment sat two points that each protruded into the Hudson, effectively pinching off the river for an easy crossing. The rebels had forts on both the east and west banks. As much as Ewald understood this tactical narrative, he was unaware of the recent developments coming out of the Patriot command to his north. In early May Benedict Arnold, the disaffected Patriot commandant of Fort Clinton, had allowed his souring opinions of the Continental Army to alter his ambitions. As the highest-ranking officer in the valley, Arnold made welcomed overtures to Clinton's department. With a willing conspirator deep within the rebel high command, the British believed that taking the entire region was not only possible but a likely outcome.

Escorted by two sixty-four-gun ships, three frigates, and four galleys, the fleet that carried Ewald's Jägers through the narrowing Hudson River valley certainly cut an intimidating sight. The intended targets sat just north of Manhattan at locations called Stony Point on the western bank, and Verplanck's Point on the east. Jutting out like an arrow from the banks of the river, Stony Point was a prime location to initiate a major maneuver that could draw the American rebels from their encampment. Its elevation offered a commanding view of the river, and the nearby King's Ferry would likewise fall under British control if all went as planned. With a victory, the British could control a vital entrance into the Hudson

Highlands, and most importantly threaten the supply and communication lines so vital to Washington's survival. There was a modest Patriot fortification on the site, but with Loyalist intelligence claiming that it was garrisoned by fewer than fifty men, Stony Point was a soft, yet highly profitable, target for Clinton's forces.[53]

The capture of the small American fort at Stony Point was by most standards anti-climactic. British ships on the Hudson shelled the tiny posts for hours, while Ewald and the Jägers applied diversionary firing from the land side. Ewald noted that the fort's stone and brick construction rendered many of their attacks useless. On June 1 the tiny post finally surrendered at midday, and most of the garrison became prisoners of war. Despite the fact that this venture is largely considered a minor footnote, for Ewald and his Jägers it was a revealing moment regarding just how much this minor rebellion had changed despite the familiar surroundings. Among the rubble they found a dead body, carefully wrapped and hidden. In the captain's mind the fallen soldier was clearly a French officer.[54]

Two days later, with Stony Point being only half of their objective, the six-thousand-man force turned their attention across the river to the primary target at Verplanck's Point, Fort Lafayette. At the end of the fruitless struggle the position fell to the redcoats, and forty North Carolinian Patriots had unceremoniously surrendered. Although it was only a small step in the complete strategy that Clinton had envisioned, he was closer than any other royal officer before him to fully controlling the Hudson River. With both sides of this coveted artery, the Crown now obtained the most vital ferry in North America; another ripe target lay only twelve miles north, Benedict Arnold's West Point.

For every minor conquest achieved by the British, more opportunity to examine the realities of war presented themselves to Ewald. His Jägers often were the first to lay eyes on the surrounding countryside as Clinton's vanguard, and the captain's fascination with partisan warfare make his recollections especially insightful; nearby villages, most notably the former rebel post at Peekskill, were now all but abandoned. Surrounding him in the days that followed their victories were a motley collection of soldiers, none of whom could be identified as Englishmen. Along with his Jägers from Hesse-Cassel, Ewald noted that much of the fighting was accomplished by fellow Germans from Anspach as well as a multitude of Irish volunteers. Ewald would have been considered a hardened veteran of wilderness combat and his Jägers in their forest green had been on the continent almost continuously with him since 1776. In contrast, the Anspachers, who spoke his mother tongue in their royal blue jackets and tall black fur caps, had only been in America for days. Those representing the Emerald Isle were assembled from within existing provincial units by the Irish Lord Francis Rawdon-Hastings during the occupation of Philadelphia in 1777. These Irish volunteers had performed so well that they were named the 2nd American Regiment. Although the American Patriot politicians desired a clear enemy to vilify, King George's imperial forces were actually something of a patchwork army.[55]

Days later it seemed that Clinton's great venture to control the Hudson was succeeding. With both sides of the river under royal control, British forces were able to move about the countryside with relative impunity. The Patriot presence that was once so strong in the area was almost gone, and if combat did occur it was nearly always sporadic, unorganized, and inconsequential; given the circumstances the light infantry Jägers excelled. Two days prior the American rebels attempted to assault Stony Point and Verplanck's Point by sending a tiny two-gun vessel up the river to antagonize the forts, and it was repelled with ease.

Indeed for the average soldier these were the times of great uncertainty. Unlike winter quarters when one could take his mind completely off of fighting, the summer of 1779 was in the midst of a campaign season. The downtime between battles often left many feeling off-kilter, never completely at ease but rarely on edge; this was the time that Ewald relished. His Jägers would spend their nights on sentry duty, but their days would be exploring the countryside and gathering intelligence. He would meet with prominent Loyalist Americans to gather information regarding troop movements, supply lines, and possible future maneuvers. All the while, however, he was keeping mental notes of the dynamic factors of change that the war brought to this strange New World. In his home of Hesse-Cassel, war was a fact of life. It was one of the great hallmarks of Old World Europe that land was obtained at the highest of premiums, and with one's greatest enemy only across a weak border, fighting was an almost annual occurrence. In this regard Ewald noted there were very few individuals whose hearts and minds were undecided, and most partisans's loyalties went back generations.

America was a completely different world, and Ewald was fascinated by the developments that the revolution produced. On June

6, less than a week since the British assumed their new position, already the game seemed to be changing. While the captain was preparing his *chasseurs* for their nightly duties, word spread across the camp that a new stranger had requested sanctuary from the wild frontier. His clothes were tattered, his skin was bruised and blood-ied, and by best estimates he had walked over fifty treacherous miles in his wretched condition. Ewald sought him out immediately.

Ewald noted that the man was strong and well-built, yet his physical appearance clearly revealed that he had suffered an ordeal. He was a Loyalist ranger in the service of the king, and it seemed that Ewald's encampment was a welcomed respite. He explained that he had been captured in Pennsylvania's Susquehanna River val-ley, and held as a prisoner of war in Poughkeepsie, New York, by a band of Patriot rebels. He escaped days earlier and traveled by night to make his way south to friendly dispositions. Ewald penned that despite his terrible experience he could observe by his conduct that he was a resolute man.[56]

At the fireside, Ewald sat with this stranger and began to inquire into his life. Since the war began the American colonies had divid-ed themselves into contrasting ideological camps. Yet between the Patriots and Loyalists there sat a great number of individuals either undecided or uninterested. At the outset of hostilities this middle ground was quickly extinguished by the extremists on each side. If there was a known Loyalist village nearby, Patriot militia would raid and destroy the homes and farms and imprison those against their cause. Loyalist partisans retaliated in the same fashion. All neutral or undecided parties were considered enemies. The man sitting with Ewald was clearly a perpetrator of that style of thinking.

It was soon revealed that this mysterious Loyalist ranger was in the service of Lieutenant Colonel John Butler, and he had seen more than his fair share of action. Butler, a native of New York's war-torn Mohawk River valley, was for many the face of the Loyalist movement in the colonies. He led dozens of his "rangers" across the frontier, raiding Patriot homesteads and villages with extreme preju-dice. Fighting with Butler in the service of the Crown were the war-riors of the Seneca, Cayuga, Onondaga, and Mohawk nations, col-lectively known as the Iroquois Confederacy. The Iroquois had been longtime allies of the British Empire before the conflict, and follow-ing the defection of the Oneida and Tuscarora to the Patriot side they were almost fully aligned with the king. The unified forces of Butler's rangers and the Iroquois warriors saw some of the most brutal fighting of the entire war, and were considered a vital part of Britain's overall strategy for success in the colonies.

Ewald was familiar with the exploits of men like Butler and Joseph Brant, sachem of the Mohawk, and his guest claimed to have served alongside both. Ewald proceeded to inquire into his experiences, and as a testament to his deep interest made a nearly exact transcription of their conversation in the glow of the campfire that evening. He began by asking about Butler's overall strength; the man replied that he had fifty Loyalist Americans and upwards of five hundred Indian warriors on hand.

The tactician Ewald could not help but inquire as to how they supported such a large force of men in such difficult wilderness conditions. The ranger explained that in the beginning they lived entirely on the wild game hunted by the Indian warriors. As soon as they reached the borders of Pennsylvania and Maryland, though, they found provisions in abundance. It was clear to Ewald at that point that this man must have had a range of hundreds of miles during his guerilla campaign. But what of the ferocity of the Indians? The Jäger captain was a man of modern European military training, and the tales of the Indian fighting style was as ferocious as they were legendary.

The stranger explained that they rarely took prisoners, and every man, woman, or child was either cut down or carried off. He continued by claiming that the dwellings were plundered, devastated, and burned. He concluded his conversation by recalling that he and his Indian allies killed two entire regiments along the Susquehanna River with no thoughts of taking a single prisoner. To Ewald this was a great affront. The European tradition of war grew out of medieval chivalric values under which men who surrender were allowed the dignity to live to fight another day. The Indian tradition of war, however, was largely in place centuries earlier. It seemed that 1492 and its aftermath could do little to redirect it.

While the mixing of European and Indian cultures on the American frontier did contribute to a unique frontier style of warfare best expressed by the Loyalist rangers and their Indian allies, the core of the martial tradition was unchanged. It was those differences that offended Ewald's sensibilities. He asked his guest if he had ever scalped a man, to which the ranger laughed heartily and claimed to have mutilated so many bodies that he was often bloodied up to his elbows, and that when living among his native allies it was only a fact of life.

The ranger slowly revealed his own past. His father was born in England, and after coming to America was a gunsmith on the frontier amongst the Iroquois. As a child the man was raised alongside the children of the Haudenosaunee, and chose to defend their worldview against the terrible corruption that he viewed as the Patriot rebellion. Ewald listened intently and recorded their conversation as the man continued by explaining that Colonel Butler could do nothing to stop the harsh realities of Indian war, and that he had understood that it was a weapon best wielded in his name rather than against it. Ewald struggled with this justification, and begged one final question: Don't the Indians ever give quarter?

The ranger coldly replied that it never happened. He informed the Germans that if a man is spared on the battlefield it was only to save him for later tortures as a means to celebrate the victory. He continued by describing a gruesome scene involving a Major Adams in which the warriors stripped him naked, tied him to a tree, and flogged him for hours. The Hessians were appalled by the tale and cringed when the ranger continued that after the beating the warriors cut pieces of the American's flesh off his body and left him bound for three more days as a part of the terrible spectacle. Finally they killed him, a death in which the ranger said was entirely devoid of honor.

Before him sat the true nature of partisan warfare, the topic that Ewald pored over in his mind for so many restless nights. The ranger before him was as natural an American as any other describing the torture and death of his fellow countryman. Their divide was not nationality nor ethnicity, not skin color nor heritage; this man's death was attributed only to the divisive politics of the age. Ewald penned finally that the stranger's heart seemed to rejoice with this tale, and it grew darker during their conversation.[57]

After three grueling weeks of positioning along the Hudson, Ewald and his Germans were recalled south to New York. The captain noted that a change in strategy must have been afoot as the six-thousand-man force at King's Ferry was slowly dismantled and floated down river to their original base of operations. By June 28 the Jägers were on their way back to their encampment and they officially rejoined their comrades two days later.

Although seemingly counterproductive to his main goal of controlling the Hudson River valley, Clinton believed that removing the majority of his forces would serve to fulfill his ultimate ambition—drawing Washington out of his camp. It had always been the primary objective of Clinton's army to force the Patriots into a showdown on their own terms, and the general hoped that with a paltry 750 men left under the control of Lieutenant Colonel Henry Johnson, the rebels would be enticed out of their hiding. As time would tell, it certainly lured Washington's forces in, but not in the manner that the British had hoped.

The men that remained behind at Stony Point were a mixed assortment made up of members of the 17th Regiment of Foot, the Grenadiers of the 71st Regiment, and a company sized contingent of Loyalist Americans. Approximately fifteen pieces of artillery defended the high ground, and for good measure the two-gunned sloop *Vulture* patrolled the Hudson to defend against any possible amphibious rebel assaults. With the vast majority of his men in and around New York, Clinton hoped that if Washington's army would reveal itself he could easily squash them and, perhaps more important, redirect his attention to a necessarily weakened Continental camp at Middlebrook. It was a gamble to say the least, and little did Clinton know that General Washington was well aware of these developments.

Stony Point presented a particularly cumbersome dilemma for the Patriots. The Hudson River had always been a key place of contention early in the war, and by controlling both banks of the waterway the British could potentially expand their advantage. Also, Washington dreaded the thought that the enemy was a mere twelve miles from West Point. Sacking and disrupting the domination of the King's Ferry would be essential for Patriot success, and given the steep rocky slopes of Stony Point a conventional assault would simply not be possible.

Washington used an advantageous peak nearby called Buckberg Mountain to calculate the strength of Clinton's remaining men. He saw that their numbers were small, and although the fortifications at Stony Point and Verplanck's Point were merely wooden abatis complemented by cannon positions, a frontal assault in broad daylight would likely be catastrophic. Like his most famous victories from months before, Washington would need to bend the rules to achieve victory against the world's mightiest armed force. He would need a commander of great virtue, with unquestioning adherence to orders from superior officers, and he found him in Anthony Wayne, a Pennsylvania brigadier general. Wayne was uneasy with Washington's plan of attack, but his commitment to execution was his reason for leading the upcoming charge.

The primary weapon the rebels wielded against their British foes on July 16 was the element of surprise. Knowing the strength of Stony Point, Wayne followed Washington's instructions to the letter by leading the charge in the dead of the night. With Stony Point surrounded by water on three sides, the Patriots would need to focus their attack on the landed side of the peninsula, and wade their way through a mucky swamp as stealthily as possible. The swamp was described as passable in theory, but the water was reportedly chest deep. The forward columns of the rebel attack, ominously dubbed "Forlorn Hope," would lead the charge with white pieces of paper attached to them so as to distinguish them from the enemy in the midnight pitch.

The Battle of Stony Point was a benchmark in the now growing Patriot lore. Wayne led his men against seemingly impossible odds, and earned the moniker "Mad" Anthony Wayne. The fortification at Stony Point fell, and the conquering general wrote to Washington, "The fort and garrison, with Col. Johnson, are ours. The men behaved like men determined to be free."[58] At Washington's wishes, with Stony Point under rebel control, Wayne turned his attention across the river to Verplanck's Point. The Patriot command hoped to capture each side of the King's Ferry, and after a booming cannonade the opposite position remained. The shelling was not entirely ineffective though, as it did manage to chase the sloop *Vulture* back to its nest in New York. All told the Americans suffered less than one hundred casualties, and the British saw nearly 550 men taken prisoner. Captain Ewald, who was now some thirty miles south at Long Island, wrote of the strange commotion at his former posts, and he guessed that the assault had taken place.[59]

Although it had been a rousing success that still rings in the annals of the American Revolution, the Patriot victory at Stony Point has produced debatable consequences. Washington's men claimed the position as their own, but after failing to capture Verplanck's Point they simply stripped the site of ammunition and supplies and abandoned their conquest. By June 18, two days after the midnight attack, Clinton dispatched members of the 42nd, 63rd, and 64th Regiments to reclaim the position without a shot being fired.

From his home on Long Island, Johann Ewald could only watch as a bystander while the American Revolution evolved around him. Since the capture of Stony Point weeks earlier, there had been a decided lack of enthusiasm amongst his Jägers. Washington's army was posted at West Point, and aside from the occasional harassment by rebel guerillas, the primary fighting of the war had slowly relocated to the American South. It was now early fall, and aside from his normal tepid duties Ewald and his men could only wait intently as news from the multiple fronted war poured in to New York. In October Clinton's army received word that a joint Franco-American attack had been repulsed at Savannah, Georgia; in reality the British had fended off a month-long siege that would have been disastrous to their southern strategy. By moving operations into the agricultural and sparsely populated colonies of the South, British administrators hoped to turn the tide of the war by enlisting the help of its seemingly abundant Loyalist population. The entire campaign, however, hinged on capturing and controlling the critical port cities of Charleston and Savannah. Led by the French Admiral Comte d'Estaing and the Patriot General Benjamin Lincoln, the siege fended off a calculated counterattack that ultimately cost the French and Patriots over 950 casualties. The victory was a hopeful indicator for success, and from New York Sir Henry Clinton wrote, "I think that this is the greatest event that has happened the whole war." In London the streets rang with celebratory cannon fire with news of the victory.[60]

It seemed from Ewald's perspective that this northeastern rebellion was going to alter his destiny as well. For almost four years he had spent his North American career in the cities of New York and Philadelphia, chasing the wily Continentals in a frustrating and emotionally draining cat-and-mouse game; in his mind this change in strategy was only a sign of poor leadership abroad. Rebellions such as this one needed to be stamped out swiftly, and the longer and more expensive the conflict became the worse it was for the dominant party. If the British Empire was willing to reallocate forces southward en masse after four years of hard fighting in the north, in Ewald's mind it meant that the rebellion which he was assigned to stop was slipping through their fingers.

Ewald remained alert to any opportunity to add to his experiences in the New World, and a chance encounter on a chilly October night gave him a valuable perspective on the American conflict. That evening Ewald sat and talked with a deserting soldier he identified as Diwizow. Unlike himself, this well-traveled adventurer embodied the mercenary cause of the eighteenth century. As was often the case, Ewald was aware that Patriot politicians had

labeled his Hessian comrades as "mercenaries," or soldiers of fortune. For this reason many Americans despised the German auxilar-
ies that fought alongside him. It was no secret that the Hessians had
no real practical issue with the American rebels, and Ewald was only
serving the British king under the wishes of his own Landgraf
Frederick II. A mercenary, in contrast, fought for his own material
gain and epitomized opportunistic soldiering in this period.

Yet Diwizow was quite different as he was not German, Irish, or
British. He asserted that he was a Cossack from the Don River valley in southern Russia. Ewald's interest was piqued at this development. Diwizow explained that he was already well into his fifties,
and the thought of retirement was simply not tenable. He had battled in one way or another for his entire life and as war was his primary income he was looking for a fight. At Ewald's inquiry, the
Cossack explained how his travels brought him to America. He had
spent twenty-four years as an officer with the Don Cossacks, and
had battled the Prussians in the Seven Years' War. Ewald first saw
action in that same conflict and his curiosity grew. Diwizow continued by claiming that his mercenary travels took him far and wide,
from the jagged lands of Ottoman Turkey to the rich valleys of
Poland. He fought for no flag and no country, merely for raw economic gain. Twenty years earlier Diwizow battled against the
Polish, and as recently as 1774 alongside Yemelyan Pugachev, the
royal pretender who led a massive revolt in Russia against Catherine
the Great. If there was ever a mercenary in North America, it was
this hardened Cossack.

The man and Ewald spoke throughout the night ranging from
topics including combat styles to future plans. Diwizow stated that
before his arrival in the New World, he had once run a postal station in Astrakhan on the Volga River near the Caspian Sea. After his
station closed, he heard talk about the American war during a stint
in the sprawling St. Petersburg. He soon traveled to Germany and
enlisted in the army of Duke Karl I of Brunswick-Wolfenbüttel, and
although he was denied a commission as an officer, he was so desperate for funds that he accepted a noncommissioned post in the
Jäger Corps.

At the Battle of Saratoga two years earlier, Diwizow claimed that
he was taken captive by the Patriots, and having no true allegiance
other than to his own purse he joined the rebel army. While it seems
unusual, German defections had actually had begun to take their
toll. Earlier in the war, American policy makers attempted to entice

disinterested German soldiers to defect by offering them a guarantee of fifty acres of American land if they abandoned their comrades. Despite his Asiatic background, Diwizow would have certainly qualified for this endowment, but his general distaste for North America prompted him to desert the Americans and seek out Clinton's base at New York to rejoin the cause of King George. From Ewald's experience a man was only as good as his allegiance to his country, and though this soldier fought for very different reasons he still considered him a man of honor. This man, he wrote, was as close to a true adventurer as he had ever had the privilege of meeting.[61]

With chance engagements and interesting conversations becoming the norm, Ewald prepared for the close of a fourth campaign season with no major victory to speak of; the unsatisfying year 1779 was set to close. The encampment which had been the empire's primary base of operations was now stirring, and orders had trickled down from the high command that a massive invasion of the American South was set for the next year. It appeared that whatever gains had been tallied over the last seven months were effectively being left behind; Ewald and his Jägers would be sailing down the coast in only a matter of weeks. General Clinton had ordered King's Ferry, which had been captured and recaptured from the rebels, to be abandoned; thus the battle for the Hudson River was lost. The British command had been bested by an insurrectionist force in conditions that should have easily favored the redcoats. In Ewald's mind the entire season had been a series of costly mistakes, and after a four-year rebellion the balance was now due. From his vantage point on Long Island looking out over the cold gray North Atlantic the captain quietly vented his frustrations. He believed that the events of the previous months were nothing short of disastrous, and after a year of hard campaigning he felt that the blame rested fully with the incompetency of his commanding officers. From his perspective the British army was no better off than it was a year earlier, and there were no signs of improvement.[62]

## South Carolina

*February–May 1780*

On February 11, 1780, the shores of Simmons Island were rife with activity. For nearly a month and a half the men who now rustled across the marshy landscape had been at sea preparing for a landing into an unusual new country, including Johann Ewald and his troops.

The reason that his and no other German chasseurs were in South Carolina was due to his great valor already displayed in the service of the king, and a little help from an old friend. At the request of Charles Cornwallis, and with the approval of General Clinton himself, Ewald's contingent of light infantry was chosen exclusively and specifically for a full-scale assault on the city of Charleston. This was not the first time that Ewald had been recognized by Cornwallis, but it certainly was the most significant. He greatly admired the British commander for both his martial skills and his generosity, and with the sun setting and the rhythms of the waves at his back he was prepared to do whatever necessary to achieve victory. As his Jägers set up camp on this unfamiliar terrain, he recalled an event in 1777 in which Cornwallis visited his men personally. Seeing the poor condition of their clothes and lack of supplies, the distinguished gentlemen promised to restock the Jägers out of his own pocket. For this, and the sterling letter of commendation written to him three years earlier, Ewald was forever in his debt.[63]

Their current position was approximately thirty miles south of the rich target that was the Patriot stronghold of Charleston, a city that would not be easy to take over. Charleston sat as a peninsula, surrounded by water on three sides like a great fortress of mother nature. Though the Americans under the command of General Benjamin Lincoln had held the position since the start of the conflict, both Clinton and Cornwallis recognized that the city's defensive fortifications were crumbling and that a well-placed army could choke the South's most populous city into submission. The siege itself would be textbook; however, reaching the peninsula had all the potential of being a disaster. Known collectively as the Sea Islands, the coast of South Carolina was shredded and split by a myriad of rivers, streams, inlets, and channels. From their landing point at Simmons Island Clinton's army would need to traverse this difficult and foreign terrain.

For this, and the siege to come, Clinton would certainly need an impressive force; he spared no expense. Following the decision to venture southward, Clinton amassed an impressive force of over 8,500 men (including one Jäger company) and left his remaining fifteen thousand men under the command of the Hessian General Wilhelm von Knyphausen in New York. Those select few sailed through the terrible conditions of the North Atlantic in winter, and battled large pieces of floating ice and debris and cold weather along the entire way. So treacherous was the passage that it was not uncommon for ships to be damaged and men to be harmed. In many cases the conditions were so harsh that most of the army's horses were injured in the chaos and had to be put down before ever reaching their destination.[64]

With the hardship of seafaring behind him, Ewald ordered his men to begin preparations for moving northward to their target. The foliage was thick, Ewald wrote, and much of their time was spent hacking and slicing their way through the desolate swamp until finding their first actual road. Although the situation was difficult, Ewald understood the strategic value of their position. The captain wrote that there was no enemy to be seen for miles around, for even he could not foresee any other force even attempting to land in such a remote and desolate area.[65]

The American South was a very different experience for the Germans than the bleak country that they had known in the Northeast for the previous four years. Its open spaces were vast, and the slave plantations had really only existed in their minds before they touched the sandy shores of South Carolina—where approximately half of all residents were in a state of bondage. Even the trees seemed like something out of an imaginary tale, the Spanish moss hanging gloomily all around. Although common throughout the South, it was like nothing the Germans had ever seen before.[66]

Despite all the challenges that this new colony posed, for Britain to reconquer it would be a turning point in the war. The American South had turned into a great "what if" for policy makers in London, and as news of Washington's escapes filled their chambers from 1776 to 1778 its prospects only became more enticing. It was largely believed among the hawkish members of Parliament that the southern colonies were filled with Loyalist Americans. That belief, combined with the development of strong popular sentiment against expanding the war, pushed those in power to pursue a southern policy in search a great victory to reinvigorate their cause.

To regain the South and hopefully ignite a wave of Loyalism that could sweep northward would require the capture and capitulation of two major port cities. The first, Savannah, Georgia, had fallen in December 1778. Georgia was a logical starting point for this new invasion as it was the least populous southern entity, and save for the still-developing Augusta, controlling Savannah would effectively subdue the entire colony. The city fell with relative ease and as predicted the rest of Georgia soon fell in line. Those who had remained loyal to the empire emerged from the shadows, and those who had supported the Patriot cause quickly suppressed their rebellious inclinations. The royal governor was reinstated soon after, and it seemed that this new "southern strategy" was the great change that the hawks in London hoped it would be. Aside from the ideological benefits of such a conquest, the jagged coastline of the South with its penetrating waterways allowed the mighty British navy to support the war effectively for the first time with reinforcements and artillery bombardment.

Despite the obvious good will that the victory at Savannah won the British at home, all parties recognized that the road to true success unquestionably ran through Charleston. At the dawn of the revolution South Carolina stood out as a massive producer; some estimates place its output totaling 29 percent of the empire's entire revenue stream. Along with fellow agricultural giants like Virginia and Maryland it could represent half of Great Britain's global wealth. For this reason the city of Charleston was recognized as the single richest city in British North America, and to capture it would vindicate the invasion's advocates in Parliament.[67]

For Ewald and his Jägers it was one thing to discuss an invasion of the South, but it was another to cut through the tangled mess of marshes and swamps of South Carolina. The British had a clear plan to attack the troublesome Patriot officer Benjamin Lincoln at Charleston, but in the days after their great landing thirty miles down the coast they found that South Carolina herself was equally unforgiving. The coast of the colony was sliced into tiny islands by a number of rivers; most notable among them was the Stono River. In order to reach the landed side of Charleston, Clinton would need to move his twelve thousand men in a northeasterly direction through the long stretches of swamp as well as across the Stono. In the process they would move from Simmons Island to the much larger Johns Island and ultimately touch James Island. From there he would turn his entire army opposite northwest to cross the Ashley River and position themselves across the neck of the Charleston peninsula. Armies moved at a tedious pace by their very nature and battling the twisting vegetation would only add to the misery.

Without question, Ewald's Jägers would be at the vanguard of this force. It was a unique position for the captain, as he and his company were specifically requested by British high command to be the tip of this royal spear. If any group could manage it was thought to be his. One of the great advantages that the German light infantry possessed was their ability to move much more quietly than a company of regulars. They had far less equipment and could maneuver through difficult positions with relative ease. As the first boots on the ground for much of this campaign, Ewald was quick to note that things had been eerily silent for his Jägers. For the two days after their initial landing there was not a rebel to be found, and in Ewald's experience that likely meant that an encounter was soon to occur. Minute by minute, and hour by hour, the hanging Spanish moss of South Carolina and silence of the forests had lulled his men into carelessness. With every footstep being a careful one, on February 13 Ewald's spell was snapped as he witnessed Patriot cavalry in the distance along the banks of the Stono. He did not know how many men were on hand, but he did recognize two critical facts: he was outgunned and unseen. The Jägers very soon realized how precarious their situation had become, and Ewald sternly ordered his men to move with the utmost care.[68]

These were the first American rebels that Clinton's twelve-thousand-man army had encountered in South Carolina, and understanding their strength was essential to calculating a plan to neutralize them. With the thought of potential promotion and reward in mind, Ewald took it upon himself to gather intelligence. To risk scouting out the enemy position in clandestine fashion carried a high probability of being noticed and potentially engaged. A clever ruse seemed like the only means to reconnoiter the location safely. It was true that the Patriots had not seen him yet, but they soon would and he insured that it would be on his terms.

Ewald approached the Americans openly by calling to them and waving a white handkerchief in the air. He hoped that these soldiers would understand his call for truce, and honor the traditions of European customs. It was a risky venture, but in the months to come bending and breaking conventional norms would become the hallmark of the American guerilla war effort in the South. Ewald was granted immunity and as a friendly gesture the rebels removed their hats to converse with him. The Jäger captain's plan was a simple one; he would present himself in search of an old friend that could be serving in the enemy camp. All the while, he was counting heads and memorizing troop arrangements and strength.

The uniforms of the men he encountered were undeniably familiar to him—they were the men of Pulaski's Legion. The legion was formed in the year 1778 by the Polish freedom fighter Casimir Pulaski, whose story was unique in the entire revolutionary period. Pulaski had earned his fame in Europe by fighting the forces of tsarist Russia as one of the leading officers for the Bar Confederation in the Polish-Lithuanian Commonwealth. When the rebellion began to crumble, the young officer sought asylum in France. While he was absent from his homeland, political opponents found him guilty of regicide, stripped him of "all dignity and honors," and sentenced him to death if he ever returned. Always seeking a cause, Pulaski next ventured to the Ottoman Empire to replicate his uprising in the Russo-Turkish War, but the resistance collapsed before his attempts could take hold. For Pulaski, the transition from famous to infamous was a difficult one, and he was content to live out his exile in Paris. He desperately sought a fight, but no European army was interested in such a known agitator. While in the City of Lights, however, the Pole had a momentous encounter with a kindred spirit named Benjamin Franklin; the two men discussed the emerging rebellion in America and Pulaski was recruited to the cause.

Casimir Pulaski was a world-renowned cavalry commander, and his impact on the Continental Army could only be described as transformative. He believed in the spirit of the American rebellion and detested royal authority even more. In 1778 he petitioned General Washington for the creation of an independent corps of foreign volunteers, and Pulaski's Legion was born. Pulaski himself was killed in 1779 during the abortive attempt to recapture Savannah, but Ewald and his Germans had long awaited the chance to finally meet this treacherous legion. From the German perspective there was a deep disdain for any continental European who would join in a rebellion like Washington's. While neither Ewald nor his Jägers had any real allegiance to King George, they did believe in a well-defined social hierarchy. In truth many of the Germans utterly detested the English way of life, but a rebellion such as this one was a direct affront to their own worldview. Ewald, like many of his countrymen, believed that if there was no forceful leader in a nation, the rule of law and security of its people would be in jeopardy. Simply put, for the Germans to support the American rebellion would be to support anarchy.

Still operating under the pretense that he was seeking out a man named "Leopold" with whom he had served in Saxony, Ewald felt confident that this particular rebel force was an outlier, and no meaningful threat to the advancement of Clinton's army. Before returning to camp, the rebels warned him to be mindful of the alligators and joked that some were twelve to sixteen feet in length.

The following day Ewald rushed the information that he had gathered up the chain of command to General Clinton and by his own boasting claimed that he was handsomely rewarded.[69]

Two weeks later Clinton's twelve-thousand-man army was progressing through the brush at a measured pace; the force crossed the Stono toward James Island, and by February 25 Cornwallis himself ferried the tidal river. The British stripped the coast of South Carolina as they crawled toward Charleston, collecting supplies and slaves along the way, and with each passing day the vitality of this new campaign seemed to grow. As a result, a pattern began to emerge with each new mile that they covered. Clinton's men encountered plantations abandoned by their owners in the path of the oncoming army, and the remaining slaves sought out the British on a daily basis. Some were seeking refuge, others support, and for the price of small bits of intelligence it was likely to be theirs.

At the vanguard of the army though sat Ewald, and his experience was much more harrowing than his allies several miles behind him. The front of this massive army saw regular skirmishes as it pressed its way toward Charleston Harbor, and the enemy was none other than the men of Pulaski's Legion with whom Ewald had conversed days earlier. In this single campaign in the wilds of the New World two forces comprised of Old World Europeans did battle, reminding all parties involved as to the interconnectedness of the imperial powers around them. The Legionnaires harassed the Germans at random intervals in an attempt to slow Clinton's progress, and before long the exchanges became common occurrences. To some, the Jägers and Legionnaires were fighting their own small war at the head of the British column, yet most of the redcoats involved in the campaign would describe it as a bore with the greatest danger coming from mosquitoes, not rebels.

For Ewald the constant harassment by Pulaski's soldiers gave him the chance to gather intelligence on his enemy by learning his tactics and predicting his tendencies. In the days that followed the Jäger captain learned that Chevalier Pierre-François Vernier had taken command of the unit following the death of Pulaski a year earlier; the thought of the Frenchman directing assaults against his men enraged him. Vernier, however, was an experienced soldier and both he and Ewald amassed distinguished European histories years earlier. Vernier was born in Belfort, France, and began his military service in 1752. In the Seven Years' War he saw action at St. Cast in 1758 and at Vildungen, Germany, in 1760 until finally in America he served as a major in Pulaski's Legion. During his stint in North America Ewald faced many challenges, but for the remainder of their journey toward Charleston it seemed that this French expatriate would serve as his primary nemesis.

Ewald carried an intense distaste for Vernier, but an unmistakable curiosity about his legendary former commander. The events of February 26 highlight this cat-and-mouse game with great detail, as well as the legion's tactics. That afternoon a British detachment strayed away from the mass of the army on a foraging mission, all the while trailed by Vernier and his men. As the men collected their spoils, the rebels sprang out from all sides and began to open fire. The British detachment was caught off guard. Ewald next described how his Jägers rushed to the aid of their vulnerable comrades, and wrote that upon their appearance the enemy turned and ran. He estimated that without their swift arrival it was likely that the entire party would have been killed in the wilderness.[70]

Ewald was now well versed in the guerilla, hit-and-run style of his enemy, but he never stopped believing that his classical training would reign supreme over the deceitful tactics of the rebels. Their problem was in the execution, not the strategic principles themselves. It seemed that Vernier had no qualms about attacking the advancing British when they least expected it, and the captain burned at the thought of such dishonorable tactics.[71]

The attack on Charleston required an intimate knowledge of the terrain, and maneuvering across the myriad waterways would be critical to surrounding the city. The city of Charleston sat on the edge of a peninsula carved out by the Ashley River to the west and the Cooper River to the east. As the two rivers merged they formed Charleston Harbor, a direct opening to the vast Atlantic Ocean. The conventional wisdom of the age stated that any attack on the city would come from the sea; therefore, the mouth of the bay was guarded by two forts. Fort Johnson sat on James Island, and Fort Moultrie was on the opposite side of the bay. For Clinton to execute a land-borne siege he would need to disable Fort Johnson for certain, and some well-placed fleets of ships could likely handle its twin. Yet, as important as these outposts were to protecting the city, Ewald and his Jägers were shocked at their dilapidated condition and lack of manpower when the British eventually took them over in late February.

From Fort Johnson on the southern edge of Charleston Harbor, Ewald scouted out both Fort Moultrie and the city itself. In his opinion both of the forts appeared to be quite sturdy in their design but utterly decaying in their present form, and their primary target was not much better off. Charleston was a city of roughly ten to twelve thousand people, and they were as diverse as colonial America itself. The population of Charleston was English by an overwhelming majority, and as much as they clung to their leisurely aristocratic traditions even the conservative crown jewel of the South was pushing the boundaries of cosmopolitanism. Along with its English base the city had small yet growing numbers of Spaniards, African slaves, French, and even the occasional German. Ewald concluded that most of the wooden buildings were home to the commoner, and the wealthy plantation-owning class tended to reside in the large stone mansions along the rivers.[72]

Ewald's men remained in the vicinity of the captured Fort Johnson for the first three weeks of March, and although progress toward the city was slow it persisted at a constant pace. On the 18th the encampment was surprised by a deserter from Pulaski's Legion, a Prussian who strode confidently among the soldiers seemingly devoid of enthusiasm for his volunteer effort. Ewald described him as a reasonable fellow dressed in a Polish uniform who clearly had come from the European tradition of horsemanship. There was no doubt this newcomer was of traditional European stock, and as he seemed to be anxious to divulge information Captain Ewald gave him an audience. The Prussian informed him that they could expect a cavalry attack on their current position in the coming days, yet curiously enough it was not this vital intelligence that Ewald transcribed. Instead, the captain inquired into the character of the late Count Pulaski, and his Prussian guest obliged saying that he feared nothing in the world and was cut from the cloth of the great nobility of an age gone by.

Although the remnants of Pulaski's Legion had been firing on his men for several weeks by then, Ewald's thirst for knowledge of this recognizable figure makes this exchange one of the more intriguing encounters of the entire Charleston campaign. He certainly admired the legendary rebel and his place in military history, yet Pulaski's affront to the order of the world offended him on a personal level. Ewald wrote that the eulogy was a fine one and certainly the type of homage that all officers hoped to receive from their subordinates; yet he had no respect for a man who would participate in such a dishonorable revolt.[73]

After the troops spent more than a month moving through the Sea Islands of South Carolina, scenes like this were growing more common by the day. Days later Ewald recorded an instance where an American rebel fired upon his Jäger company despite being hopelessly outnumbered. After gunning the Patriot down, Ewald questioned the wounded man as to why he would attempt such a foolish act. Wincing and fading in and out of consciousness, the soldier, who identified himself as van Waik from Boston, replied that General Washington personally promised him an officer's commission if he could collect intelligence regarding Clinton's forces. He next requested to speak with Ewald's surgeon to determine if his wound would be fatal. The answer was yes. Upon receiving this news the young partisan claimed that he would gladly die for his country and for its just cause.

After hearing these words Ewald handed him a glass of wine and wrote that the soldier drank it down with relish and died an honorable death. This instance troubled Ewald, and for the next several days his skirmishes with the rebels took on a more somber tone. In his writing these engagements were never celebratory, but he was disdainful when describing his enemies. In the days that followed, however, his disregard for the Americans seemed to melt away.[74]

In the final days of March the last major hurdle between Clinton's army and the city of Charleston was cleared. The Ashley River, which created the western shore of the peninsula, was beginning to be crossed by the British. While it was secured as early as March 26, it was not uncommon for a river crossing by an army as large as Clinton's to take days, and those who passed first had specific duties to complete while their comrades caught up. The Jägers were one of the first companies to pass over the Ashley, and in typical fashion Ewald took it upon himself to secure the area and locate the enemy before the entire British force was caught in a maelstrom of musket fire. He singled out a large plantation just north of the city, its owners having remained inside. Unlike most plantation owners at the time, these Americans stayed behind and Ewald understood that they were likely to be armed; he ordered a volley of shots fired into the mansion's windows to present his terms of surrender.

The door slowly opened and the owner came out with his sobbing wife clutching his arm. Elias Horry was in his early seventies and was a well-known member of the planter class in South Carolina. He had three children, all grown, who were each deeply involved in the Patriot cause. One son was in Philadelphia at the time as an aide to the Continental Congress, the other was current-

ly serving under General Lincoln only miles away from their present position. Though Ewald had no idea who this man was, or how
greatly he was aligned with the rebels, he began his interrogation
without pause. Horry slowly revealed that the army in Charleston
was well supplied by the French, and with forty-two guns placed all
around the harbor, a siege would be impossible. Again though,
rather than recording this valuable intelligence in his journals,
Ewald pressed him with questions of a different nature, on why he
would allow his son to join the side of the rebels but not defend his
own kind; Horry replied that his family was never political in
nature, and neither the king nor the Continental Congress ever
reached out to him in any way. Earlier that summer, he continued,
General Prevost arrived and plundered every estate that he could
find with no regard for friend or foe; after the British left his son
hurried to the American army to avenge his father's losses. While he
did not know it at the time, the captain was hearing about a dramatic turn in the southern colonies that had occurred en masse.

Ewald's response to this revelation was merely to shrug his shoulders. He continued by saying that, despite the sad story, he was prepared to take Horry to General Cornwallis personally, but the clearly distraught, crying man was not worth his efforts.[75] Although
seemingly inconsequential in the mind of the Jäger, this story more
than any other strikes to the heart of the American Revolution in
the southern colonies. The South was always thought to have been
the great secret in the back pocket of Parliament's war hawks to
ending the rebellion. They believed that the abundance of Loyalists
would rush to their aid and Washington's army would be isolated
and squeezed into submission. King George, ever boastful, was even
rumored to have claimed that he believed that the North
Carolinians were his most faithful subjects in his entire empire.

Yet, despite these supposed advantages, British forces received no
heroic welcome, and saw no mass volunteerism to their cause. In
fact, the southern colonies soon crumbled into a mess of random
partisan bands that would torture Clinton and Cornwallis incessant-
ly. Many historians believe that policy makers were foolish to
believe that such strong Loyalist support ever existed in the South,
but in reality there was a natural tendency to favor the shared conservative traditional English values that the redcoats represented.
This would be an opportunity wasted by the empire, however, as
Elias Horry's testimony confirms, British soldiers stripped and
spoiled their way through the South. The old adage of history that

has stood for many years was that ideologically Americans were divided into thirds: Patriot, Loyalist, and undecided. A more accurate measure (if one can ever exist) would be that 25 percent of Americans were deeply partisan on each side, and the remaining half quite simply supported whichever army happened to be marching through their front yards, and ultimately, held them in the highest regard. In other words the British army's ill treatment left many southerners feeling that they little choice but to fight them, if only to defend their personal property and honor.

None of this mattered to Ewald. He knew that preparations were necessary before Cornwallis and Clinton crossed over the Ashley to begin their siege. By day's end Charleston was now well within sight, and there was much work to be done before it was fully at their mercy.

By late April, General Henry Clinton and his twelve thousand troops had reaped the benefits of their long and difficult march through the coast of South Carolina. Before him, sitting like a small outlet surrounded by the ocean on either side, sat the city of Charleston. Since April 8 the British army had besieged the city, and it was clear by the end of the month that the Americans trapped within stood little chance of breaking free of Clinton's grasp. Across the landed side of the central peninsula on which Charleston rested the British had constructed a powerful siege line. At the beginning of the month the Americans had constructed their own defensive line in anticipation of a British attack consisting primarily of a canal that stretched the length of the neck of the landmass capped on either side by very weak redoubts. At the center arrangement was a structure known as the citadel, or "old royal work," that was made of tappy, a local product of consisting of shells, lime, sand, and water.

When Clinton first approached this almost laughably feeble earthwork in late March, he assigned his best siege master, Major James Moncrieff, to begin preparations to move toward and eventually break through the American line. Moncrieff, a Scottish Highlander who served in America during the Seven Years' War, was most recently responsible for the defenses of Savannah. Given his past achievements, creating a strategy to capture the poorly defended Charleston would be considerably easier. At the outset of the siege the two lines were separated by approximately eight hundred yards; to close the distance would not require any genius strokes but merely an application of clearly defined European siege warfare. As with their initial approach to Charleston, slow and steady would win this race.

Moncrieff began by digging a large trench known as the first parallel that crossed the width of the central peninsula and that would be far enough away from the enemy line that few artillery shells could disrupt his progress. This was easily completed by April 1, yet it was only a small step in a much larger process. When the first parallel was fully dug out, Moncrieff ordered his men, including an assortment of local slaves, to then dig perpendicularly toward the American position; on April 13 a second parallel was dug that cut the initial distance between the two lines in half. Progress would then continue in a similar fashion until the third parallel placed British forces directly against the American canal that only weeks earlier was their primary defensive position. Moncrieff was applauded with great vigor among the British high command, yet others had their doubts. Having had two weeks to watch this massive trench network carve its way through the peninsula, Ewald noted that it was an impressive feat, but weak when compared to others he had seen.[76]

Whether or not Ewald's low opinion of the British engineer's abilities was warranted, he would not have been the first individual to be critical of Britain's history of siege warfare. The siege was an ancient practice designed to conquer well-fortified cities by isolating them from support and choking them into submission. It had been practiced seemingly as long as cities had walls and by the eighteenth century there was a clear methodology to apply. In Ewald's time it seemed that every nation in Europe had its own specialized ability; for the British it was their navy, the Prussians their cavalry, and the siege was the exclusive property of the French. In the Seven Years' War, the French had executed a number of masterful sieges around the globe. While Major Moncrieff was accomplishing his task, he hardly met the standard of the day. Some Old World sieges lasted for months, even years, but given its wretched condition Charleston would likely fall in weeks.

If one were to have viewed the siege of Charleston from the air, it would have seemed like the British were crawling their way toward a stationary and hopeless Charleston. A siege is one of the most effective and foolproof ventures that an army could undertake, and unlike most battles, victory was not achieved with the musket and bayonet; the hallmark of the siege was the chorus of clanking shovels, picks, axes, and spades. A siege could certainly fail, there are numerous examples of that throughout history, but so long as the offensive force has certain resources the success rate was nearly 100 percent. Those commodities were precious, but undeniable: time and money. If the approaching army has a sturdy position and remains well supplied, a besieged city could do very little to save itself.

In Charleston it seemed Clinton had all the time in the world. Developments since the siege began gave Clinton very high hopes for success, yet like any besieged city Charleston could only fall if it was totally and completely isolated from the outside world. On April 8 the British fleet entered Charleston Harbor, cutting off any hope of an escape at sea, but blockading the Atlantic was not enough. Since the siege began, the British had failed to secure the eastern coast of the peninsula created by the Cooper River; for that reason the American rebels were able to receive information and supplies from the north. With the siege lines completed, General Clinton sent Brigadier General Banastre Tarleton, one of his most trusted subordinates, northward to disable this line of communication. On April 14 at the Battle of Monck's Corner Tarleton did just that and gave Clinton's army full control of the Cooper. From this point onward the city of Charleston was completely on its own.

With the lines pressed nearly against one another in the final days of May, one of the major obstacles that separated the two armies was the hastily constructed American canal that was filled with sea water. Holding the canal in place and keeping it filled was a dam, and if the dam gave way the canal would be instantly emptied and easily passable. To break down this construction would require a small party of men to charge the position under heavy fire and attempt to dislodge it while still returning shot of their own. It was by all accounts an undesirable assignment that bordered on suicidal, and without hesitation it was Ewald's Jägers that received the assignment. On May 5, Ewald entered a harrowing description of his efforts to burst through the clogged artery while fending off the myriad rebel sharpshooters who plagued his men's progress.[77]

A day later the dam was pierced through and the drainage process begun. It seemed now that the end was near for the Americans, and General Benjamin Lincoln requested that he be able to surrender with honors, and that his army be able to leave on their own terms and conditions. Clinton scoffed at this idea as the rebel city was essentially hopeless, and he confidently turned down the offer. Unconditional surrender was the only escape for the city of Charleston. With the canal drained, the British army began to pour fire and lead into the city. Though time worked against the South Carolinians, Clinton wanted to expedite the process by blasting them into compliance. The watchful Ewald questioned why they were wasting ammunition when the conflict seemed it would end naturally, to which the siege engineer Moncrieff responded that the cannon fire was only meant to frighten the Americans. Ewald accepted this answer, but would later write a scathing critique that while he respected the man for his candor, he would be nothing more than an errand boy for the great German generals of Europe.[78]

Criticisms aside, on May 12, 1780, the white flag finally flew over a burning and beaten Charleston. After more than a month there was no more food, there were no more supplies, and the Continental Army had been pushed to the breaking point. With dreams of battlefield glory shattered by defeat General Benjamin Lincoln saw no escape for his men or the city that he commanded. Upon his surrender that day the British Empire had achieved its greatest victory of the entire war, and nearly broke the ideological back of the American Revolution.

The fall of Charleston was a disaster of epic proportions for the Continental Army. Although casualty rates were relatively low for a month-long siege, eighty-nine dead and one hundred and thirty eight wounded, it was the count of the survivors that rocked the Continental Army to its core. Over five thousand soldiers were taken prisoner by Clinton's army, along with nearly three hundred fifty pieces of artillery, six thousand muskets, and thirty thousand rounds of ammunition. The blow that it delivered nearly wiped out the entirety of the Continental Army in the South, and in London many spectators believed that the victory at Charleston would likely bury any ill will regarding the defeat at Saratoga; it was momentous occasion.[79]

Although the combat operation was over, the horror of war had not revealed itself fully. Three days after the prisoners had been taken and the city had been securely occupied, a loaded musket was casually thrown into a small outbuilding where the confiscated Patriot powder was stored. The resulting explosion was horrifying in its destruction. Six homes were reduced to ashes, and two hundred people lost their lives. Among the dead were Americans, redcoats, and Germans; catastrophe killed indiscriminately. Ewald, who narrowly missed the explosion, wrote that the scene was the most terrible he had ever witnessed. He saw limbs spread across the camp and burned victims writhing in pain; the field after a battle was a terrible sight, but the aftermath of the explosion so unnatural that it was horrifying beyond belief.[80] In the end the random blast killed twice as many people in Charleston as the siege itself.

Upon securing the greatest victory of the entire war, Sir Henry Clinton confidently left the southern theater in the hands of Charles Cornwallis. The men had famously been at odds for most of the Charleston campaign, but Clinton trusted the judgment of his subordinate. Sensing that his work was done, and more pressingly that the French navy might attack in his absence, Clinton announced to his men that he would be returning to New York to rejoin his army. Along with four thousand troops and an abundance of supplies, Clinton once again requested that Ewald's Jägers join him on the journey. On June 2 the Germans were back onboard their cramped vessel sailing northward again for Long Island. The war had already been seemingly endless, yet in many ways it felt as though time had hardly moved at all. On the long journey Ewald's mind kept returning to the terrible accident that claimed so many lives, and he wondered at his own mortality. He wrote that so many men go into battle fearing death they hardly give notice to the potential hazards that existed around them every day. He concluded his entry by asking plainly, "Was all fear in vain?"

VIRGINIA

*January–October 1781*

For over a week Johann Ewald had been at sea. On December 20, 1780, the Jäger captain received orders to board a waiting shop off of Long Island, New York, as part of a sixteen-hundred-man special operations force to invade the Chesapeake Bay. The soldiers that he sailed with were a select assortment of light infantry, Loyalist rangers, and light dragoons hailing from all corners of Europe. There were Scotsmen from Edinburgh, Loyalists from New York and New Jersey, and British regulars. For all the diversity onboard the ships that sailed him southward along the Atlantic Coast, however, there was one fact that weighed on his mind; his Jäger Company were the sole German representatives on this mission, and just as on his last venture into the American South he was requested specifically.

While he sailed with Charles Cornwallis and Sir Henry Clinton en route to Charleston, he now found himself under the command of one of the most ambitious and controversial figures in the king's army. Benedict Arnold was born in Connecticut in 1741, and from the outset of the American rebellion served valiantly against the forces of Great Britain alongside General Washington. He was held in the utmost regard by his command and country, and was often given overblown monikers for his past glories like "the American Hannibal" and "the Hero of Saratoga." However, after being passed over for a promotion by the Continental Congress and feeling slighted by his high command, the thirty-nine-year-old Arnold had decided that his services were no longer reserved, but would be sold to the highest bidder. As the commandant of West Point, Arnold had begun selling information to the British in 1779 with the hopes of turning over the vital location to the British soon after. In 1780, however, when his clandestine correspondence was discovered by Washington, he fled down the Hudson as quickly as possible to the safety of the ship *Vulture* and the waiting arms of Sir Henry Clinton.

He agreed to join Clinton, and along with an annual pension and one-time sum of £6,000 (roughly $350,000 today) he was commissioned a brigadier general in the king's army. To show his loyal fervor, he purchased a home near the commander-in-chief in New York and clearly stated that he would do whatever necessary to prove his allegiance to Great Britain. In December 1780 he got his chance.

Since the siege of Charleston ended in May, the British Empire's grasp of the southern colonies had deteriorated badly. While they intended to exploit and recruit honest Loyalists throughout the South, their presence also served to stir up the emotion and ambitions of latent Patriots; for that reason rebel numbers swelled as well, and the summer of 1780 was a brutal and bloody one. All across the South partisan bands raided and bludgeoned one another, and pitched battles like Camden and King's Mountain shook royal policy makers to their core. Although their primary focus had been Washington to the north, figures like Francis "Swamp Fox" Marion and Thomas "Gamecock" Sumter became legends in their own time for their unique ability to register terrible blows to the British Army through guerilla tactics. Hoping to reassert his dominance over the region, Sir Henry Clinton believed that an increasing British presence in Virginia would be the key to his success.

For this duty he gave the hopeful Brigadier General Benedict
Arnold a chance to prove his mettle. Clinton hoped to increase his
presence in the Old Dominion and Arnold's mission was to land in
Portsmouth, a position previously held in the Chesapeake Bay on
the James River. He instructed his newest officer to sail to
Portsmouth and establish a foothold along the coast that would help
address the growing naval presence of France. On December 20,
1780, Arnold assembled a contingent of sixteen hundred troops to
accompany him. Among them were servicemen from every corner
of Clinton's army in New York, and Ewald's now highly regarded
Jägers would be considered essential for operational triumph.
Arnold was given a fairly straightforward set of orders, as Clinton
understood that the American had a nasty independent streak and a
history of making executive decisions that all too often compromised his original mission. Henry Clinton intended on keeping the
brigadier general on a tight leash, but with echoes of "traitor" and
"villain" being attached to his name, Benedict Arnold was hungry
for revenge, and Virginia would be his retribution.

Arnold's fleet left New York on December 20, and by Christmas
day 1780 they were sailing along the shores of Maryland. The next
two days, however, were marred by an unexpected and violent
storm. By the 29th Arnold was able to rally his force at Cape Henry
on the northernmost tip of today's Virginia Beach, but much of his
army was unaccounted for. Somewhere in the melee brought on by
the weather Arnold lost ships containing over four hundred men
and one heavily armed escort vessel. From his vantage point the
Chesapeake Bay was his for the taking, yet losing 25 percent of his
total manpower placed him in a difficult position. Sensing that time
was of the essence, and rationalizing that a surprise attack force of
twelve hundred men would be just as effective at taking the colony
of Virginia as his original strength, Arnold ordered his men to press
on. By December 30 he finally dropped anchor at the mouth of the
James River near Newport News.

Arnold's objective was clear: take Portsmouth. His desire for personal gain strongly guided his administrative compass as well.
Arnold was well-versed in the riches of Tidewater Virginia and
knew that North America's wealthiest plantations were within his
reach. To move further up the James River the American general
would need to downsize his fleet as the waterway grew narrower. He
soon ordered his twelve hundred men, including Ewald's Jäger
Corps, to disembark into smaller, more mobile craft to make their
way more stealthily up the coast.

Like a great serpent the James River twisted and turned its way through some of the most fertile and prosperous communities in the Old Dominion. In Arnold's mind moving up the coast gave him his choice of plantations to raid. Even more it could give him the chance to capture the capital city of Richmond. By early 1781 the colony of Virginia had been mostly untouched by combat. Jefferson had moved the colonial capital from Williamsburg to Richmond a year early in the hopes that it would more sturdily fight off an invasion. Taking Richmond would be a tremendous boost for Arnold's reputation, and a timely assault would still allow him to return and take Portsmouth with minimal disruption. On December 31 Arnold captured a small fortune worth of tobacco at Newport News from local merchants. While his recent acquisitions were being loaded for transport, the general next instructed his men to fan out across the nearby countryside and reconnoiter any possible enemy positions. When they returned he discovered that the rebels had men posted on both banks of the river that he planned on sailing up.

Sensing that his progress could be impeded, Benedict Arnold called on Ewald's Jägers to storm the enemy position despite not knowing the number of rebels on hand. Ewald wrote that he took forty men with him to climb the banks of the river, and upon reaching the enemy seemed to have caught them by surprise. When the Jägers first burst into view, Ewald was shocked to see that he was outnumbered by what described as "hundreds." Nevertheless the captain ordered his men to unleash a volley into the much larger but unprepared camp of Americans, and though they did return fire the disorganized militia broke rank and fled. Against the odds it seemed that Ewald had won the day, but he burned with resentment that his specialized force had been utilized so carelessly. He recorded that on that day he began to question the martial instincts of his new commanding officer.[81]

He continued by adding that he felt compelled to let the insult pass without ever bringing up his concerns given Arnold's previous actions; he feared that the insolent commander might formally reprimand him out of spite. Even Ewald sneered at Benedict Arnold for his betrayal. From the German's first experiences in America he felt little regard for the capabilities of the rebel command, and he unhappily found himself now at the whims of a man born of that very school. It was growing more difficult to hide his disdain.[82]

On January 2 Arnold's flotilla continued its journey to Richmond, and just south of Williamsburg he encountered a small force of resistance. Two American vessels were attempting to ferry the James River, and Arnold approached with full confidence that they would surrender at the sight of his much greater strength. Under the white flag of truce General Arnold sent an officer onboard the ships to request their capitulation, and the American officer stood defiant. He asked if it was truly Benedict Arnold who had sent the demands, and was adamant that he would under no circumstances give up to a traitor. He further instructed the general's messenger to relay that if he were to get a hold of Arnold, he would hang him up by the heels. As Ewald recalled, the messenger repeated the threat verbatim, and Arnold became visibly disturbed. Sensing that Richmond was still his desired goal and probably feeling more than a little humiliated, Arnold allowed the rebels to go free and proceeded north. At that point, whether the Americans had any actionable intelligence or not, Arnold had certainly revealed his hand. The colony was fully aware that the British were on the move in Virginia.[83]

Within days Arnold had found himself in striking distance of the colonial capital, but to make an assault from the James would be impossible. If he were to take his men via the river, he would be surrounded and outgunned; to take Richmond would require an attack on foot. As a testament to the interconnectivity of the age, Arnold had a sturdy plan in his back pocket. Just a few miles south of the city was the Westover plantation, headed by a widow who was the cousin of Arnold's wife, Peggy Shippen. The widow Mary Byrd gave Arnold's men shelter and a temporary base of operations.

By January 5, 1781, Arnold's Loyalists and redcoats were marching into Richmond with Ewald's Jägers at the front. To capture a colonial capital would send a direct message to the inhabitants of the area that the British Empire was in full control. It would also draw out any pensive Loyalists and hopefully push the Rebels into hiding. Aside from that obvious military benefit, though, a successful sacking would elevate Arnold's name in the eyes of his superiors, and even possibly allow him to capture some of the high-value targets. Most notable among these conspirators was Thomas Jefferson, the acting rebel governor of Virginia and the very man who penned the much maligned Declaration of Independence five years earlier. To capture the city would also likely put his men at unnecessary risk. For Arnold there was a fortune to gain, and almost nothing to lose, except for a handful of replaceable soldiers.

Finding Jefferson would be high on Arnold's agenda. A day earlier on January 4 the governor received intelligence that Arnold's army was drawing near and made the executive decision to flee the capital. Along with the governor many of the city's residents fled as well. Before leaving, Jefferson supervised the relocation of valuable documents and supplies to a foundry at Westham and waited to see exactly how the invasion he anticipated would play out. From his vantage point of Manchester on the southern shore of the James River he could have seen Arnold's force enter the city on January 5.

Upon entering the city, Arnold saw that the capital was weakly defended. To his left an enemy force had established a line on a hill, known locally as Church Hill and Shockoe Hill, with artillery in tow, and to the right a large party of American riflemen used thick brush as cover. Arnold instantly turned to Ewald and shouted that removing the rebels was tailor made for his German troops. The Jägers rushed up the hill and after one half-hearted volley the rebels quickly dispersed; it seemed that taking Richmond would be a mere exercise in practicality. After finishing, Ewald was directed to march on the foundry eight miles north and destroy everything there.[84] When the Jägers and the Loyalist Queen's Rangers made it to the strategic locale a few hours later, Ewald took note of the position and began his course of destruction. In the process the Germans took all of those present as hostages and damaged the machinery beyond repair. The destruction of the foundry was total and along with the vital stores countless documents, including the wartime papers of Jefferson, were left in ashes. Soon after, Ewald wrote that he was called to return to Richmond where Arnold's forces would be making camp for the night.

When the Jägers rejoined their comrades they found Richmond in a state of unrest. Arnold's men had located the vacant home of Thomas Jefferson and ransacked it, they next began to pillage, plunder, and burn buildings of any strategic value in the city. Ewald was taken aback by the wanton damage being done as buildings of all kinds from churches to private residences were being put to the torch. The invasion of Richmond may have loomed large in the strategic resurgence of Benedict Arnold, but in reality it devolved into a drunken melee perpetrated by a disorganized and undisciplined army. As a man of tradition Ewald believed that this kind of raucous activity and unacceptable behavior was the result of weak leadership, Arnold's in particular. While the Jägers certainly participated in the drinking, they largely stayed away from the vandalism. Ewald wrote that the actions of the troops were on par with any great pirates and scoundrels seen throughout history, and he was especially disgusted to witness even churches being raided and sacked.[85]

The following day, January 6, Arnold ordered his men to load the booty that was collected from Richmond onto ships; Ewald counted forty-two fully loaded vessels in total. At mid-day Arnold made the short trip back to the Westover plantation. Ewald complained that his men moved slowly because they had imbibed too much of the city's beer and liquor stores. He wrote that they made such a commotion that he guessed they could be heard from at least two miles away. It was no matter, however; the conquest of Richmond had been completed, and Arnold now sought to accomplish his actual mission of establishing a base at Portsmouth. In Ewald's words they marched leaving a broken city in their wake "with half the place in flames."[86]

MAY 1781 WAS A MONTH UNLIKE ANY OTHER FOR JOHANN EWALD. Since mid-March he had been crippled by a rebel musket ball that shredded his left knee, and was now recovering peacefully away from his men in Norfolk. From across the Elizabeth River he could see his Jägers toiling away at Portsmouth, yet the distance was difficult to overcome. Every day Ewald thought about the fateful engagement that left him in such a feeble position, and not an instance went by when he did burn with rage at the man that he felt was most responsible. Brigadier General Benedict Arnold had not only ordered his men into harm's way but had proceeded to strip the Jägers of the honors that were rightfully theirs. Ewald wrote that he would have gladly given his life for the English cause, as he believed in the order of an imperial world, but he detested Arnold so much that it took the entire spirit of his being not to personally admonish the general. It was likely that had Captain Ewald been any less of a soldier he certainly would have been brought forward on charges of insubordination.[87]

The wound that Ewald suffered, and that nearly ended his military career, came as a direct result of Arnold's botched occupation of Portsmouth five months earlier. Shortly after the sacking of Richmond on January 5, Arnold led his twelve hundred soldiers back along the James River toward their original targeted designation of Portsmouth. His goal was to take command of the post that the British had held there earlier in the war, and reinforce it to make it strong again. Portsmouth had been considered a vital outlet of the

Chesapeake Bay, and occupied up until 1780 by the forces of Henry Clinton. After the march on Charleston, however, the men who were stationed there were relocated down the coast to strengthen the siege. As there was really no action to speak of in Virginia, there was no risk in moving these men. Since the spring of the previous year Portsmouth had been vacant, and Arnold's sole mission was to retake and reinforce the post. There was no fight for Arnold in reasserting British control at the city, and because of the constant downtime the American turncoat used it as a base of operations to raid the countryside of Virginia. While Ewald saw little value in having his elite Jäger Corps utilized to take private property, the results spoke for themselves and the riches poured into the encampment. Throughout February and early March, however, Arnold neglected his duty to build up the position and left it vulnerable to outside attack.

In New York Henry Clinton was aware that Arnold had achieved his objective, but he was not privy to the fact that the rebel high command was informed as well. From his northern headquarters General Washington had developed a plan to uproot Arnold from Portsmouth, and it would involve an amphibious operation between American and French forces. The overall objective of this joint mission was to remove the British under Arnold from Portsmouth, thereby freeing the mouth of the Chesapeake Bay, and their intended means of doing so was by instituting a siege by land and sea. Washington began by ordering the young upstart Marquis de Lafayette to march a small army southward into Virginia to approach Portsmouth by land out of Newport, Rhode Island, and the French Admiral Destouches would complete the siege by sailing his fleet along the coast to blockade the port by sea.

Following each other's movements like strategists behind a chessboard, the British responded in kind by sending Admiral Mariot Arbuthnot to the Chesapeake Bay to meet the incoming French force. As Arbuthnot was sailing from New York, and Destouches from Newport, the British fleet was able to arrive before their enemies and achieve superior position. The ensuing naval battle on March 16 was known as the Battle of Cape Henry, and while both sides sustained heavy casualties, at day's end the British Admiral Arbuthnot retained control of the bay; Arnold and his post at Portsmouth were safe. Washington called off Lafayette's land attack, but the young French officer stayed in the countryside for a possible later strike.

It was the aftermath of this battle that brought Ewald to his fateful wound three days later. With one of the largest naval battles of the entire war now completed, Arnold finally took it upon himself to begin construction on fresh, new defenses around Portsmouth. For days he suspended his raids and focused nearly all of his attention on modernizing the defensive fortifications of this now invaluable post. While the majority of his men worked, the Jägers handled security; it was yet another example to the captain of poor time management. Ewald noted that it seemed as though Benedict Arnold wanted to make up for his weeks of inefficiency all at once, and though he disagreed he ordered his Germans to work around the clock.[88]

On March 18, a party of Jägers brought a prisoner they had captured to Ewald for interrogation. After some stern questioning, spiced by the threat of summary execution, the rebel divulged that a corps of over five thousand men under the commands of the Marquis de Lafayette and the Prussian Cavalry General Baron von Steuben were bearing down on his position. Ewald rushed the intelligence to General Arnold. The general, he wrote snidely, took his intelligence very seriously at the risk of being hanged. Indeed Ewald was correct, as only weeks earlier General Washington issued an execute-on-sight order for anyone who should locate the now infamous traitor.

As the men discussed options to deal with this now advancing threat, Ewald heard a sudden explosion of gunfire. In a frantic dash the captain ran for his men, and shouted for any Jägers on hand to join him. When he reached the causeway that surrounded the outpost, he was shocked to see the entire opposite bank lined with rebel militia, and with his Jägers in tow Ewald charged the position. With swords drawn the Germans rushed into a wall of gunfire, and the captain led the way. The pattern that developed was soon evident: the Americans charged to the head of the causeway to fire, but the sturdy line of Jägers impeded their progress to the point where the rebels had to fall back. After regrouping they would charge again, fire, and retreat. In the chaotic and turbulent exchange Ewald dropped when an American musket ball zipped through his left knee; he immediately called to his men to hold firm. He tried to remain composed and shouted that as long as a Jäger lived no "damned American" would cross the causeway.[89] Indeed they did not, and the Americans slowly melted back into the countryside and Portsmouth survived.

For Ewald this great stand at Portsmouth was a shining example of the fighting prowess and discipline of the Hessian Jäger. He had received many commendations in the war to that point, and this great stand was sure to be among his greatest achievements. He penned proudly that one Jäger fought against thirty Americans and boasted of their courage. Yet when the orders of the day were passed down, Ewald heard nothing from Benedict Arnold. He waited longer and still received no commendation for the actions of his men. Was it possible that Benedict Arnold, a man who turned on his own nation for the simple fact the he felt that he was not adequately appreciated, was denying the Jägers? It seemed so.

The captain was highly critical of the general from the beginning, and took careful notes of his actions. He wrote that Arnold always carried two small pistols in his pocket so that in the event of his capture he would take his own life rather than face the gallows. Ewald penned vindictively that any time the rebel force advanced, Arnold became anxious and worrisome, and the German took great delight in declaring that he was not the "American Hannibal" that he pretended to be. Ewald was filled with resentment toward his commanding officer, and while he never openly stated it, he scribbled insults with a furious rancor.[90] Ewald's left knee was destroyed, but all was not lost. Surgeons thoroughly examined the wound and determined that only rest and perseverance could allow the captain to rejoin his men in time. For the next two months Johann Ewald, the honored captain of the Jäger Corps, would watch the war play out from a window across the Elizabeth River in Norfolk.

Although he was sidelined by his injury, satisfaction did come Ewald's way a few days later when he received word that General William Phillips had sailed into the Chesapeake via New York with fresh reinforcements. More important for the Hessian was that Phillips primarily came to assume control from the unhappy General Arnold. While there was no confusion in the ranks as to who was in overall command, Arnold argued that he had never technically been relieved of his post so he stayed at Portsmouth as a co-commander; for Ewald, the difference between the two men was as pronounced as day and night. While General Phillips carried on as a true officer should, Ewald explained that Arnold did things in what he described as the less formal "American fashion." As a result the efficiency of the post increased dramatically and the captain was convinced it was due to the change in leadership.[91]

For all of April General Phillips worked his men tirelessly to transform Portsmouth into an adequate defensive post, and all that

Ewald could do was watch the action from a safe distance. With time, however, the captain's knee improved and doctors were pleased with his progress, but the rest of his army was not so fortunate.

For much of the first half of 1781 Charles Cornwallis had been wrestling with partisan guerillas and the reunified Continental Army for control of the Carolinas, but with each passing day it seemed that winning the colonies was becoming untenable. The British had been battling rebel militia seemingly from the beginning, but the relocation of the Continental Army under the American General Nathanael Greene was pushing Cornwallis to his breaking point. The Battle of Cowpens in January was a disastrous defeat for the Crown, and the Battle of Guilford Courthouse was a calculated yet costly draw that sapped five hundred casualties from Cornwallis's two-thousand-man force. Greene had developed a keen strategy for winning the American South, leading Cornwallis on an endless run throughout the frontier regions of the Carolinas. Far away from their supply stores along the coast, the British were forced to raid local farms for sustenance and with every homestead that they pillaged a new enemy was born. It seemed that the original southern strategy employed by commander-in-chief Clinton would need to be reevaluated, and complicating matters even more was the development that Cornwallis was surpassing his commanding officer back home in the eyes of London. By April 1781 Cornwallis conjectured that the majority of supplies and reinforcements that were troubling him so much were flowing from Virginia; with a stable body of men already in place at Portsmouth the general fashioned a plan to move into the relatively untouched colony. It was a drastic change of strategic direction, and for certainty Cornwallis had it verified with the Secretary of State Lord George Germain. Cornwallis was about to move his army into the Old Dominion with the approval of London, and Sir Henry Clinton was bypassed completely; it seemed that even the British high command was in disarray.

Cornwallis left Wilmington, North Carolina, on April 25 and wrote immediately to General Phillips at Portsmouth to assemble their armies at the designated meeting point of Petersburg, Virginia. While the two forces did converge on schedule, tragedy soon struck. In the weeks leading up to their scheduled arrival, General William Phillips fell ill with what could have been any number of common maladies of the humid and muggy South; he died on May 13. A week later Cornwallis arrived at Petersburg to receive this bad news and placed himself in full command of all British forces in Virginia. Arnold, who had been acting commander in the wake of Phillips's demise, was soon dismissed out of hand and quietly slunk back to New York to finish out the war wrestling with a troublesome spell of gout.

For Ewald, the arrival of Cornwallis was enough to lift his spirits and motivate his return to service. He had always admired the general, and he would not miss an opportunity to serve him again. With the bad taste of Benedict Arnold's command still in his mouth, on May 29 the Hessian crossed the Elizabeth River and returned to duty in Portsmouth. Once back to operational capacity he penned a letter to Cornwallis personally stating that he was perfectly healthy and longed to get back to his Jägers.[92] It was indeed Ewald's pleasure to be back, and his men welcomed his return.

By August, Cornwallis's great raid into Virginia was revealing the strains between himself and his commander in New York, Sir Henry Clinton. Since his arrival in the colony the commander had encountered stiff resistance from local populations, and for his grand plan of drawing Loyalist support to come to fruition he would need to establish himself in a stable, defensible position. In July Clinton had ordered Cornwallis to make this maneuver sooner rather than later, and with some debate the small port city of Yorktown became the empire's great hope for victory on the Chesapeake Bay. As a location it offered a much needed respite for Cornwallis's army. Since their arrival in Virginia three months earlier they had been plagued by the maverick Marquis de Lafayette. In July, Cornwallis laid a trap for the young officer by crossing the James River with hopes of drawing his enemy near. The Battle of Green Spring was a major British victory, but like nearly all others in the year 1781 it fell into a startling trend; Cornwallis was winning the battles, but losing the war. With every passing victory it seemed that the most valuable resource—the loyalty of the people—was turning against him. At Yorktown Cornwallis hoped that he could be easily reinforced, readily supplied, and begin to turn the tide of a conflict that had raged for the last six years.

Ewald's role with the army had not changed much. The Hessians often found themselves at the front of the force as it crawled its way

through the colony, and all along he took notes of the peculiar practices of the region. One particular development that troubled him
was Cornwallis's interactions with the runaway slaves. Ewald
observed that the general allowed each captain to keep four horses
and two slaves for personal service. By the time Cornwallis reached
Yorktown his army had over five thousand slaves in tow, most of
whom having fled to the British anticipating freedom. In a rare
admonishment of his commander, Ewald noted the army appeared
more like a wandering Arabian or Tartar horde than a modern
European fighting force.[93]

Upon their arrival at Yorktown that fall, Cornwallis would
employ these runaways to begin to fortify the small city in preparation for a potential attack. In exchange for their services, they were
all promised freedom at the end of the war. Day and night, Ewald
wrote, the enslaved dug and picked their way through the Virginia
soil to defend the British army, and when finished Yorktown was as
protected as any other site in British North America. Cornwallis
believed that he had at least six weeks of provisions on hand, with
full and ready access to the Chesapeake Bay; if that vital outlet to
the Atlantic was ever lost, though, Yorktown could very well be the
general's last stand.

While the British seemingly organized a tolerable defense in
Virginia, the rebel high command was divided. Since the summer of
1781 General George Washington and the French commander the
Comte de Rochambeau had been engaged in a heated debate
regarding where to confront their mutual British foes. While
Washington believed that a joint American-French assault on New
York was the best option, Rochambeau was less than convinced.
Their tenuous strategy sessions changed, however, in August when
the French commander received a message from the French
Admiral Comte de Grasse. In his letter de Grasse claimed that he
was en route to Virginia with twenty-nine warships and over three
thousand troops, but with hurricane season at hand and other pressing matters in the Caribbean, he could only remain until October.
Time was now of the essence, and Washington and Rochambeau
believed that if the Admiral de Grasse could blockade Chesapeake
Bay with his fleet, Cornwallis could be trapped at his new operational headquarters of Yorktown. On August 19, 1781, Washington
and Rochambeau began their march to Virginia; it would be the
first time that the American commander had been home in over six
years.

By October 14, the scene that was playing out at Yorktown was the stuff of legend. The Admiral de Grasse had successfully blockaded the Chesapeake Bay, and the city itself was surrounded by almost nineteen thousand American and French soldiers. Like a great wall they fanned around Cornwallis's forces, trapping them on all sides, and with de Grasse's fleet in place the British were completely cut off from the outside world. For more than three weeks this had been the setting for General George Washington and the American rebels' finest hour. It was also a welcome opportunity for the French to deliver a crushing blow courtesy of their world-famous brand of siege warfare.

Inside his headquarters in the besieged city, Cornwallis was growing desperate. His ramparts were being descended on at a rapid rate, and his food supply was running low. Clinton had sent reinforcements southward, but they would be unable to break the French blockade over the Chesapeake. To save vital stores for his men, Cornwallis had taken to extreme measures in a futile attempt to hold out for support. With supplies running low, the general ordered that all of the army's horses be slaughtered at once and thrown into the York River. Ewald wrote that within days the tide brought the bloated carcasses back to shore, and his Germans were haunted by the somber and chilling sight.[94] In the waning hours of what would be his last battle in North America, the British general took his desperate attempt to hold out a step further. After killing the camp's livestock to save grain for his men, Cornwallis looked to further eliminate any usage of food that he considered unnecessary. His next demand though would trouble Ewald more than nearly any other experienced yet in America.

On October 15 the general ordered that all slaves, with no discrimination between men, women, or children, be expelled from the camp. In a wave of frenzy these people were thrust from behind British lines and abandoned in the no-man's-land between Cornwallis and his besiegers. As the enslaved families scattered in the confused melee, Ewald could not sit back and watch. On his own initiative, the captain and his party of Jägers leapt from behind their defensive lines to drive the abandoned people to safety. Ewald recalled the event with great vigor and explained that he led a party of his men into the teeth of the firefight at their own risk. He continued by stating that in hindsight the order was far too dangerous to justify at the time, but he and his Germans could only think of the young families in harm's way. They were overcome with the desire to usher them to safety.[95]

On October 17, 1781, the white flag of truce flew over the British position at Yorktown and Cornwallis had surrendered. On the brisk, fall day of October 19 the official capitulation of over seven thousand men was signed and agreed upon; Lord Cornwallis, claiming illness, was conspicuously absent from the proceedings. For Johann Ewald, captain of the Jäger Corps, it seemed that his American Revolution would end here along this desolate river as a prisoner of war. While preparing to spend the remainder of the conflict under enemy control, however long that it might last, this hardened soldier of the Old World penned a startlingly clear New World revelation: "With what soldiers in the world could one do what was done by these men, who go about nearly naked and in the greatest privation? Deny the best-disciplined soldiers of Europe what is due them and they will run away in droves, and the general will soon be alone. But from this one can perceive what an enthusiasm—which these poor fellows call 'liberty'—can do."[96]

# II

# Frederika Charlotte Louise von Massow

*Baroness von Riedesel*

*Brunswick-Wolfenbüttel*

1776–1778

ENGLAND

*May–December 1776*

IN HER THIRTY YEARS FREDERIKA CHARLOTTE LOUISE VON MASSOW,
Baroness von Riedesel, had never left the continent of Europe.
Now, in the northern French port city of Calais she could see the
White Cliffs of Dover, England, only thirty miles away. She prepared her daughters to board the ship that would ferry her across
the narrowest point of the English Channel, their next stop on the
journey to North America. Frederika often thought of her husband,
and the first time that they met when he was a twenty-one-year-old
officer stationed along the banks of the Weser River in 1759 and she
was only thirteen. Yet as happy as this memory was, she inevitably
drifted to the time when she last saw him several months earlier.


IN 1776 THE BARON FRIEDRICH ADOLF RIEDESEL WAS A COLONEL IN
the army of the Duke of Brunswick. Only one day after the agreement was signed between the British Empire and the Duke Karl I,
the thirty-eight-year-old was given full command over the first
armed force headed to America; for Frederika the promotion had
been a gift from God. While it would require Friedrich to be far
from home, both husband and wife knew that service to their king
would translate to elevated wealth and status when the American
Revolution was over. This separation was a cross that the baroness
knew she would have to bear as the wife of a soldier. Frederika was
born in 1746 as the daughter of the Prussian Lieutenant General
Hans Jürgen Detloff von Massow, and she was raised with the
understanding that the peculiarities of a military life were also the
realities of her own. She met her husband, the Baron of Eisenbach,
during the fiery days of Europe's Seven Years' War, and the young
couple was married three years later. They settled and purchased a
home in the Saxon city of Wolfenbüttel, and by 1776 they were the
parents of two children.

Before leaving for America, Friedrich promised, after his wife's
incessant pleading, that she and the children could follow him to the
New World as long as certain precautions were taken. When he left

in February, she would still be seven months pregnant; his stipula-
tion was that she would not begin her great journey across the
Atlantic until the baby was born. Frederika agreed with her husband, and also that she would travel with a companion "lady of quality" on the ocean voyage to ensure her safety. Shortly before departing Wolfenbüttel with his men, the baron informed his depressed
wife that he had been promoted, and revealed his surprise by calling her "Mrs. General."[1]

While it was not uncommon for soldiers' wives to join their hus-
bands on such exotic deployments, this practice was not always
accepted by Frederika's peers. Immediately prior to her departure,
the baroness wrote to her mother explaining her plans. Infuriated
that she would be so rash as to take a newborn baby on a transatlantic voyage, Mrs. von Massow openly forbid her daughter from
going. Frederika curtly replied to her mother that she would have
to disobey her deliberately for the first time in her life.[2]

And so with her husband an ocean away in May 1776 Frederika
and her three daughters began the long and arduous journey to
America. They set out by carriage from their home and passed
through dozens of German villages en route to the Netherlands. All
the while the baroness maintained a poised exterior that disguised
her inner fears of the unknown. She had seen most of Europe in her
youth attached to her father's camp, but the idea of traveling thousands of miles to British North America was something that she
could not prepare herself for. "They represented to me not only of
the dangers of the sea, but that we might be eaten by the savages;
the people in America ate horsemeat and cats; yet all this frightened
me less than the thought of going into a country where I could not
understand the language."[3]

Putting her mind at ease, however, was the fact that she would
not be alone. Aside from the wonderful opportunities the journey
would give the four-year-old Augusta, two-year-old Frederika, and
the infant Caroline, the baroness was also traveling with her long-
standing personal footman named Röckel. While he was far less
experienced than his mistress, Röckel was often the calming influence on the long, strange trip; in truth he was her primary support,
and she was thankful for him.[4] Soon after crossing the Dutch border, Frederika would already see how vital his service really was.

After crossing into the Netherlands, Frederika was warned by
locals to be vigilant in her travels, and avoid moving at night if at all
possible. The road on which they traveled had seen a dramatic flare-

up of attacks in recent weeks of criminals and bandits preying on the passing carriages of wealthy aristocrats like herself. Frederika informed Röckel that she would only travel by daylight, and that she wished to always begin her day precisely at dawn. During her first morning of travels through a dark forest in the country, with the sun still not yet risen, Frederika wrote of a strange object that crashed into her door. It smacked against her outside window frightening the entire family, and upon further investigation it was the body of a criminal still swinging from its noose.

That evening, passing through that same forest, the family Riedesel rested for the night in a desolate inn; it was the only one seen by the baroness for miles. As she tucked her children in for the night, Röckel rapped on her door. He explained that he unwittingly discovered a room full of weapons and that their hosts were not to be trusted. Seeing that Frederika was unsettled, Röckel declared that he would personally keep watch outside their door until they awoke.[5] They continued the next morning at four o'clock, with no hardships to speak of. Their journey, though at times frightening, was a true tour of Europe. They passed through Brussels and Cassel before crossing the French border into St. Omer. The children blossomed and Röckel provided for their every need; for Frederika it was a ray of hope for their travels ahead. By her count they passed through thirty-two different villages, and enjoyed the regional specialties of all of them.[6]

By the end of May Frederika and her family arrived in Calais. Only thirty-four miles separated England and France at Calais, and the English mainland was clearly visible from the shores of its French neighbor to the south. At this port on a warm spring day the baroness boarded a ship that would carry her one step closer to her husband. While France had already publicly sympathized with the American rebels, they had yet to send any actual provisions to the colonists. During this time the usually heavy packet-boat traffic across the Channel was slowed, but not stopped; Frederika was one of the fortunate few to book passage.

Unlike Friedrich's utilitarian military vessel that carried him across the Atlantic to Canada, his wife's ship was the picture of opulence. Frederika's cabin, she wrote, had a total of eight beds. The accompanying furnishings were made of pure mahogany and brass that shone. By all accounts the children loved the voyage, and took to the crew right away. Watching her daughters take charge of the packet-boat the baroness laughed as she described her daughters gleefully offering their arms to be escorted by the sailors onboard. The crew was enchanted by the young girls almost immediately. After only five hours of sailing, the Riedesel family landed at Dover.

Frederika had heard that the cities of England were alive with activity, but as she stepped off her ship and into Dover she was overwhelmed. As usual when a new passenger arrived, a rabble of innkeepers stormed the docks in an attempt to attract new customers to their lodgings. Frederika quickly gathered her family, and with Röckel in tow they hurried their way to the nearby customs house. To avoid the cumbersome routines and regulations of travel, she produced a letter from her home government that stated her intentions. The inspectors apologetically backed away and stated that had they known of her husband and of her elite family status they would have never troubled her.[7]

By the afternoon of June 1 the baroness was in a carriage en route to London. Frederika took a moment to read some of the correspondence received from her husband. Each began with "Dearest Wife," and all expressed his great longing to see his young family once again.

As the letter continued, Friedrich further implored his wife to be sure to never travel alone, and stated that he had arranged a partner for her voyage. The woman that Frederika was to meet with in England was a Mrs. Harriet Van Horne Foy, the wife of the adjutant-general of Canada, Captain Edward Foy. She and Mrs. Foy were to meet in the city of Bristol, from whence they would make the journey to North America together. Trusting her husband's judgment, Frederika looked forward to making Mrs. Foy's acquaintance.[8]

Upon her arrival in London the baroness ushered her children into their temporary lodgings. Small and terribly dark, her cabin made Frederika shudder, and she quickly set about seeing this immense new city. That evening she dined with many familiar faces, including General Martin Ernst von Schlieffen and Captain Karl August von Kutzleben. As she did not speak English, supping with fellow countrymen and speaking her native tongue was a welcome respite. These men, though foreigners like herself, were power players in the metropolis and very well connected—General von Schlieffen was the Hessian ambassador to London and Captain von Kutzleben was the resident minister.

To illustrate just how politically aligned these individuals were, one need to look no further than the extraordinary lengths that they took to ensure

Frederika's comfort during her stay. In the initial days of her London visit, the baroness began to suffer a malady of the eye, which had become terribly inflamed. She soon called General von Schlieffen for assistance and within two days she was paid a visit by Queen Charlotte's personal physician. The royal oculist raised a small palate of powder and suddenly blew the contents into her face. The pain was indescribable, she wrote, but her condition began to improve within hours. The unnamed doctor then gave her a prescription, and charged her three guineas. When she protested the cost, General von Schlieffen interrupted, saying that she could not pay less as the physician was the oculist to the queen.[9]

The Riedesel family quickly made themselves at home in the city that summer. Their afternoon routine often included taking a carriage ride to St. James Park, where Frederika would nurse the infant Caroline and the girls would watch the people as they went about their business. On one occasion, the baroness recounted particular excitement at seeing the private and illustrious sedans of King George and Queen Charlotte pass by. In 1776 St. James Park was in the heart of London's Westminster, and it was capped on each end by 10 Downing Street and Buckingham House, today's Buckingham Palace. Frederika seemed astounded at the sheer volume of patrons that ventured to the communal site each day, and guessed that there had to be over five thousand regular visitors. St. James quickly became her respite from the business of the city and stress of being so distant from home. While the children busied themselves in the hot London afternoons she took the time to write to her mother and was relieved to see that the tensions between them began to melt away.[10]

In early June, the baroness was invited to dinner at the home of Hanoverian minister Herr von Hinüber, to which she gratefully obliged. After their engagement, the wife of the minister suggested that since Frederika and her family were so fond of St. James Park, they should enjoy a walk together to cap off their meal. But unlike previous times, on that occasion they found themselves being ridiculed and snickered at by the socialites around them. Frederika, who prided herself on being a woman of the highest pedigree, grew quite embarrassed. As it turned out, the clothes that she and her daughters were wearing that night, while very beautiful, were clearly in the French style. As the French and English were much at odds during the age, she drew unwanted attention to herself and her family. In her diary she recounted, "The following day I went out again, and we were all of us dressed throughout in the English fashion, I thought that we would not be especially noticed. But I was mistaken, for I again heard the cry 'French women! Pretty girl!' I asked the valet de place why they called us French women, and was informed it was on account of my having put ribbons upon my children. I tore them off and put them in my pocket."[11]

At that moment Frederika learned the importance of blending into her new surroundings, and it was a hard lesson that most Continental Europeans had to face when visiting England for the first time. In her home of Wolfenbüttel she was highly regarded for her fine appearance and fashionable parties, but here in London that same cultural sophistication would be a curse upon her. There had always been certain practicality to British society, one that valued substance much more than the sizzle of their French and German neighbors. In this way her experience was not different from that of the multitudes of Germans who served the Crown in the fight against the American rebellion. For the baroness did not speak the language and, despite the kindness of those who welcomed her, as long as she was in England she would feel like a stranger.

Before leaving for America Friedrich had conveyed very carefully designed plans to his wife to ensure her safety on what was sure to be a difficult and challenging journey. Among them was an almost step-by-step itinerary from her arrival in London to her embarkation for the New World. While she could have sailed out from any number of ports toward the North Atlantic, the Baron von Riedesel was insistent that Frederika stop in the city of Bristol before taking her leave ultimately from Portsmouth. Sitting approximately one hundred and twenty miles from London, Bristol was a bustling port that had everything in place to accommodate the family's needs. Most important, though, was the woman that Friedrich selected to travel alongside his wife on their arduous Atlantic crossing.

Mrs. Harriet Van Horne Foy, or Mrs. Foy as Frederika would refer to her, was a member of Bristol's social elite; like the baroness she was also the wife of a military officer. When Frederika and her children arrived at the port city Harriet was one of the first people that she met. With her husband away it would befall Harriet to be a shining beacon of English life for her foreign guests and see that they were given all the hospitality that she could afford. In reality, however, the women had very little in common. Aside from the obvious linguistic differences their reception was warm, and Harriet cordially invited her new guests back to her home. One of the finest attributes that Frederika noted about her hostess was that she spoke enough French that the two women could communicate on a basic level. It seemed that as finished as her exterior appeared, Frederika was embarrassed by her inability to speak comfortably to the people around her. She was utterly overwhelmed by her perceived inadequacies, and spent the rest of the evening sobbing alone in her chambers.[12]

In Bristol Frederika found a suitable situation while waiting for the ship that would take her to Quebec. She rented a room for her family near the cathedral that offered a commanding view of the College Green, although it was no St. James Park. Here the baroness immersed herself in the English tradition, and after many long weeks of exploring and spending time with Mrs. Foy she grew accustomed to the new country. As a testament to her openness and personal comfort, she wrote that she dedicated herself to mastering the English language in a mere six weeks.[13]

Indeed London was England, yet it seemed that not all of England was like London. Bristol, she wrote, was very different than the capital, and the people were rough and working class. It was not suited to her taste. In one instance during her stay in the later summer, Frederika's hostess knocked on her chamber door to inform the family that a delightful spectacle was occurring outside. The children rushed to the window to look down into the street and saw a crowd gathered. While she was initially confused, Frederika was aghast at what she saw. "The very day after my arrival, my landlady directed my attention to what she called a most charming sight. As I stepped to the window I beheld two naked men boxing with the greatest fury. I saw their blood flowing and the rage that was painted in their eyes. Little accustomed to such a hateful spectacle, I quickly retreated."[14]

The baroness's reaction to a very ordinary bare-knuckle boxing match among anxious sailors probably drew a silent laugh from her hostess. For a woman of nobility like Frederika, the common brutality of plebian life was simply too much. This however was life in England, and if the mere sight of an exhibition between young men could so offend her then the prospect of witnessing the terrible war in America might just overcome her.

Days after the event that so scarred her, Frederika walked with Harriet Foy and related the story; her confidante was not impressed. Nevertheless her strolls through the city helped the baroness practice her English and gain a better understanding of British customs. One startling difference between the women was that as much as Friedrich occupied her thoughts, it seemed that Harriet almost never spoke of her husband. The women discussed the difficulties that an American journey might bring, but it always seemed that Mrs. Foy was much more concerned about the social gossip of her homeland than a reunion with her distant spouse.

Frederika was learning a great deal of English culture, but she had not quite mastered it, and one story reveals just how much she still had to learn. On this occasion the baroness and her daughters had met Mrs. Foy for an early supper and proceeded to walk to the College Green; Frederika wrote that she was wearing a chintz gown trimmed with green taffeta, which probably seemed outlandish to the people of Bristol. Seemingly so, for as she passed a large party of sailors awaiting departure they "pointed at me with their fingers, at the same time crying out 'French Whore!'" In her embarrassment Frederika rushed her daughters into a nearby store and immediately bought a more understated ensemble. Mrs. Foy remained silent on the subject, likely because she was amused by her German friend's discomfort.[15]

Upon her return that day Frederika got rid of her gown, as it seemed there was no place for its ostentatious presence in this new country. She next gave it to her cook, who was delighted to have it. Bristol was a much coarser place than she was used to back home, but she always tried to make the most of her travels. Upon Mrs. Foy's recommendation, Frederika ventured to nearby Bath. The heated pools of Bath were a premier winter destination in the region, but as the baroness visited in late summer she was the sole visitor. It seemed that even with all the trappings of aristocratic life in one of the busiest cities in all of Europe, Frederika was almost entirely alone. Mrs. Foy was helpful but self-absorbed, and the only company the baroness sought was a world away. Frederika received regular letters from her husband in Canada, but they were frequently several months delayed. In a June post, Friedrich explained his view of the American rebellion to his wife. He wrote that in his estimation only a handful of wealthy elitists directed the entire rebellion and the lower classes flocked to fight a war, from which in his vantage point, they stood to gain nothing. He continued by writing that the entire affair was unsustainable for this reason of inequality and the rebels would soon capitulate in the face of the Crown.[16]

By the time Frederika received her husband's June correspondence she and her family had already been in England for almost five months. While her stay was pleasant, England was merely a stopover point until she could accomplish her true wish of being reunited with her husband. She desperately longed to leave the country and begin her voyage, but the circumstances that kept her in place were both frustrating and revealing. Long after he arrived in North America the Baron von Riedesel remained adamant that his wife never travel alone, and his wife's attachment to the name of Mrs. Foy became a near obsession in his letters. There was scarcely a post received that did not mention her, and considering the two women's shallow relationship it certainly troubled Frederika. But all the same, the baroness was beholden to her husband's wishes, and she refused to travel without Harriet Foy in tow.

This was perhaps the greatest source of tension between the two army wives. For Frederika to finally set sail to America, she desired to do so from Portsmouth; it was not that she had any attachment to the place, but the overwhelming majority of German auxiliaries funneled through that particular English port before leaving for the New World. Before she could take that first great step though, she would need to convince her travel partner Mrs. Foy to prepare to disembark as well. Portsmouth sits on the very southern coast of England and was roughly a ninety-mile journey from Bristol; while the Riedesel family was more than ready, Harriet Foy was obstinate.

Harriet Foy was settled in Bristol and she had very little enthusiasm about leaving it behind. Also working in her favor was the fact that it was nearly October, and to set sail across the Atlantic at that time would be foolish for a civilian party, as they would spend most of their journey fighting off an icy, unforgiving winter. It seemed Mrs. Foy was content to wait out the proverbial clock. The longer she made Frederika wait, the more likely it was that their window to travel would close. In Harriet's mind, they would sail the Atlantic, but not until the following spring of 1777, and by then the war could be over and the women would not need to travel at all. But, for all of her naivety regarding transatlantic travel, Frederika had been informed by her friendly acquaintances that her prospective journey would need to be before October. With this deadline in mind she grew weary at Harriet's stalling tactics.[17]

So close to finally seeing her dearest Friedrich, the baroness was not content to sit idly by and let her opportunity pass. She soon drafted a note to Lord George Sackville Germain, the British secretary of state. By 1776 Lord Germain was heartily occupied trying to draft an overall strategy to suppress the American rebellion, until Frederika's letter arrived. In his obligatory response, the ambivalent

Germain offered his suggestion that late September was too late for a lady of Frederika's stature to sail, and that she should wait. If she could convince Mrs. Foy to join her though, he would provide a ship. While largely inconsequential, the episode revealed a futile attempt by a hapless aristocrat to call upon one of the single most powerful men in the world to solve a rather mundane dilemma. With the secretary of state's offer in tow, Frederika was determined to extract Harriet from her entrenched position. She wrote that the closer the proposed date of departure drew, the more resolute her associate became. The baroness was insistent, until finally in late September the Riedesel and Foy families left Bristol for Portsmouth.[18]

When the party arrived in Portsmouth, the two women seemed to be miles apart. The evening before they were finally to set sail, Harriet Foy and her sister had a lively get-together with some old acquaintances in the city while Frederika took special care to tuck her daughters into bed; their ship was to leave port at eight o'clock sharp. The following morning the Riedesels were up at dawn and prepared for the daunting journey that would reunite them with their father, and Harriet Foy was nowhere to be found. Sensing urgency, Frederika rushed to the Englishwoman's chambers to discover that she was not prepared in the slightest.

Mrs. Foy proceeded to tell Frederika that the gentlemen she and her sister had spoken to that previous evening insisted that to travel this late in the year would be far too dangerous and that she had elected to simply forgo her voyage; even worse, Mrs. Foy had taken the liberty of sending all of the Riedesel family's baggage on a carriage back to Bristol the night before. At this announcement, Frederika was crushed. The suddenness of the deception stunned the baroness, but she was quick to point out that as they argued a large sum of money was being loaded onto what should have been their ship . . . how dangerous could the journey be? The women began to quarrel with raised voices and the tension between them grew.

Harriet Foy and her sister did in fact return to Bristol, and, sensing that she had no other option, the broken-hearted Frederika followed soon after. She slowly came to terms with the dismal fact that she would not see her husband for another six months, and poured out her sorrow to him in her letters.[19]

THE BARONESS RETURNED TO LONDON DAYS LATER, AND SWORE TO herself that she would continue to make the most of her time in England. Since her great disappointment in Portsmouth, Frederika continued to refine her language and engage in the customs of the day. On several occasions she dined at the home of Admiral James Douglas and slowly grew to understand the English style of dining. One particular tradition that Frederika could not avoid for long was that the English drank wine at every meal. As Frederika was still nursing the seven-month-old Caroline, she was running out of polite excuses to avoid drinking and she did not want to stand out.[20] After her horrid interactions with Mrs. Foy, Frederika was pleased to be surrounded by such accommodating hosts. As a token of her appreciation the Riedesel family even accompanied Admiral Douglas and his wife to a church service; it was loud, musical, and different that anything she had experienced in Wolfenbüttel.[21]

Despite her misgivings and misadventures Frederika began to grow quite fond of England, and in late December she was offered the chance of a lifetime. Since falling out with her previous company, the baroness had rapidly reinitiated herself into the high society of London; one of her closest new confidantes was the wife of Lord George Germain. Under her tutelage, the baroness was introduced to a multitude of debutantes and aristocrats from all corners of the empire, and each of them marveled at her plan to cross the sea with such young children in tow. Her greatest honor, however, came in mid-December when she was offered the chance of a lifetime: a personal invitation to meet the king and queen.[22]

It was an amazing opportunity for Frederika to meet the royal family, and the pain of being far from her husband was momentarily minimized at the mere thought of it. In preparation for her regal audience she had a dress specially created by the finest maker that the city had to offer, and the Lady Germain would officially present her. On New Year's Day 1777 the baroness and her daughters were escorted to St. James Palace. Originally built by Henry VIII in 1531, the red-brick Tudor style palace was a sprawling complex that contained four courtyards. This impressive structure was the principal residence of George III. Its main entrance faced north and was the door that the baroness would have entered; it was highlighted by two mock battlements on either side. Frederika remarked "I found the castle very ugly and furnished in an old fashioned style."[23]

In this way the baroness was not unreasonable. As a general rule continental Europeans tended to place great cultural value on intricacy of design; the English however often preferred quantity over quality and strength over sophistication. Nevertheless Frederika was thrilled at the prospect of meeting the sovereign of the British Empire. In typical fashion all of the guests that joined her formed in a circular arrangement beginning on either side of the door that the Royal Family would enter. Moments before His Majesty was announced, the baroness sought some last-minute advice from her presenter. Frederika had heard that the king would kiss all of the women upon first meeting them, and she wondered if this would also happen to her. "No," Lady Germain replied, "only English women . . . and the only thing to do is stand quietly in place."[24]

In the next instant King George arrived through the door accompanied by three courtiers; his wife Queen Charlotte followed behind him. The king began his official pleasantries to the right of the room while the queen ventured left; they made it a point to welcome each guest to their home. After speaking with each person, the monarch and his wife switched sides to complete the circuit of guests.

When the king approached Frederika, she did as instructed and held perfect form; before she could speak, however, King George placed his lips on hers. "I was greatly amazed, and turned red as fire, since it was so entirely unexpected," she wrote. The king went on to inquire as to whether she had heard from her husband, and assured her that he had personally made special inquiries into the baron's station and condition, finding that he was doing very well. He then moved on, leaving Frederika in a state of bliss. Following their official meeting the baroness turned to Lady Germain and stated that she now felt as though she was "naturalized." Before long Queen Charlotte approached her and offered a warm greeting, and surprisingly inquired into her plans to travel such a great distance with her young family.

"Do you not then fear the sea? I love it not at all," the queen asked.

"Nor I either," Frederika replied, "but I have no other means of again seeing my husband; I shall therefore, joyfully make the journey."

At that point the queen gave pause, smiled, and responded, "I admire your mettle."[25]

The North Atlantic

*April–June* 1777

At the city of Portsmouth, winter had melted away into spring, and Frederika, her servant Röckel, and her family were full of joy. For much of the last year the Riedesel family had lived in England for what was supposed to be a temporary stopover en route to Canada where their father awaited, but all that was behind them. On April 15, 1777, the 32-gun warship *Blonde* now sat ready to take them to Quebec; as fate would have it the same ship had carried her husband a year earlier. The baroness was pleased with the arrangements and grateful for the favors that made it possible.

The upper crust of English society had taken on the baroness's journey as a sort of pet project, and likely equated supporting her with supporting the British suppression of the American rebellion. After her initial meeting with Queen Charlotte in January, Frederika and her daughters made regular appearances at St. James Palace and the queen wrote to her regularly in the weeks leading up to her journey. Lord George Germain, the secretary of state, was also instrumental, as he arranged a meeting with a prominent member of Parliament, Sir Brook Watson, to supply her passage. Frederika even wrote that General William Howe, commander-in-chief of British forces in North America, promised the German noblewoman sixty men and two officers to provide security on her travels.[26]

At five o' clock in the evening, the *Blonde* set sail with familiar faces on board. To honor her husband's wishes, Frederika contacted Mrs. Foy to accompany her on the journey, to which she accepted; all was forgiven. In total more than thirty ships were in the fleet that sailed, and after stopping at St. Helen's just east of the Isle of Wight they headed for the open sea. A transatlantic journey of this sort was a grueling affair and an assault on the senses. Not only was the voyage upward of eight weeks long, but the lack of fresh provisions made it a difficult traveling with young children. Many sailors had vitamin deficiencies during their travels, but with Frederika's Caroline barely one year old she would need to pay close attention to her condition, as the threat of scurvy was ever-present.. Because of the extended nature of the voyage, there was no way to maintain perishable items on board; meats may be salted, but most of the protein consumed would need to be caught from the ocean. Likewise any fruits or vegetables would spoil in a matter of days, and factor in the constant rocking and swaying of the seas, and near total lack of fresh water, and one could easily see their health rapidly decline.

Only a week after hitting the high seas Frederika was already seeing their effects, but fortunately feeling none herself. She wrote that most of the passengers around her were falling sick; however, she kept so busy with the children that the motion of the ship did not affect her. And indeed she did; she maintained a rigorous schedule that included eating more than five times per day, and sewing or embroidering when time allowed. The children seemed to take to the sailor's life right away and often danced to the tune of a fifer on the top deck. When the children did fall ill, their mother found that tending to their needs was the best remedy for fighting off her own motion sickness. And still as she sailed on the same route and ship as Friedrich a year earlier; her thoughts turned to him. She believed that her faith in God would guide her, and wrote that as a family the children prayed every night and renewed their promise never to go back to Germany without their father.[27]

By May 1 the *Blonde* had sailed over six hundred and fifty miles into the vast sea, and the baroness was astounded to see how normal life could be in such an unusual setting. Aside from the daily meals and general pleasantries, the crew of the ship made it a point to hold regular church services. Despite the terrible conditions of the sea, the entire crew attended the vigil and offered a tremendous sight as they all knelt simultaneously in prayer. On one occasion the waves were so abrasive that in mid-ceremony the ship rocked so terribly that the faithful were sent crashing to the ground. Frederika herself fell numerous times, and her daughters received cuts and scrapes as well. For the Riedesel family, prayer was a regular occurrence on the great sweeping voyage, and Frederika ensured that her daughters all practiced nightly petitions for safe travels.[28]

In early May on an especially tumultuous night at sea, Frederika wrote that she could not sleep because of the storm. As she inspected her daughters in their beds, she saw the four-year-old Frederika awake, and seemingly in mid-prayer. When the child finished, her mother inquired into what she was praying for, and the girl responded, "I long to see my dear Papa soon." The baroness next asked what she would pray for when they were finally reunited, to which her daughter replied, "I would pray to God every day that He never more would separate us." Frederika later wrote that she was so touched that she wept the entire night.[29]

On May 6 the fleet had caught a favorable wind and traveled one hundred and thirty miles in a single day. After nearly a month at sea everyone, including the aristocratic Riedesel family, was adjusting to life aboard the vessel, and small measures were taken to make the baroness feel at home. One of the pastimes that the fleet would engage in was for two ships to pull directly alongside one another so the crew or passengers could shout pleasantries and pass a variety of goods back and forth. It was during one of these changes that Frederika was surprised to see the ship *Henry*, with one hundred and thirty men onboard, align its crew on the deck to address the family. "Long live the dear wife of our general, and the good general himself!" they all shouted. The flattered baroness called back, "Long live the entire ship!" to which they all cheered "Hurrah!"[30]

It was a small pleasure, but rather insignificant occurrences such as this went a long way to help pass the time. One of the other ships that sailed alongside the *Blonde* was named *Porpoise*, and it also carried its own distinguished guests. The captain of the vessel was formerly a lieutenant and was recently promoted upon the recommendation of Baron von Riedesel himself only a year earlier. Frederika was thrilled by the irony and felt her husband's effect in the heart of the cold North Atlantic. On board the sister-ship also sailed Colonel Philip Skene, who before returning to England was a high-ranking official of both Fort Ticonderoga and Crown Point along the shores of Lake Champlain. He had held the position in North America since 1774 before returning home to retrieve his son. In 1777 he had decided to volunteer his services again to fight the rebellion and made the journey with his son Andrew Phillip. The colonel and baroness first met in Portsmouth before boarding their respective vessels, and, seeing that she was traveling alone, he offered her whatever money she might need. While Frederika misunderstood him as being governor of Georgia, probably due to his posting near Lake George, she wrote that she would never forget his kindness.[31]

Although Frederika was finding her travels to be relatively uneventful, the terrible realities of such a trip during a time of war were soon evidenced. On May 8 she was alarmed to hear that a lone ship was spotted on the horizon; it was likely an enemy ship. While the American rebels possessed only limited naval power at this time, they had found great success in arming privateering vessels to raid British shipping. Already by the spring of 1777 men like John Paul Jones were becoming household names in England and America for his raiding exploits; although his true star was still to rise, the fleet knew enough to be wary of such a renegade development. The baroness wrote that she was frightened and had no desire to witness a battle at sea. Fortunately for her, and more likely for the American ship, the enemy crew decided against a maneuver toward a British war fleet that had it outnumbered thirty-to-one, and it quickly disappeared.

Sailing was a dangerous undertaking, and the baroness soon discovered how simple mistakes could costs lives, with or without a war. Shortly after the American vessel disappeared, a snapping sound ripped across the deck of the *Blonde* and four seamen were flung into the water. While the crew rushed to their aid, Frederika averted the eyes of her children as only one was recovered, and the other three were drowned.[32]

Finally after weeks of endless ocean, the crew of the *Blonde* spotted land. On May 22 a steady rain had poured all day and surrounded the ship with a dense fog. Through the mist, however, Frederika saw what would be her first glimpse of North America. Though they were still weeks from their destination, the forested coastline that made its appearance to the baroness was the eastern shore of Newfoundland. She was far from the shore, and sixteen hundred miles from England, but Frederika finally understood the great value of the New World. What lay before her was a veritable wilderness, and while it seemed dark and mysterious to her, in the eyes of a capitalist it was an endless fortune of timbers and furs. The coastline would be a reliable guide for their sailing, but the dense fog made their thirty ship convoy a terrible liability. At times some of the vessels would begin to drift away from the main body of the fleet, and the *Blonde* fired booming cannonades on the hour to draw its comrades back to their place. The blasts, Frederika wrote, frightened mother and children alike.[33]

It seemed to Frederika that she was now closer than ever to her husband, and after two thousand miles they would be reunited in this strange, foreign land. Yet as far as she and her family had traveled and as distant as anything in England now seemed, she couldn't help but be reminded of the litany of bad experiences left behind. Harriet Foy and her sister had been on board the *Blonde* since Bristol, and it seemed that no matter how hard the crew tried to satisfy them, nothing was enough. It was true that the ship's amenities were a far cry from the luxurious lifestyle left behind in the British Isles, yet most of the passengers somehow managed.

Most, that was, except Mrs. Foy. In her world, as a member of society's upper crust, she expected to be the center of attention, but the ship was a community that operated along different rules. Even more galling to her was the fact that technically Frederika was considered of a much higher status than she, and when extra attention was expended it often went to the baroness and her daughters. While always present, the tension was noticeably thick between the two women after six weeks at sea. "I had much more reason to regret that I took her with me," Frederika wrote.[34]

On May 26 the feud which had repressed itself so well on the voyage spilled over into an open argument—over a fish. One of the greatest single resources that Canada's eastern seaboard had to offer was its world-famous cod fisheries, and for almost two centuries prior it had enriched both the French and British empires. The early Frenchmen who sailed the region discovered a fishing ground the likes of which they had never seen before, and following the Seven Years' War in 1763 the British Empire reaped the benefits in their stead. By May 1777 all of the sailors on board the *Blonde* knew that when they reached the Canadian coast they would be enjoying some of the largest and finest cod on the planet; even sweeter was the fact that it was all-you-can-eat or, rather, all-you-can-catch.

While the crew anxiously awaited their meals, the ship's cook arose with a very large fish in hand and presented it directly to Frederika. She was flattered by the gesture, and because of her fine and cordial nature the crew understood the ceremony. But, as she was about to accept the gift, the captain of the *Blonde* rose to his feet; he stomped angrily in her direction, snatched the cod, and threw it overboard. At that moment the crew, who were perplexed at the tense scene before them, went back to their duties with the understanding that they probably would not be dining on cod that night. It was a strange moment but it would soon be clear why the captain had taken such offense at the gift.

Over time it was also revealed that the captain of the *Blonde* was a former lover of Harriet Foy, that they reignited their old affair during the voyage despite her marriage. When the cook presented his prized catch to Frederika, the captain took offense at the fact that it was not offered to Mrs. Foy first. Frederika described it: "Madame Foy's old intimacy with the Captain of our ship . . . was the reason of her not daring to refuse him those liberties to which he had formerly been accustomed." The codfish incident came to a conclusion when the *Porpoise* pulled alongside the *Blonde* and passed along four massive cod from their own supply as a gift to the baroness. The fish, it seemed, were a repayment from the grateful

captain of the *Porpoise* for Baron von Riedesel's earlier recommendation, and the baroness treated all of the souls on board to her gift
as though nothing had happened.[35] It was never revealed whether or
not Mrs. Foy partook in the feast.

For Harriet Foy the codfish incident was just the beginning, and
with every passing day she became more unpopular with the sailors
on board the *Blonde*. Frederika recounted a specific incident in which
Nancy, the lady's maid of Mrs. Foy, began to engage in some unsavory behavior below decks. It seemed that Nancy had been carous-
ing with the crew for some time, and when the captain's personal
wine cache was broken into, a great hullabaloo soon developed.

Harriet Foy, her sister, and Nancy all claimed that Frederika's
footman Röckel had been the culprit; in truth even the baroness was
not certain of his innocence. But fortunately for the Riedesels' faithful servant the truth came to pass. Frederika explained that one
evening on an especially turbulent sea the maid was thrown to the
ground in front of a large crowd, and as she stood up there were
beneath her two shattered bottles. When the officers came to sort
out the trouble, Nancy pleaded that an unnamed sergeant had been
enticing her to steal the wine, and they often enjoyed it together.
Furthermore, it was also revealed their favorite spot to carry on
their affair and imbibe themselves was most often the baroness's
own cabin while she was occupied on other parts of the ship.

On June 4, like a great gateway on the distant horizon, the mouth
of the St. Lawrence River came into view. The great river that
served as an artery of North America was finally before Frederika,
and on the other side was her waiting husband. By her calculation
they had traveled almost two thousand eight hundred miles in
approximately eight weeks, and for the first time on her entire journey both sides of the ship were surrounded by land. She made note
of the mountains to her left, and the passing ships to her right; the
St. Lawrence was the launching point to the North Atlantic, and
while she was just beginning her adventure many more were ending
theirs. When the ships rushed by the *Blonde*, Frederika pictured her
Friedrich onboard headed due east for Europe, possibly because the
war was already finished. She wrote that many other passengers
troubled her greatly with reports that they had seen German soldiers on board, and she was overcome with grief at the thought of
missing the baron.[36] Her husband, however, did not leave, and in
fact was waiting for her. Despite the fact that she may have had
indeed seen soldiers going home, the American rebellion was far
from over. In many ways it was just beginning.

## QUEBEC

*June 1777*

The Gulf of St. Lawrence was impressive in its size. As the location where the enormous river bearing the same name flooded into the North Atlantic it stands as one of the largest estuaries on the planet. But for European colonists of the seventeenth and eighteenth centuries it was much more than a river, it stood as a superhighway into the heart of a dark and dangerous continent. For the empire of New France (now gone since 1763) it had been like the great artery of their North American dominion; if a fur trader or trapper were to brave its waters they would be thrust into the Great Lakes, further connected to major rivers like the Ohio, and eventually extend their imperial grasp to the Mississippi and almost to the Rocky Mountains. It was immensely valuable waterway and after the Seven Years' War, George III took command of the continent and maintained the passage as one of his primary entry points to a land that was home to almost untold natural riches.

It was for all of these reasons that the British had not razed the cities of Montreal, Trois Rivières, and Quebec that made up the administrative heart of New France. When British forces stormed the Plains of Abraham some fifteen years before Bunker Hill, they fully expected to conquer, absorb, and continue the prosperity that King Louis had enjoyed for so long. The result was a unique and eclectic land that combined many worlds into one, and gave rise to the official British province known as Quebec. While it can be confusing at times, "Quebec" for the average Briton in 1777 would have most likely been taken in reference to the city, rather than the massive province that stretched from modern Labrador to the shores of the Mississippi. When speaking of that particular polity the term "Canada" was most often employed. Whatever the nomenclature, what is now Canada was a melting pot of eighteenth-century life, consisting of French Catholics, British colonists, and a myriad of Indian peoples; all told, however, only 2 percent of the population spoke English. Together they formed a brand new society, though rarely peacefully, which made Canada unlike any other place in the world.[37]

Canada was of the highest priority for Britain, and the empire maintained half of its army there under the command of Governor Guy Carleton, 1st Lord of Dorchester; its other half rested at New York City with William Howe. Carleton was a veteran of the Seven

Years' War where he first defended Hanover from French incursion, but it was in Canada that he earned his stripes. He was on hand for the Battle of Quebec, and after wresting the continent from the French he was appointed lieutenant governor of Quebec Province in 1766. Two years later he was sworn in as governor of half of British North America. Although Quebec and Montreal had been of the utmost importance decades earlier, by the time of the American rebellion the focus of the conflict had shifted, making Canada all too often a forgotten front when compared to New England to the south.

For most Britons, Canada represented a great wilderness. It was a land of fresh air and open spaces that held a special importance to their national spirit. First, it was all British territory and therefore a great boost to imperial power and wealth, and second, it stood as the latest reminder of their greatest victory over their natural French enemies. Whereas much of Europe saw Canada as an untapped resource, in those same forests could be found the true spirit of expansion that Britons craved. It was for all of these reasons that Friedrich von Riedesel had spent a year there, and why his wife and three daughters were now only days behind.

The St. Lawrence River valley was a completely new experience for Frederika, for the country was sparsely inhabited. In Europe, land was a valuable commodity, and old family grants claimed every square inch. Yet here in Canada it seemed that settlements hugged the riverbanks and rarely expanded either north or south. The land was so great and so vast that it seemed to her that it could take centuries for anyone to fully explore it; little by little she was beginning to understand the mysterious charm of this wilderness realm. She wrote of her observations: "The houses are painted white, giving them a most beautiful look, especially if seen in passing through the St. Lawrence, for then their appearance, in the distance, is even more splendid. Each dwelling has a little fruit garden; and at evening the herds returning homeward present a most charming sight."[38]

The population of the land that she was seeing was not large; a census produced in the year 1740 listed just over forty-four thousand inhabitants in the entire river valley, and by the 1770s that small number had only grown to eighty thousand. In her time though the vast majority of the Canadians were residing in one of the three major cities: Montreal, Trois Rivières, and her intended destination of Quebec. On June 10 the city of Quebec appeared on

the banks of the river, and after two months aboard the *Blonde*
Frederika was elated to see it.[39]

In 1777 Quebec would have looked more like a fortress than a
city. Its surrounding walls were large and dominated the capital, and
had protected it for over two hundred years. The original founder
of the site was Jacques Cartier in 1535, and since then each new
generation had added their own stamp to the distinctly European
city. By the time that Frederika's ship approached its docks more
than eight thousand people lived there, and despite two hundred
years it remained a relatively small city by North American standards. While the walls had defended the tiny population of Quebec
from everything from Indian raids to British bombardment, the
restrictive nature of its design greatly hampered the city's expansion.

Yet for all the importance that the empire placed on the region,
and for all the strength that its walls produced, the American rebellion had only limited effect on the city. In the aftermath of the
Seven Years' War and its great victory over France, Britons around
the globe grew accustomed to using the phrase "British North
America" to describe their conquests. Not only had they secured
their hold over what would come to be called the thirteen American
colonies; they also snatched up East and West Florida from the
Spanish and of course all of Canada. Therefore at the start of the
American rebellion many separatist sympathizers assumed that once
all of the thirteen colonies finally rallied together, it was only natural that the population of the Quebec Province would follow suit as
well. But the debate was not without its ideological detractors. One
of the greatest fears amongst the white, Anglo-Saxon Protestant
elite of colonial America was the undeniable fact that over 90 percent of Quebec's population was Catholic (and therefore beholden
to the pope), and, most distressingly, Francophone to the core.
While the discussion of religion is all too often minimized in geopolitical matters, part of the historical animosity that Britons felt
toward their French counterparts centered around their rich tradition of Protestantism and inherent distaste for papal authority to
which the French submitted. There was no doubt that the
Canadians could be valuable allies in the war to come, but many in
the Continental Congress saw the Quebecois as more of a looming
cloud of Catholicism than as friendly neighbors to the north. What

Congress did not account for were the recent liberal developments of the British Empire toward its Canadian holdings, most notably the Quebec Act. Passed in June 1774, the Quebec Act was an unlikely attempt by royal policy makers to appease and adapt to its ever-growing and highly diverse empire. Among other factors, this new law guaranteed the rights of the residents of the former New France to practice their Catholic faith. Though it was not exactly a protection of religious freedom in the modern sense, it was enough of a concession to make the French-speaking *habitants* far less inclined to participate in any rebellion that might creep up from New England.

It can be said that the American Revolution was the greatest political campaign ever undertaken, and the methodology of convincing a populace to turn Patriot was the end result. To win the war, rebel leaders like George Washington and Benjamin Franklin knew that fighting battles was secondary, for the true revolution and instrument of change was found in the hearts and minds of the people. Simply put, to win the war one must win over the people, and true independence would eventually follow.

In 1775 during the earliest stages of the war, the rebel cause was ragged and not unified. All thirteen colonies were joined in the political effort, but the rebels themselves had yet to find a common cause. The taxation of the coastal colonies mattered little to the Indian fighters of the frontier, and the result was a diverse collection of bands and militias that often fought the same enemy for very different reasons. In that way 1775 was a year of coming together, and out of the rabble was formed the earliest conception of a Continental Army. In June they had found their commander-in-chief in George Washington, and now all they needed was a fight.

By the summer of 1775 Boston had been besieged for three months and the rebels had been firing on the British since Lexington Green. War was a reality, not an option. The importance of Canada was never lost on the Continental Congress; in fact, they had twice invited the residents of Quebec to join them at their proceedings in Philadelphia and received no response. While the Congress debated the merits of taking Canada by force, intelligence had indicated that Governor Guy Carleton was actively fortifying vital routes into the seditious colonies that could prove to be potentially disastrous. The decision to invade was essentially made for them.

The invasion of Canada was a two-pronged assault; one force left Fort Ticonderoga under the command of Richard Montgomery in

August while the other left Cambridge, Massachusetts, led by Connecticut-born Colonel Benedict Arnold. Montgomery, who was operating under the orders of the Continental Congress, moved swiftly to the British Fort St. Johns where he besieged the post and eventually captured it; with that fort gone, Montreal was effectively open for the taking. By November the American rebels had captured the city, and Governor Carleton had fled upriver to Quebec after nearly being taken prisoner by the Americans. It was behind that city's massive defensive walls that Carleton hoped to make a stand.

The force that would test Quebec was well on its way. Earlier that summer Benedict Arnold had hoped to lead the force that captured Montreal but was denied the post; as a result he sought out a commission from General Washington himself. After pleading his case, Washington granted Arnold of force of eleven hundred men designated for an assault on Quebec, and that fall the colonel set sail. Arnold took his men to Fort Western on the Kennebec River in present-day Maine, where he marched directly toward his heavily defended target. By November he had reached his destination. Although his army made it to the city walls, Arnold had underestimated how unforgiving the wilds of Maine could be, and after a four-hundred-mile trek his original eleven hundred had been reduced to a paltry six hundred men.

The original plan of besieging the city was now unfeasible, and Arnold instructed his men to move to a position away from Quebec where they would await reinforcements. The troops that would fill out his haggard force were none other than Richard Montgomery's men from Montreal. The rebels had made an easy conquest of Montreal, but it became apparent by December 1775 that the administrative heart of Canada and its true prize was Quebec. Therefore Montgomery abandoned Montreal and focused all of his efforts on supporting Benedict Arnold's six hundred men to capture the rough frontier city.

On December 31 the American rebels stormed the walls of Quebec in the midst of a blinding snowstorm just before dawn. The plan of attack was to use two separate forces to capture the lower city before focusing their joint efforts to storm the heavily defended upper portion of Quebec. The results, however, were disastrous for the Americans. Early in the engagement Richard Montgomery's men received heavy fire, and the general himself was killed after being struck in the head by a blast of grapeshot. For Arnold, the attempt at taking the city proved equally problematic as his men were also beaten back and he was wounded in the leg. By 10 A.M. the battle of Quebec was over, and nearly fifty Americans were dead and over four hundred and thirty were taken prisoner. It was the first defeat suffered by the Continental Army.

Still seeking out greater glory despite the loss of two-thirds of his army, Colonel Benedict Arnold was determined to continue his campaign. Knowing that another frontal assault would probably finish off his men entirely, he instead opted for the original plan of an extended siege. Typically a besieging army would rely on its superior numbers and greater lines of supply and communication to suffocate its target, but by the winter of 1776 Arnold had none of these on hand. While his men froze and starved on the outskirts of the city, the British within Quebec largely went about their business as though there were no siege at all. All told, the abortive siege of 1775–1776 was a haunting indicator for what kinds of challenges the American insurgency would face in the future.

The American experiment in siege warfare was coming apart at the seams by the spring of 1776, and the command structure was falling apart. Benedict Arnold wrote of his troubles to the Continental Congress in Philadelphia, asking that they send a more capable commander to execute the siege in addition to the reinforcements they had already sent. By April the American force numbered almost three thousand men, but only a quarter of them would have been considered fit for duty. Disease, malnutrition, and discontent had taken their toll on the army, and the situation for the rebels only worsened. After Arnold slipped down the St. Lawrence to Montreal, the Continental Congress selected Boston siege veteran Major General John Thomas to replace the discontented colonel; upon arrival he began to organize the retreat from Quebec.

By June 2, 1776, John Thomas would be dead. He, like many of his men, contracted a strain of smallpox that took his life. It seemed that the American invasion of Canada had been a failure, but it was not an isolated incident. Across the Atlantic in London, Prime Minister Lord North began a campaign to ratchet up British strength in North America in order to suppress the rebellious colonists. He garnered a force of over fifty thousand soldiers from all corners of Europe, and sent them across the sea that April. While the majority of them sailed for New York, eleven thousand headed directly for Canada to address the failing siege of Quebec; among them was a contingent of Brunswickers headed by Baron Friedrich von Riedesel.

By June 1 these fresh European troops were in place, and their commanders were anxious to tackle the ragtag American army that threatened the Canadian frontier and had already started their retreat. The baron wrote a letter to his wife that June claiming General Carleton had driven the rebels from the vicinity of Quebec and was pursuing them.[40] A week later, when it seemed that the threat to Quebec was neutralized, he further described the defeated American army as rascals that were so wretchedly provided for that she should never fear losing her husband to such deprived souls.[41]

The Americans had never seemed so desperate by mid-June. With word that these reinforcements were coming, Benedict Arnold abandoned Montreal and attempted to burn the city. The other American force, after being soundly routed at Trois Rivières, continued their retreat southward down the Richelieu River where they waited at Fort St. Johns, the very post they captured to begin the campaign. There, after combining their forces, they pressed onward to Crown Point on Lake Champlain to finally signal the invasion of Canada a failure. Isaac Senter, a surgeon who had seen much of the conflict, described his experience as "a heterogeneal concatenation of the most peculiar and unparalleled rebuffs and sufferings that are perhaps to be found in the annals of any nation."[42]

Whereas the invasion of Canada ended in a complete loss from a military perspective, perhaps the greatest casualty of the campaign was the effect that it had on the local population. As originally conceived by its instigators, the American rebellion could succeed only by obtaining and keeping the loyalties of the people. In theory the venture into the St. Lawrence River valley was designed to do just that; however, in practice it was terribly botched. The American invasion of Canada was not different in its conception than the British invasion of the southern colonies two years later. Both hoped to exploit friendly participants to their advantage, but just as the British mistreatment of southern colonists prompted a push toward Patriot sympathies, so did the American mistreatment of Canadians send them running to the Royalists. When Montgomery captured Montreal it seemed that the original plan could hold, but whatever sympathy the rebels garnered was surely lost after the six-month siege of Quebec.

The conclusion of the expedition was the St. Lawrence River valley, still essentially all of Canada, and its people would never join in the American rebellion. The invasion had the exact opposite effect of transforming the vast land into a British stronghold and major base of operations. Despite the best efforts of the Continental Congress, capped off notably by the sending of a party of delegates including Benjamin Franklin and Jesuit heavyweight John Carroll to Montreal, it seemed that the anti-imperialist uprising would remain unique to the thirteen colonies.

As fate would have it though, the failed invasion of the St. Lawrence River Valley may have been a blessing in disguise unfortunately for the Americans that could only be seen in hindsight years later. While the rebels slunk their way out of Canada, Governor Guy Carleton prepared his great counterattack in the spring of 1776. With fresh reinforcements, including General Friedrich von Riedesel and his Brunswickers, Carleton began a campaign to chase his attackers southward into the thirteen colonies themselves. With his attack in motion, the governor hoped to not only trap the Continental Army but to take command of the extraordinarily vital Hudson River.

Moving north to south the Hudson is a three-hundred-mile waterway that begins just south of Lake George and eventually empties into the Atlantic at New York City. Although the Hudson runs entirely in the state of New York, at the time it was traditionally considered to be the great divide between the middle colonies of New York, Pennsylvania, New Jersey and the New England colonies to its east. By 1776 it was well ingrained in the minds of English policy makers that the American rebellion itself was almost wholly isolated to New England, and if they were able to isolate those seditious colonies from their southern brethren they could effectively contain and stamp out the revolution before it even began. It was for this reason that General William Howe stationed one half of His Majesty's forces at New York, and the other in the St. Lawrence River valley.

From Quebec, it was hoped that a massive invasion force could sail down the Richelieu River into Lake Champlain and continue through Lake George and ultimately into the Hudson River valley. When this circuit was completed, the British hoped to have created an impenetrable wall keeping New England and its troubling brand of upheaval from spreading; at this stage the rebellion was in its infancy, and many Britons still used the term "Bostonian" to differentiate a rebel from an average American Briton. After the failed invasion of Canada and broken siege of Quebec, Governor Carleton believed that he would be the man to see this large-scale imperial pipe dream come to pass, and he immediately sent his new arrivals in pursuit of the Americans limping southward.

The man who would lead this great charge on behalf of Carleton was also fresh off a transatlantic journey. General John Burgoyne was the picture of the modern Briton. He was raised the son of a British captain and educated at the prestigious Westminster School. Known for his distinct appearance and affluent nature, Burgoyne joined the Horse Guards in 1737 and donned the ostentatious uniforms that were their trademark. He lived wildly for most of his twenties and ultimately racked up a troublesome gambling debt. In 1751 he eloped with the daughter of the highly influential Lord Derby and spent the early years of his marriage traveling abroad and making a home in France and Italy. Burgoyne would ultimately return to military service in the Seven Years' War, where he served the crown in Portugal before being promoted to major general. By the time he arrived in America two decades later he was considered one of the empire's most prized assets and relished in his new moniker "Gentleman Johnny" Burgoyne.

Carleton's great offensive led by the newly arrived Burgoyne was sound in its conception, but proactive steps by the retreating rebels disabled it thoroughly. As Benedict Arnold moved south, fresh off a promotion to general, he did so in a deliberate fashion, making sure to score whatever meaningful blows he could to any imperial presence on Lake Champlain. Although he was technically in retreat, Arnold instructed his Patriot rebels to burn and destroy any ships or equipment that they left behind so it would not be of use to the enemy. Although these actions could have been viewed as a self-inflicted wound, Arnold's plan made an immediate British attempt at the Hudson River valley impossible. Guy Carleton in Canada now was faced with the reality that if he was going to execute his grand maneuver to sever the colonies, he would need to rebuild a navy first.

By October 1776 Carleton's small but essential navy was completed, and Benedict Arnold oversaw the construction of an American fleet at Crown Point on the western shore of Lake Champlain. Since the retreat from Canada had begun, the Continental Army had posted the vast majority of its men at Fort Ticonderoga, and left approximately three hundred men at Crown Point under Arnold's command. These two points, about ten miles apart, had been long understood as the critical linchpins to holding and controlling the Champlain Valley and therefore the most direct line into Canada; for decades the French, British, and now Americans fought over these vital positions. On October 11 Carleton's newly minted fleet clashed head on with Benedict Arnold's smaller rebel counterpart at the Battle of Valcour Island, and as expected it was a sound British victory. Arnold was significantly outgunned and overmatched, and after losing the battle he was forced to abandon Crown Point altogether. He and his men rushed to Fort Ticonderoga to rejoin the bulk of the army.

By October 17 Carleton's forces had occupied Crown Point and seemed as though they were in place to march down the corridor and into the Hudson, but as winter was approaching such a venture would be impossible. It is one of the great ironies of the rebel invasion of Canada that as mismanaged and ineffective as the actual attack was, the retreat was actually a great success. When Benedict Arnold took the time to disable the leftover shipping during his recoil south, he effectively guaranteed that whatever retaliation Carleton had planned would be terribly delayed. Had the British obtained access to those vessels in the summer of 1776, they could have easily continued their march and delivered a potentially fatal blow to the American rebellion that year. Instead, a small fleet had to be constructed, and the attack did not begin until fall, by which time it was simply too late in the year to do anything but settle in for the harsh northern winter.

Sensing that his window of opportunity was closed, Governor Carleton ordered his men back into Canada on November 2, 1776, to await the spring thaw. His campaign had gone exactly as planned, but he had simply run out of time.


In modern times the city of Quebec has been described by North American visitors as the most European city in the Western Hemisphere, but to the Riedesel family in June 1777 there simply was no comparison. Quebec sits high above the banks of the St. Lawrence River and is protected by its massive walls, but unlike its European counterparts there was little account for aesthetics. The city itself was divided into two parts, the Upper and Lower Towns, and a great wall separated the two. The Lower Town was the domain of Quebec's busy harbor, and it was the first part of the city that Frederika entered; like most harbor towns, this area of the city was far less cosmopolitan than its counterpart and was bustling with sailors and merchants anxious to strike a deal. The Upper Town within the defensive fortifications was the heart of Quebec itself, and its narrow cross-streets steadily climbed up an elevated slope that in the future would become the hallmark of the city.

The city of Quebec tried desperately to present itself as a modern European capital of the eighteenth century, but it could not hide its colonial roots. Situated on the northern bank of the St. Lawrence River, Quebec jutted out on a parcel of land shaped like an inverted triangle with its point facing east. The entire city was surrounded by a stone wall, with the longest, far western edge defended by a series of noted posts including the Potasse Demi and Saint-Jean bastions. In some parts a defensive ditch was dug to protect the city against the unlikely event of a land invasion; the river itself was the primary threat. Although Quebec was considered one of the largest forts in North America, its true heart was the inhabitants inside. Most of the city consisted of small, crowded homes and shops, but it retained a distinctive French presence from its larger buildings such as the Chateau Saint-Louis and hospital. Perhaps the most alien things to Frederika though, and to most Britons who visited, were the Catholic institutions that embodied the original French spirit. At the city center was located the Jesuit College and resident halls and just north was the Ursuline Sisters College.

The baroness recognized the rustic charm of the capital of Canada, but was not quiet about her opinions, claiming that the city was ugly and its streets were far too steep for leisurely strolls. But despite these complaints, she did not travel eight weeks to sightsee: she was in North America to find her husband. As she disembarked from the *Blonde* and prepared to take her first steps onto this new continent, she was met with the utmost pomp and circumstance. In the harbor all of the vessels greeted her arrival by firing their cannons, and twelve British sailors dressed in perfect white with green sashes and silver helmets stood guard as her welcome party. Despite their formal nature, these men carried little that was of significance. They did deliver a small bundle of letters, all from Friedrich.

Dating from the year previous to her arrival, the letters contained her husband's entire thoughts on her stays in England and beyond. They were warm, often painful reminders of the many months that they had been apart, and though she was reading them long after their intended time, it offered her peace that she would soon be with him again. The letters that she wrote while on board the *Blonde* had not been delivered for obvious reasons, but Frederika still relished the chance to read the baron's responses to her earlier travails, as well as some of his own. In a letter dated April 16, 1777, Friedrich wrote that he had received disingenuous word that Frederika and his daughters had arrived safely in Quebec while in reality they were still in transit. He was heartbroken by the deception. Although they were only scribbled on a bundle of folded, stained letters, his words rang in her heart as though he had spoken them alongside her.[43]

As much as she enjoyed reading her husband's letters, her daydream was short lived. Upon reaching the shore of Quebec she learned that Friedrich had departed almost a week earlier farther inland to the city of Trois Rivières; it seemed that their great reunion would need to wait a few days more. Frederika broke the news to her children and shared a somber moment, but was surprised to see a carriage waiting for her at the dock. The carriage, she learned, was sent by Lady Maria Carleton, the wife of Governor Guy Carleton, to usher the baroness and her family swiftly to the executive residence where they would stay during their brief time in the city. Lady Maria Carleton was uniquely positioned in British North America to see the development of the complicated politics of the continent. As the wife of the governor she had enjoyed certain privileges, and while her husband defended the empire she was able to travel as an attachment to his army. She was present during the French and Indian War and kept a diary that still stands as one of the most complete and rich accounts of vital battles such as Louisbourg, Havana, and the capture of Quebec. While it is unlikely that either Frederika or Lady Carleton knew exactly how precious their journals would be, it certainly would have shaped their brief time together in Canada that summer.

Shortly before departing the *Blonde* for the final time, the ship's captain stopped the baroness with hat in hand. Clearly embarrassed by his earlier display during the fish incident, the officer begged forgiveness of Frederika and petitioned her for a final favor. His request was a common one for a man in his position, and offers a revealing look into the state of the British navy in 1777. The captain's fear lay not in the safety of his crew but its retention. His great fear was that the most capable and able hands on deck would be impressed into service of the Crown, a maneuver that would dramatically decrease the effectiveness of the *Blonde* for its return journey. Impressment was a harsh fact of life for a seaman of the eighteenth century, and more and more the empire was relying on its controversial methods to restock its navy. Typically, impressments occurred while merchant vessels were at port, and while their crews toiled away in the taverns of their respective ports of call they would be forced on board Royal Navy ships and absorbed into the crew. Technically these acts were legal, albeit sketchy, and more and more in England by 1777 impressment was becoming a major topic of debate. But the results spoke for themselves. The British Royal Navy was the greatest force to ever sail the oceans, and the average Briton thumped his chest at the thought. While the forced servitude, sometimes in the form of kidnapping, was often decried, it was considered a sacrifice that most Britons were able to ignore. From her vantage point, Frederika personally saw little problem with the merits of impressments (the German feudal system did not place a high value on individual freedom), but she granted the captain's wishes regardless.[44]

After finding themselves ashore for the first time in eight weeks, the Riedesel family rode through the rugged and bumpy streets of Quebec until finally arriving at the home of the governor. Frederika wrote fondly of her dinner at two o'clock that afternoon with Lady Carleton, and in typical form focused more on the pleasantries of the conversation; it was highly unlikely that any information of strategic value regarding the upcoming campaign was ever mentioned. Among the topics was the unique fashion worn by the women who accompanied Lady Carleton. "The Canadian fashion for a woman's dress is a very long cloak of scarlet cloth. The rich wear them of silk, and without this garment they never go out." It seemed like the wilds of Canada had their own special effect on even the most refined of European ladies, and at her meal Frederika had plenty of examples to cite. In total, seventy-seven women accompanied the soldiers from Brunswick and many were undoubtedly with her that night. "The Ladies were astonished to see me dressed like an Englishwoman," she wrote. It seemed for Frederika that no matter where she went, she was out of place; she was criticized for her German style in England and later for her English style in Canada.[45]

She did not know it at the time, but that same evening downriver at St. Johns, Baron von Riedesel was sitting down to dinner with General John Burgoyne and Governor Guy Carleton to discuss the upcoming campaign of 1777. Unlike the previous year when they were stifled by the harsh winter, Carleton and Burgoyne now devised a plan to move by June and let nothing stand in their way. The venture they planned was a herculean one, and if accomplished it would capture the Hudson River valley and quarantine the seditious New England colonies and their rebellion. In total Burgoyne would lead eight thousand troops from across Europe through the colony of New York and with luck connect with General Howe's army in New York City before August. While the stakes were high for the government in London, the baron's mind was distant; he wrote to his wife that night to be patient, for they would soon be together again.[46]

Frederika's dinner at the Carleton residence was a great privilege, but after having an audience with King George and Queen Charlotte she was likely unimpressed by dining with the wife of a governor. The baroness's visit to Quebec was not for pleasure, but a stop on the long journey to find her husband. While Lady Carleton was warm and opened her home to the family, Frederika simply could not waste another second in a foreign city when Friedrich was so close. She speedily made arrangements to sail farther into the depths of the continent, and she and her daughters were on board by six o'clock that evening.

## TROIS RIVIÈRES

*June–July* 1777

After spending less than ten hours on dry land Frederika was loading her family onto another ship. Following her meeting with Lady Maria Carleton, the baroness booked passage down the St. Lawrence River where she would meet with her beloved husband for the first time in fifteen months, and her family was giddy with excitement. Although the Canadian wilderness was an unfamiliar place for the baroness, her husband had seemingly been nearly everywhere she went. As she read through Friedrich's months-old correspondence she could not help but feel like she was following in his footsteps.

For every new town or city that she passed onboard her tiny transport vessel, she found a corresponding description or experience that her husband had written about months earlier. In fact, not only did the baron give her detailed accounts of what challenges and places lay ahead of her, but he also left behind a trail of acquaintances who seemed to await her at every turn. The ship that she boarded was one that her husband had used for months, and its captain was the same man that originally ferried Friedrich and the Brunswickers across the Atlantic in 1776. Philemon Pownall was the former captain of the *Blonde*, which brought the baron and his men to America. Pownall repeated the transatlantic voyage in 1777 aboard the *Apollo* which brought General John Burgoyne. He warmly welcomed the baroness and made it a point to comfort and pamper the Riedesel family at every opportunity.

Her ultimate destination was yet to be determined, but in all likelihood it would be Fort Chambly, an outpost situated due south of Montreal and just north of Lake Champlain. General Burgoyne's eight-thousand-man army was now on the move into the colony of New York, and Frederika and her family were faced with having to race to catch up with the baron rather than simply rendezvous along the way. While there was too much uncertainty to determine a meeting place beforehand, Frederika understood that her husband was an army officer, and in the midst of a campaign he would have to honor his strategic obligations first. It was a sacrifice that she had made her entire life; she was, after all, the daughter of a general. Before she could arrive there she would need to take virtually a grand tour of the province of Quebec by stopping at specific points to break up her travels and to more easily navigate the often treacherous North American landscape. Her first stop would be Pointe-aux-Trembles, followed by Trois Rivières, and finally the grand city of Montreal.

One of the most stringent and stressful elements of her journey that summer was the great measures that it took to reunite with Friedrich. Aside from the two months crossing aboard the *Blonde*, Frederika was cautioned that traversing the one hundred and sixty-two miles between Quebec and Montreal was itself going to be a battle of wills. She was onboard the ship and she was quite content there, but the captain warned her that her comfort would not last long. After landing at Port-aux-Trembles, the baroness would need to travel by land for a brief time until finally entering Trois Rivières in a wooden canoe. The thought of such a venture terrified Frederika, but there were few alternatives in British North America. She quickly resigned herself to her fate and prepared herself for whatever new adventures awaited her; by midnight their ship docked at the tiny hamlet of Pointe-aux-Trembles along the St. Lawrence where she was greeted by beautiful moonlight and splendid music. After putting her children to bed at a tiny inn she joined the adults and remained awake drinking tea until they departed again at 2 A.M.[47]

That morning Frederika received her first taste of the enormity of the province of Quebec, and more notably the gentle hospitality of the Quebecois that made up the majority of its population. As their next destination would be the city of Trois Rivières, Captain Pownall informed her that her trip would be greatly shortened if she and her family were to travel by land rather than by river. To this she agreed, and she was soon met by a carriage unlike any she had ever seen before. The horse-drawn transport that awaited her was known locally as a *calèche*, and was much smaller than any she had ever ridden at home in Wolfenbüttel. The calèche was pulled by a single horse, and due to its lightness made for travel at very rapid speeds; the driver would sit on a small bench in the front while the passengers could sit comfortably, although usually only in pairs, in the back. For Frederika, though, the prospect of leaving one of her three daughters to ride separately with a maid in such a hostile place was one she would not entertain. In response to her maternal instinct the baroness fastened the toddler Frederika to her side, situated the oldest, Augusta, on the floor between her knees, and held the tiny infant Caroline on her lap. The open-air carriage made them a spectacle for all to see en route to their destination.

Like a blur the Riedesels coursed their way through the rolling countryside of Quebec, with the powerful St. Lawrence River always to their left. As the calèche strode along, the baroness was tickled to hear her French-speaking driver shout commands of endearment to his horse like "*Allons, mon prince!*" and "*Pour mon général!*" In one instance, the driver even went so far as to shout "*fi donc, madame!*" and, assuming that he was addressing her Frederika responded, "*plaît-il?*" After some embarrassment, she noted with amusement, "The Canadians are everlastingly talking to their horses and giving them all kinds of names."[48]

Although her jaunt through the countryside was brief, the baroness was immediately taken by the modest and hardworking people of the region. Like her coachman they were very friendly and made their affection for her well known. As the party approached their destination the sun was finally rising and the small Quebecois villages were beginning to stir; in the morning light Frederika saw how the other half lived on the other side of the world. Each tiny village that they passed would have looked the same with log-hewn homes sitting side by side, typically made by the persons who lived there. At the center of most communities was a Catholic church adorned with a large, if somewhat crude, crucifix.

Unlike the peasantry of Europe, the people of Quebec often had large plots of land to farm and tend, but unlike their colonial neighbors to the south it was unusual for a resident to own their acreage.

Since the earliest colonization of the region by the French over a century earlier, the property system in Canada effectively transplanted the Old World feudal economy into North America. While the British Americans to the south basked in the glories of land ownership and property rights, in New France farmers and laborers toiled under the old, top-down-style economy that so defined Europe for centuries. Known as the seigneurial system, this ancient practice oppressed the general populace while centralizing power in the hands of the few. Though it was thoroughly galling for many Americans, for Frederika this was the natural order that maintained her status, and many of her German brethren fought to defend it. The seigneurial system was never under attack during the British takeover of Canada, as the Quebec Act of 1774 only strengthened and validated it, but in the eyes of many landed gentry the troublesome American rebellion could endanger their comfortable way of life.

Despite these stark differences, in a rare flash of genuine interest it seemed that Frederika was taken by the rough-hewn style of the *habitants* that whipped past her carriage. She wrote down the smallest encounters that she had with the people of Canada, even down to their hunting practices. But of all the sights and sounds of this New World, there is no question that it was the people that stole her affections. She explained that they were friendly, and she noted that they all lived in homes that were virtually identical and typically white, a striking sight from the St. Lawrence River. Each tiny home was accompanied by a garden and fruit tree making for a charming scene.

During her journey Frederika recounted that peasants would often shout at her passing calèche "We love you!" and "There goes the wife of our dear general!" Before long she waved to the habitants as she and her family strode by. At midday her overcrowded carriage finally came to a stop at the tiny village of Batiscan, and she was informed that her travels by land were now finished. Awaiting her party was a large wooden canoe and an explanation that it was the only way to the city of Trois Rivières. Frederika had no interest in climbing into the wooden structure, and tried everything in her power to buy her way out of it. "I begged an implored, and offered money upon money." she wrote. Before long, the negotiations were rendered moot by an oncoming storm and the baroness, in all her refinement, loaded her perfectly dressed children into the rocking canoe.[49]

For most Canadians, traveling by canoe was less an inconvenience than a fact of life. To navigate the country often required traveling great distances through empty stretches of forest, and if a water passage was possible it was always preferred. Traveling in a normal boat by Frederika's standards was simply impossible after moving past the city of Quebec, as the rivers and streams quickly become rocky, narrow, and peppered with deadly rapids. To successfully traverse the rushing waters would require the same system that the native peoples had used for centuries, and out of this comes one of the great societal developments of British North America. Surviving in North America often meant that European settlers and native residents had to borrow from one another until eventually they formed their own new unique way of life. While the Quebecois were raised in this fashion, Frederika had little interest in adopting the ways of the frontier.

Aboard their slick and maneuverable new vessel, the baroness and her children sat on one side facing Röckel and her other servants. Soon rain began to pour and the smooth waters became perilous. With the children upset, and Röckel trying fruitlessly to calm them, the canoe sliced though the current and wind with surprising ease. A larger vessel could have never passed through the shallows, and the experienced pilot navigated the dangers with expert prowess. Her middle child was on the verge of hysteria and Frederika could only hold her close and suppress her own fears when her pilots told her that any sudden movements could overturn their precarious vessel. For the baroness, it was one of the most traumatic experiences of her entire voyage to the New World, but it was a necessary introduction to the tribulations and sacrifice of provincial life.

Situated at the mouth of the St. Maurice River, the small post of Trois Rivières was a testament to the ever-expanding and often fleeting ambitions of European empire in North America. Originally founded in the 1630s by early French explorers, Trois Rivières (Three Rivers) was given its name due to the unique pair of islands that sat at the confluence of the St. Maurice and St. Lawrence rivers. Although technically only two, the dual islands presented the appearance of three, and it was on that location that the administrators of seventeenth-century New France decided to make their second bastion of settlement to complement Quebec. While Trois Rivières had high hopes, time soon rendered the position useless as the new settlement of Montreal replaced it as the far western edge of the French empire in North America.

While it could be considered as the city that time forgot, since the dawn of the eighteenth century Trois Rivières had proven itself to be a useful stopover for weary travelers making the journey from Quebec to Montreal. When Frederika arrived with her family it was the official winter quarters for all German soldiers who were stationed in Canada. Prior to leaving the city, Friedrich outlined to his wife that he had made arrangements for their arrival, including maintaining his vacant officer's quarters for them to use during his absence. Although their stay would be short, the Riedesel family would be provided with all the comforts that Trois Rivières had to offer. The city was considered the lesser of a three-part triumvirate featuring Quebec to the east, and Montreal to the west, but like its two larger cousins it too retained a uniquely French character in a very British world. It housed numerous religious institutions, including the Ursuline sisters' convent, school, and hospital as well as the mission of the highly influential Franciscan order called the Récollets. Where it differed though from its neighbors was in its fortifications; while Quebec was supremely defended with stone walls and Montreal equally so, Trois Rivières had been left exposed since the previous century. One hundred years earlier the city withstood a major assault by a band of six hundred Iroquois warriors, but upon the completion of Montreal it was determined that there was no strategic value in fortifying a post other than serving as a stopping point. Since then, its original twelve-foot-tall wooden palisade had been left to rot, and Trois Rivières faded from importance.[50]

When Frederika stepped out of her canoe the city seemed as though it had been awaiting her for days, and in many respects it had. A party of officers and local debutantes greeted her enthusiastically, but also expressed a sigh of relief when they found that her entire party had arrived safely. When they finally reached the city the resident commanders were shocked to see that the pilot would dare to deliver such important civilians in such terrible weather. As it turned out, during the very same storm that so troubled Frederika, two Canadian fishermen had been drowned in the rushing currents.[51]

Her fearful emotions did not last long. Soon after making her way into the city, Frederika was introduced to Pierre Garreau, the

Vicar General of Trois Rivières. Known locally as Monsieur St. Onge, Garreau was well recognized as the highest-ranking Catholic clergyman in the city. Born in Montreal in 1722, Garreau had been a close associate of Friedrich while he was stationed in the city. Despite his high personal standing and the Quebecois' strong attachment to the Church of Rome, Garreau was viewed with great mistrust by the residents of Trois Rivières. In 1775 and 1776 when the American rebels invaded and briefly captured the city, Garreau did everything in his power to show that he was hostile to the occupation. It was a bold statement for the vicar, for as adamant as he stood against the rebels, the majority of his proverbial flock seemed to welcome the Americans. It was through this conflict, priest versus parish, that the true political power of a high-standing clerical office is revealed. Taking direct orders from the bishop of Quebec, Jean-Oliver Briand, Garreau demanded that the Catholics of Trois Rivières participate in an endless number of novenas, benedictions, and processions to honor and strengthen George III. It was clear that Garreau was satisfied by the Quebec Act of 1774, but the habitants of Trois Rivières were far from convinced.[52]

For the baroness, however, Garreau's arrival was a godsend. In his letters Friedrich had repeatedly stated that he would be her primary contact during her stay at Trois Rivières and, much like his insistence that his wife closely shadow Mrs. Foy while in London, the baron was equally adamant that she not stray from Garreau. As the vicar led the family to their quarters he spoke very openly of his fondness for their absent father, and highlighted some of their more personal moments during his stay in the city. Garreau informed the family of just how dearly their father missed them, and how often his anxiety for their travels dominated their conversations. In one instance, Garreau mentioned that Friedrich had received erroneous news that Frederika had boarded her ship in England only to change her mind and return to Wolfenbüttel; worse yet, he was later stricken when he heard that a vessel with a woman and three children on board sank in the cold North Atlantic. It was then, in their bleak, cold lodgings with the wind and rain whipping outside, that Frederika grew most restless to see the father of her children.[53]

Garreau was accommodating, but Frederika was fixed on continuing her trip. The next morning at six o'clock, she once again hustled her children into a carriage and set off to meet her husband. While she was unsure how long Friedrich would remain, it became clear by June 12 that she would be reunited with him at Fort

Chambly along the Richelieu River, and thankfully the trip would be entirely by land. The distance from Trois Rivières to Fort Chambly was roughly ninety-five miles, and for the first time since beginning her great Canadian odyssey she would be leaving the shores of the St. Lawrence River behind. Seventeenth- and eighteenth-century North America was a world absent freeways, roads, and byways. Instead, from the view of an imperialist, it was a continent made up of natural "superhighways" around which control of the entire landmass revolved. These were not man-made structures, of course, but the rivers, lakes, and streams that coursed their way through the rough and difficult terrain.

The St. Lawrence River was the great launching point into this system, but it was by no means the only path. A series of metaphorical "exits" led to all corners of the New World. The French had realized this a century earlier, and utilized waterways to stretch their economic footprint all the way to the Rocky Mountains. But while the Great Lakes were of importance to the French, it may be said that the tiny Richelieu River, which connected the St. Lawrence to Lake Champlain, was highly prized. At just over one hundred miles long, the Richelieu acted historically as the Iroquois' main line northward into Canada in the seventeenth century, and soon after King Louis transformed it into a direct shot southbound into England's American colonies. The French built a series of impressive forts along the waterway at critical points to solidify their control in 1665, and at the heart of these new outposts was Frederika's destination of Fort Chambly.

Considered to be a point of strategic value, Fort Chambly rested in the center of the Richelieu at a series of rapids that caused the relatively narrow river to bulge outward like a serpent after a large meal. The French undertook an impressive construction project, and when it was finished at the start of the eighteenth century, Fort Chambly was everything that a French fort in North America could hope to be. Made entirely of stone and shaped as a large square, it sat as a permanent reminder that New France possessed grand designs for the New World. After the British conquest, attention to Fort Chambly only increased. Unlike many of the wooden palisaded fortifications of the frontier, Fort Chambly possessed intricate stonework including a spectacularly designed chapel and an ornate entrance gate known as a *machicoulis* that was adorned with the royal coat of arms. In many ways it had all the hallmarks of a traditional French castle. Fort Chambly had long been considered to be a mere link in the chain that had fallen to disuse after the Seven Years' War, but now in 1777 it would serve as a vital supply point to the largest invasion force that the American colonies had ever seen.[54]

While General John Burgoyne's army had begun to swarm into the colony of New York, those hundred-year-old forts along the Richelieu River were abuzz with activity. The Britons' intended target remained the Hudson River and the division of New England, but like all major campaigns of the age the overwhelming majority of the time most soldiers just idled in place. One of these idlers was Friedrich von Riedesel, and unbeknownst to him his wife and children were speeding toward him. For Frederika, now closer than ever to her long-absent husband, the speed and terrain of her Canadian travel was taking its toll. Frederika described the journey as terribly rough, and later noted that she was bruised from the uneven roadways.[55]

Before she had left Trois Rivières, the baroness was told that there were two possible routes to reach Fort Chambly, one through the walled city of Montreal and the other from a small village called Berthier. For Frederika this decision was of little concern, and she chose the route through Montreal for expediency. She slept there on the night of June 13, and at sunrise the Riedesel family was on the move again. While the baroness usually described the major cities that she visited in great detail, there was almost nothing written about her time in Montreal; it stands as a strong indicator that her stay was brief and also that she was almost entirely focused on seeing Friedrich. Finally, the one-horse carriage that pulled Frederika and her daughters completed its trip south along the rolling Richelieu River in less than a day, and it came to a stop at the rapids where they would see their husband and father for the first time in over a year.

Fort Chambly was a sight for sore eyes. It may have been rough by Old World standards, but the mere fact that Friedrich was somewhere nearby was enough to lighten the hearts of Frederika and her daughters. The baroness had left Montreal at dawn so that she would arrive at her destination by midday, and it seemed that for the first time everything had gone according to plan. Finally, just before evening was beginning to settle, Fort Chambly, the busy hub of imperial activity, came into view. While the fort itself was relatively small, many hundreds of British and German soldiers depended on it, and all around the stone walls were camps and tents filled with men just like her husband missing their kin an ocean away. Most of these infantrymen came from the lower classes of German society, impressed into service, and none of them had any chance of seeing their families until the American rebellion was over. The Riedesels' aristocratic lineage separated them from the burdens that were stark reality for their countrymen.

The baroness would have driven through a myriad of these encampments en route to the administrative heart of the army, and though she heard songs from her homeland being sung it is unlikely that she noticed them; if she did she certainly did not care. Her world had escaped the notions of fairness and social equality ushered in by the Enlightenment, and Frederika was entirely comfortable with the stark divisions of class that allowed her dying feudal system to function. Furthermore, she was entirely transfixed on finding Friedrich, and had no time for trivial exchanges of politeness amongst the ranks of her own native army of Brunswick-Wolfenbüttel. Before long she spotted a familiar face.

Standing among a group of officers outside the primary gate of Fort Chambly was the baron's personal coachman. This driver, who goes unnamed, left Wolfenbüttel with the baron in 1776 and accompanied him all the way to Canada; his presence brought Frederika closer to her husband than she had been in months. The carriage had barely stopped before the baroness rushed to speak with the coachman, and being sure to guide her daughters beside her Frederika quickly begged for Friedrich's whereabouts. The coachman was overjoyed to see his master's family, and in the case of baby Caroline it was for the first time, but after the initial excitement he began to speak to his mistress in a measured tone; bad news awaited her. "He has driven over to Berthier to meet you," the confused servant said. As it turned out, before Frederika had left Trois Rivières one of the baron's former acquaintances had sent him a letter claiming that his wife and daughters had arrived safely in the city, and that they would be at Fort Chambly within the next two days. In a flood of emotion, Friedrich hopped in a carriage and rode to intercept them. Recalling that there were two roads to Fort Chambly from Trois Rivières, Frederika felt a wave of regret come over her as she realized the error she had made. While she had taken the route through Montreal, it seemed that her husband had chosen the other road through Berthier. It was a cruel twist of fate that after being a world apart, their desire to be together delayed their reunion.[56]

Among the officers by the gate who stood and spoke with Frederika was Governor Guy Carleton. Since the spring, Carleton had been anxious to reignite his failed invasion of the Hudson River Valley, and more and more he had been forced to relinquish operational command to General John Burgoyne. Following the failed invasion of a year earlier, Burgoyne made the long sail back to England to both elevate his own status and lay blame upon Carleton for its shortcomings. In London, Burgoyne wrote a report entitled "Thoughts for Conducting the War on the Side of Canada," in which he outlined a new invasion for the year 1777. Meeting personally with the secretary of state Lord Germain, Burgoyne made a rousing case for himself to lead the new campaign, and considering that Lord Germain and Governor Carleton disliked one another intensely, the choice was easy. In May 1777 Burgoyne returned to America with direct orders from the Secretary of State that he should be the new commanding officer in the field, and that while Carleton was technically still governor, he could only exercise his authority in the confines of Quebec itself. Carleton was furious at the decision and viewed it as a personal assault on his character and tenure of office. Since they were still technically in the province of Quebec at the time, Carleton remained a strong presence among the army, but as soon as Burgoyne marched them into New York the governor had specific orders to stay behind. Distraught by the news of her husband's absence, and perturbed at the extension of her wait, Frederika expressed her sadness to the downtrodden governor; he politely accommodated her and assured the irate lady that her husband would return in less than a day's time.[57]

With full command of the army now in the hands of Burgoyne, Carleton left the Richilieu River valley to return to Quebec. That night the baroness and her children slept inside the imposing stone walls of the fortress to await any news regarding the whereabouts of Friedrich. By the next morning, Frederika awoke to find her children, as well as the dutiful servant Röckel, absent from their quarters. Upon a brief inspection she located her brood standing cheerfully along the roadway amidst the army of Brunswick-Wolfenbüttel. With every passing carriage or wagon the girls perked up with anticipation, only to be disappointed when its passengers remained strangers or when it was simply packed with supplies, but still they waited. Although she occasionally checked on them, it seemed that the baroness put her full faith in Röckel and took the time to rest in her quarters.

By mid-day Frederika could no longer remain still, and she eventually joined her daughters, until finally a lone carriage was seen bumping its way toward Fort Chambly. Like the many that passed before it this one was entirely ordinary, and as it got closer the baroness's excitement began to dissipate. As the car neared it became clear that inside the car was not a German lord, but as Frederika described "a Canadian." His clothes were not a uniform, but a tattered jacket made of animal fur that she had seen so many Quebecois wear, and his face was bearded and unkempt. Soon, the carriage came to a halt, and the mysterious provincial stepped forward. Frederika instantly recognized his eyes, and was overcome with joy to finally see her husband. He was dressed as a native and wrapped tightly in heavy furs despite the June weather; she soon surmised that he was long ill by his tremendous weight loss and gaunt face. "My joy was beyond all description," she penned. "But the sick and feeble appearance of my husband terrified me, and a little disheartened me."[58]

All new developments aside, the baroness hurried her daughters to their father, who now too had broken down in tears. Augusta, the oldest, leapt into her father's arms, yet the four-year-old Frederika remained at a distance. Her mother explained that throughout their travels she had repeatedly shown the toddler a sketch of her father wearing fine garments and standing well groomed. To the innocent child, the man before her looked nothing like the picture that she had grown so fond of. Little Frederika turned from Friedrich and shouted, "No, no! This is a nasty papa; my papa is pretty!" Undeterred, the baron removed his heavy fur and comforted his distraught child, and soon all was well. It was a reunion long worth the wait, and made even more special by the fact that Frederika was able to present their new baby Caroline to Friedrich for the very first time.[59]

The family had a great deal of catching up to do, and that night they all dined together behind the safe wall of Fort Chambly. Among many of the conversations was how they had missed one another the previous day, and the baron explained his side of the story. He claimed that he was having a meal with Lieutenant Colonel John Anstruther when a local woman overheard news from Montreal which she immediately relayed to the baron. The information was sparse, but to Friedrich's delight he was told that a woman and three daughters had arrived in Berthier. Even more compelling was the fact that she claimed to be the wife of a German general.[60]

While it was not recorded how the remainder of their reunion was spent, one could imagine all sorts of conversation; in truth the baron had a great deal to discuss with his wife. In the days just prior to their meeting at Fort Chambly Friedrich penned a ledger of his activities which included a who's who of high-profile British officers as well as daily updates regarding the position and arrangement of forces during the preliminary stages of the Saratoga campaign. On June 6 Friedrich lodged at Fort Sorel with Monsieur Saint-Onge (the vicar Garreau), and the following day he first arrived at Fort Chambly. By June 8 he had marched with the Barner and Breymann battalions to Fort St. John on the Richielieu, and by the 11th he was back at Fort Chambly dining with General John Burgoyne. In the immediate days prior to their reunification the baron supped with both Burgoyne and Governor Carleton at Fort St. Thèrese and ventured as far south as Crown Point on Lake Champlain before returning to Fort Chambly to meet his family.

In total the Riedesel family was united again for only two days until duty pulled Friedrich away. While their time at Fort Chambly was brief, for Frederika it changed her entire outlook on the continent and the war that was about to rage.

> We remained with each other for two happy days. I wished very much to follow my husband, but he would not agree to it. I was therefore forced, to my great sorrow, to go back to Trois Rivières, where I suffered yet more upon witnessing the departure of the troops against the enemy, while I, with my children, was obliged, alone and deserted, to return and live in a strange land among unknown people. . . . This time I did not move so quickly; for at every post station, which removed me further from him I loved, my heart was torn open afresh.[61]

DAYS LATER FREDERIKA AND HER DAUGHTERS HAD SAFELY MADE THEIR way back to Trois Rivières and the baron had journeyed south to rejoin the army. Since returning to the city on the St. Lawrence the baroness had been offered lodging among the Ursuline Sisters of Charity, and her family had settled in quickly to their new home. Founded in 1639, the respected religious order was one of the oldest Catholic institutions in the New World, and for one hundred and fifty years it had played a crucial role in transforming Canada into a papal stronghold. While their presence was minimal compared to their sprawling French-style college in Quebec, the sisters maintained the greatest kindness toward Frederika's daughters in an attempt to divert their attentions from their again absent father. Although they did not share any common cause with the Germans themselves, the Ursuline sisters were loyal to the imperial mission and had gained a reputation as the caretakers for the sick and infirmed soldiers of Brunswick-Wolfenbüttel during their long winter stay.

The time spent at the dark and sacred convent was therapeutic for the baroness, and in time she found the sisters to be surprisingly good humored. On more than one occasion the women drank down casks of French wine and spent their long nights laughing and sharing stories; at one point the sisters even dressed Frederika in a full nun's habit and claimed that she looked like the Virgin Mary. One particular sister, a novice, was quite set on recruiting the baroness to her order, to which Frederika joked that she would so long as her husband could reside in the convent. Despite her jest, the naïve sister actually inquired to her superiors about such an accommodation, and later was seen kneeling before a crucifix thanking God for Frederika's transformation to the Ursuline order. Yet still, despite these overall joyous times, Frederika could not help but think about her husband as he embarked on his campaign to cut down the American rebels. Her daughters had been away from home for a year, and the fatigue was taking its toll. One evening the baroness attempted to lighten the somber mood among her children and appeared at their bedside dressed in the nun's habit, but it was more than the girls could stand. Upon seeing her, young Augusta pleaded with her, "Dear mama! Do not become a nun, I beg of you!"[62]

She was safe in Trois Rivières amid the Ursuline sisters, and that was her husband's intention. But after all the travel and all the heartache, she could not concede the fact that she found herself in a foreign land within only a few days' travel to her beloved Friedrich and she was barred from joining him. She promised her daughters that they would be with their father soon regardless of his wishes expressed at Fort Chambly; she put her children to sleep and began to walk the halls of the hospital. That evening while simply attempting to clear her mind, she was startled by a figure slinking through the dark fire-lit corridors of the hospital. He was a soldier from her native country who was deemed unfit for service in the upcoming campaign.

Upon recognizing the baroness the mentally disturbed man threw himself to his knees and suddenly wrapped his arms around her, shouting, "Be my rescuer!" Through his uncontrollable sobbing he locked eyes with Frederika and uttered one desperate plea, one single wish that encapsulated the struggle of the unwilling participants that were so callously described by the American rebels as heartless, dishonorable mercenaries. "Become my deliverer! Cause me to be killed, that I may return to Germany!"[63]

## The Champlain Valley
*August–September* 1777

The time that Friedrich and his family had together was sweet, but to Frederika it had been entirely conditional. During those two days in June that the baron had shared with his wife, there were immediate and pressing concerns demanding his absolute attention. On June 14 at Fort Saint-Jean just south of Fort Chambly, General John Burgoyne was reviewing his army for what would be the largest single venture of the war for Great Britain. If successful, the campaign would sever the New England colonies, choke off their rebellion, and tighten the noose until the seditious effort collapsed; it would be the crowning achievement of John Burgoyne's ambitious career.

The army that stood at attention before the man they called "Gentleman Johnny" was an impressive sight. Representing the king's army were soldiers from across England, including the 9th, 20th, 21st, 24th, 47th, 53rd, and 62nd Regiments. At the vanguard of the force would be Brigadier General Simon Fraser commanding light infantry, and on the right was Major General William Phillips. In true North American fashion, along with the well-trained redcoats were eight hundred Indian warriors representing the Iroquois Confederacy along with myriad other nations made up of longtime British allies from wars of the past. Of the most immediate interest, however, were the three thousand one hundred Germans that comprised the entire left wing of Burgoyne's invasion force, led by Baron von Riedesel. The German forces that Riedesel commanded consisted of two brigades and a single advanced corps, the latter being led by Brigadier General Johann Friedrich von Specht and Brigadier General Walther R. von Gall. The former was headed by Lieutenant Colonel Heinrich Breymann. The advanced corps included irregular Jägers and a band of dragoons, while the brigades consisted of five regiments labeled von Rhetz, von Specht, Prince Frederick, Hesse-Hanau, and naturally von Riedesel. In total there were over seven thousand regulars and one hundred and thirty pieces of artillery under Burgoyne's command, all primed for a direct assault at the perceived heart of the American rebellion.[64]

As the overall commander of all German forces in Burgoyne's army, Friedrich had a heavy responsibility on his shoulders, and it was for this reason that his reunion with his family was necessarily brief. Therefore by June 17 as Frederika and her children rode to the safety of Trois Rivières headed north, the baron dashed toward the three thousand Brunswickers and Hanauers that awaited his command to the south. Compared to the British regulars, the Germans were almost always poorly trained and undersupplied, yet in accordance with the agreement signed between their monarchs they would act with as much a passion and ferocity as the British themselves when marching on the enemy. Despite their presence and official commitment, there was always a divide between the Redcoats and Germans. Much of it was cultural and a great deal of it stemmed from centuries of past competition in the European sphere; in the end the Germans would offer a convenient scapegoat for the failings of the war as a whole. With a grand total of almost ten thousand people when factoring in the civilian contingent that operated in support of the army, Burgoyne believed that he was well positioned to find victory quickly. He was so confident that he wagered before leaving England in early 1777 that he would return triumphant in less than a year.

Perhaps the single greatest reason for Burgoyne's hubris was the corrective design of the campaign when compared to Carleton's abortive venture the previous year. While the governor had attempted a full invasion from the north, he did not provide for any auxiliary support from any other direction. Therefore, as all his men were concentrated around the northern edge of Lake Champlain, an event as predictable as winter was enough to stymie his attempt. While in London, Secretary of State Lord Germain and the politicking Burgoyne devised a strategy that, in theory, would offer total domination of whatever rebel army they might encounter by attacking it from three different sides. While Burgoyne would lead his previously mentioned force southward along Lake Champlain, Lake George, and ultimately the Hudson River, he virtually ensured success by sending a secondary attack force venturing west to east along the Mohawk River in support. These two armies were designated to converge at Albany, and there they would meet the other half of King George's Army under the command of William Howe moving north from New York City. At least, that was the plan.

As usual politics soon replaced practicality and the original design began to fall apart. Howe believed that Philadelphia was a prime target and its occupation would be easily accomplished, therefore operating from New York he would first capture the rebel capital and *then* join Burgoyne at Albany on the Hudson River. It was a complication, but if Philadelphia was to fall as easily as Howe had calculated it would be well worth the delay. More interesting was the possible effectiveness of the secondary force that Burgoyne assigned to march eastward to meet him.

First rallying at Lachine near Montreal, "Gentleman Johnny" promoted Barry St. Leger to lead approximately eight hundred men down the St. Lawrence River to the strategic post at Oswego on Lake Ontario. From there, St. Leger would march his motley assortment of Loyalists, Canadians, and Iroquois warriors along the historically bloody Mohawk River to effectively bisect the colony of New York and rid it of any Patriot influence. The Mohawk River, which led directly to Albany, ran perpendicular to the Hudson and by 1777 the area had descended into a brutal civil war between Loyalist and rebel communities. More than any other region of North America, the rebellion had turned brother against brother and was rife with disputes that often ended in dire resolutions. The arrival of the conflict in the ancestral home of the Iroquois Confederacy made the Six Nations choose sides, and by that summer had already altered their centuries-old social order in drastic ways. For the Haudenosaunee the American Revolution would prove to be a death knell to their way of life. In total what Burgoyne and Lord Germain had fashioned was a three-pronged campaign designed to fully debilitate the American rebellion. On paper it seemed like flawless pursuit, but it all hinged on the one precious asset that Governor Carleton had lacked in 1776: timing.

With the logistical and structural problems of 1776 behind him, General John Burgoyne began his great campaign in earnest by crossing into the colony of New York and commencing his march. As was typical for an army of his size, the force moved slowly but deliberately and gauged its progress by meeting very specific bench-marks along the way. To march via land entirely would have been cumbersome, and sound military strategy dictated that traveling by water, if possible, was most desirable. In this regard, the earliest movements of the British invasion force were highly promising as both Lake Champlain and its smaller counterpart Lake George would allow for a speedy descent toward their target of Albany.

Moving down the watery and contested corridor would not be easy. As policy makers were well aware, the two vital outposts that defended the lakes would need to be neutralized before any success could be found.

The American rebellion was a product of an imperial world; and the position of the rebels was evidence of that fact. At the outset of the insurrection a mixture of regular and irregular Patriot forces made every effort to capture and command critical positions in preparation for whatever conflict would come, and their 1775 takeovers of Crown Point and Fort Ticonderoga embodied this necessity almost more than any other. Fort Ticonderoga was renowned across the empire as the "Gibraltar of North America" because of its strongly engineered defenses as well as its almost impregnable position in the Adirondack Mountains, and it was often viewed as a proverbial "key" to the continent. By 1777 its standing had not changed much, and since its original construction as Fort Carillon by the French twenty years earlier it sat high on the priority list of each respective power that contested for it. By the time that Burgoyne's army began to move on the location, however, it had been in rebel hands for nearly two years, and recapturing it would be essential to the progress of the overall campaign.

Fort Ticonderoga was not alone on Lake Champlain. Only a few miles to its north sat an important yet often undervalued location called Crown Point. While Crown Point was not home to a major fort in the traditional sense, it had served as an important supporting post to its much more powerful neighbor to the south. It was the former location of the French Fort Saint-Frédéric, and was typically an afterthought in strategic comparison to Fort Ticonderoga. Despite its shortcomings, Crown Point was a necessary conquest, and by June 30 Burgoyne's army captured the unoccupied place without a shot being fired. Although it was considered a minor footnote in the larger Saratoga campaign, the retaking of Crown Point extended Britain's line of communication out of Quebec, and reincorporated Lake Champlain into the network of waterways leading back to the St. Lawrence River valley.

But as consequential as Fort Ticonderoga was to both sides, the Americans who garrisoned it were shockingly unprepared; in reality the inadequacy was the result of an overall lack of structure in the American command. In early 1777 the Northern Department of the Continental Army was led by General Philip Schuyler, and Fort Ticonderoga was commanded by General Horatio Gates. In March the Continental Congress promoted Gates to command the entire department, and after a fiery protest by Schuyler the Congress was compelled to reverse their previous controversial decision. At that point, Horatio Gates declared that he would no longer serve under Schuyler and vacated New York for Philadelphia. Back in full command, Philip Schuyler appointed the Scottish General Arthur St. Clair as the new administrator of Fort Ticonderoga only weeks before John Burgoyne's invasion force was set to attack it. While the change in leadership was certainly confusing, it only underscored an overall lack of coherence and organization among the rebel government as a whole.

Aside from its administrative shortcomings, Fort Ticonderoga remained a formidable conquest. Situated on a peninsula on the west coast of Lake Champlain, the former French post boasted tall outer walls and was surrounded by unforgiving terrain. To its northwest sat a piece of defensible high ground known as Mount Hope, and immediately across the lake was the heavily fortified Mount Independence. Connecting Fort Ticonderoga to Mount Independence was a small wooden bridge across the water that served as a primary escape route in the event of an enemy attack, and in the days to come it proved vital to the rebels' survival. Although it was strong overall, there loomed one major chink in the armor of this stone "Gibraltar," and it was the massive peak that overlooked the entire setting. Called Sugar Loaf, but later known as Mount Defiance, it stood out as the tallest point in the vicinity and a potential threat to the security of the entire fort. For most of its occupation, American officers quibbled over whether Sugar Loaf could ever be fortified. While some including Benedict Arnold and Anthony Wayne believed that it could be, the commander St. Clair was not convinced. Unfortunately for the Americans, John Burgoyne's plans included placing cannons atop the peak; overlooking it would prove fatal for the rebel command.

On July 1, less than five miles from the fort, John Burgoyne began his assault. As the British Army was crawling toward their target, the American rebels were fully aware that they were about to be attacked; due to the clever deceptions of the king's Indian allies, however, they did not know how close Burgoyne actually was. The general plan for capturing Fort Ticonderoga was to institute a siege, for that was believed to be the most effective way to guarantee that it would fall. Burgoyne first sent General Simon Fraser's light infantry on the western side of the lake to attack the Americans at

Mount Hope, and then issued orders for Major General Riedesel to take his Brunswickers and Hanauers along the eastern shore to capture Mount Independence and more importantly the lone road that the Americans could use as an escape.

Mount Hope was soon captured by the redcoats and the Americans abandoned the site for the safety of the fort, and once there Burgoyne saw the great opportunity that stood before him. As was debated by the Americans months earlier, placing cannons on Sugar Loaf seemed to be an almost foolproof way to achieve success, and the British command began their effort to do so. For Burgoyne, timing was of the essence for the entire campaign, and the fall of Fort Ticonderoga would be no different. To place cannons atop the contested peak was a must, but to reveal his hand too soon could greatly diminish his overall effectiveness. With this in mind Burgoyne chose to take the hill in a clandestine manner and wait until Riedesel and the Germans had successfully cut off the Americans' escape route across Lake Champlain.

Unfortunately for Burgoyne, the army that he commanded was an amalgam of imperial forces, and exercising true control over all of it was proving impossible. On the night of July 4 a smattering of small campfires were lit atop Sugar Loaf and the Americans were fully alerted to their new threat. On July 5 Arthur St. Clair elected to abandon Fort Ticonderoga. While Baron von Riedesel led his three thousand Germans to cut off the retreat, logistical problems greatly delayed his march. Hours later, using darkness as a cover, the Americans loaded their supplies onto a small fleet and sailed south to safety. The majority of the garrison walked across a foot bridge that spanned a narrow part of Lake Champlain and escaped into the Hampshire Grants (modern Vermont) with no resistance, as Riedesel's Germans had never arrived. By July 6 the morning light over the Adirondacks revealed that the mighty Fort Ticonderoga was now Burgoyne's for the taking, and with the exception of minor skirmishing early on it was achieved without firing a shot.

"IT IS CERTAIN THAT WE ARE MORE APPREHENSIVE OF DANGER befalling those we love, if they are absent, than if they were near us," Frederika wrote in late July. Since her return to Trois Rivières she had sat idly as her husband marched with Burgoyne's army, and the lack of letters that she received was beginning to trouble her. She still wrote Friedrich on a regular basis, but because of her husband's constantly changing location she received no return letter, and therefore had no way of knowing if her own were getting through. While she kept him abreast of his family and their desires to see him, she had lately began pressing hard to join the baron during his march; she was adamant that her presence would not be a burden. "I therefore wrote and urged and implored my husband to allow me to come to him. I told him I had sufficient health and pluck to undertake it, and that no matter what happened he would never hear me murmur."[65]

Much to her delight soon after, she received a bundle of letters from Friedrich that stated that she would in fact be able to join him, but in due time. While it was not expressly written, Friedrich insisted that certain events had to transpire that would allow for his family to safely traverse the Richelieu River and Lake Champlain; with little conjecture it can surmised that his ultimate decision rested on the fall of Fort Ticonderoga. When Burgoyne's army recaptured the site from its rebel occupants, the baron sent word back to Canada that it was now safe for Frederika and the children to proceed south. Frederika's journey would be a short one compared to her previous travels, but it would take her to regions she had never been to before. Friedrich, though absent, was diligent as always and commissioned a personal aide, Captain Samuel Willoe, to oversee her travels. One of the realities of North America was that it was still a very wild place. Throughout her trip Willoe watched over his commander's family nervously, and at one point even stayed awake an entire night while stopped near a location called Isle aux Sonnettes, or Rattlesnake Island. One presumes that a place carries such a moniker for a reason. The next morning the family awoke to a startling sight of vacant snakeskins all round them, and the worrisome Willoe hurried Frederika on her way.[66]

Finally the Riedesel family reached Lake Champlain. Frederika had never seen a lake quite like it back in Germany. At dawn the water shone a fiery orange as the morning sun's rays bounced off its waves, and at dusk the entire valley transformed into stunningly brilliant hues of purple and pink. Not only was this body of water aesthetically pleasing to the baroness, but it was also her direct link to Friedrich, and her vessel was finally able to sail ahead at full speed, no longer restricted by the tight curves of the Richelieu River. Frederika spent the night on a nearby piece of ground called Wolf's Island (which was far less aptly named than Rattlesnake

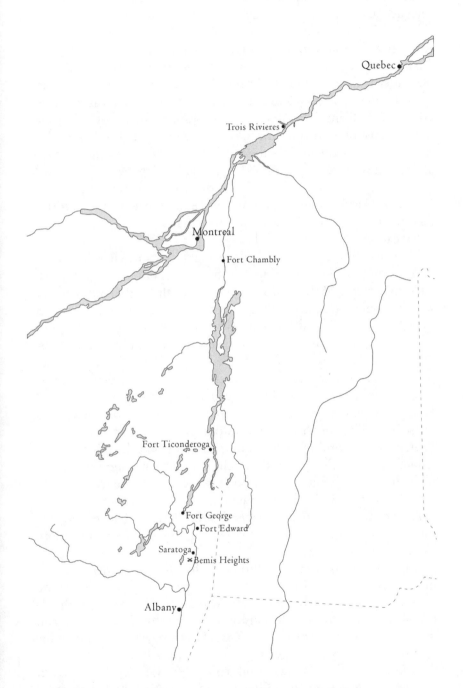

Baroness von Riedesel in the American Revolution, 1776–1778.

Island) where they waited out a thunderstorm, and the next morning she passed the recently acquired Fort Ticonderoga.

Their intended stopping point was Fort George, a much smaller fort on the southern tip of Lake George, just south of Lake Champlain; from there she would continue to Fort Edward. Ticonderoga and George had been absolutely vital forts in the conquest of New France a decade earlier, and as Burgoyne's army headed toward Albany it was equally necessary to reoccupy these old posts to ensure his own victory. As Burgoyne moved south, he gradually forced his Patriot foes to abandon these positions and regroup at forts further south; eventually, the general believed he would occupy them all. When Frederika and her daughters finally arrived at Fort Edward it was already August 14, and, true to the unfortunate theme of her journey, she was told that Friedrich had left only a day earlier.

Shortly after Frederika finally caught up with her husband's army, things quickly took a turn for the worse. One of the more fascinating aspects of the British army during the eighteenth century was the cooperation it received from its Indian allies, a unique asset as well as a potential detriment. As Burgoyne's forces moved down the valley and toward Albany, they were almost always preceded by the Indian warriors that accompanied them; the result was a series of raids that would effectively "clear" an area before the regular troops would move in to begin their operations. After the fall of Fort Ticonderoga, however, these native raiding parties became a distinct liability for the general. In one particular instance of great controversy, a band of warriors murdered a young Loyalist woman named Jane McCrea, and although Burgoyne had nothing to do with the event, public opinion soon placed the blame squarely on him. What followed was the exact opposite of what Lord Germain and other imperial policy makers desired. Rather than Burgoyne's invasion making local colonists oppose the rebellion, it drew more support for the rebels.

Even more troubling for Burgoyne than the allies that he could not control were the forces within the campaign that he hoped he could. As originally designed, his campaign was to be a three-pronged assault on the Hudson River valley from north, south, and west, but that soon fell to pieces. In the Mohawk River valley his subordinate Barry St. Leger was unsuccessfully besieging the rebel fortification of Fort Stanwix, and worse news was yet to come. On August 3 a messenger from General Howe in New York who finally slipped through the rebel lines to meet with Burgoyne delivered bad news. The correspondence that the runner carried was from Howe, indicating that he was about to move his southern forces up the Chesapeake Bay to begin an assault on Philadelphia. Although it was generally assumed that he would next move in support of Burgoyne, he implied that such a move was unlikely to occur. In sum, by August 1777 it seemed that "Gentleman Johnny" would have to take Albany by himself.

When Frederika finally arrived at Fort Edward on August 14 she was witnessing an army in the early stages of turmoil, led by a commander whose command of his troops appeared to be faltering. With the murder of Jane McCrea occurring as a result of Burgoyne's inability to control the Indian warriors that he marched with, and the news that Howe would not be joining him, the general was beginning to feel pressure, and the possibility of impending failure. After taking a drubbing in the court of public opinion regarding the American girl's death, Burgoyne made public aspersions toward *all* of the native warriors of his army, not just those responsible for McCrea's death. The vast majority of them deserted in protest. It seemed that his great plan that had made him the toast of London was disintegrating, and ordinary logistical miscalculations were about to make it worse.

One of the most effective methods that the American rebels used to slow down Burgoyne's army was to chop down trees and lay them across the roads that the British would use to march. It not only slowed the much larger force but it also greatly complicated precious supply lines. With his men finding little productive farm land in the mountainous region, murmurs began to swirl through the British camp that there would not be enough food or draft animals to continue the campaign. Growing desperate, Burgoyne called upon his fellow officers to develop any sort of strategy that could curtail this growing problem; it was then that Baron von Riedesel submitted an idea. Knowing that the Hampshire Grants were only a short distance to the east, Riedesel suggested that Burgoyne send a foraging expedition into the rolling green country to feast off its mostly untouched riches. Burgoyne agreed and on August 9 ordered one thousand men to pillage the countryside and bring back any valuable goods that they could find.

Although Riedesel did not join the expedition, he used the break to venture back to Fort Edward and rejoin his family. The reunion was a much-needed respite for Friedrich, but his stay that began on August 15 was not to be a long one. The following day Riedesel received word that a terrible disaster had befallen the troops that ventured into the Hampshire Grants: they were met and defeated by local American militia near the hamlet of Bennington. As it turned out, when the rebels under Arthur St. Clair vacated Fort Ticonderoga a month earlier, they began a campaign amongst local populations to form militias to stifle the oncoming storm, and while Burgoyne paid little mind to it at the time, it was these irregulars that soundly defeated his men at the Battle of Bennington. In total, Burgoyne sacrificed nearly all of the one thousand soldiers that he sent on what was designed to be a mere foraging mission. It was the worst of the crushing blows that Burgoyne's great campaign had suffered.

The baron was crestfallen by the defeat, but the loss did allow for Burgoyne to temporarily bring his army's march to a halt. Friedrich returned to Frederika and his daughters on August 18 and happily spent the next three weeks with them at Fort Edward. Frederika typically did not write about the affairs of the army, and up until that point she never cared to pry, but the Battle of Bennington must have weighed heavily on her husband's mind, as she mentioned it by name. Describing it carelessly as the "unfortunate affair at Bennington," the baroness expectedly downplayed the major American victory. She was also very forthcoming with her opinion that the defeat was a blessing in disguise as it gave her three weeks with her husband while General Burgoyne calculated his next move.[67]

For those final weeks of August 1777 the Riedesel family stayed on the occupied John's Farm between Fort George and Fort Edward, and enjoyed the mountainous green landscape that was so different from their German home. Their cottage was known among the camp as the Red House. While the German nobles were certainly accustomed to much finer accommodations, the Red House was the modest home of a provincial farmer. It had one main room, which Frederika, her husband, and all three daughters shared, while her maids slept in what she described as a sort of hall. Alongside the larger room was a small study that the baron would use to read and respond to official letters sent from the army, but for the most part the house was a place of rest, not war. She wrote that when the weather was fair they had their meals under the shade of the trees, but when it was not they dined in a nearby barn. She also wrote that it was under those conditions that she sampled the true tastes of American life, including bear meat, the local specialty. She was gracious in these times and claimed that even though they often went without, they were happy to be together as a family.[68]

The calm shared by the baron and baroness at the Red House was rare in the unforgiving season of combat, and while they rested their commanding general was not so fortunate. With the hardships of a failing campaign beginning to catch up with him, John Burgoyne's hand was being forced; and major decisions were being made. The defeat at Bennington was a disaster for the empire, but a survivable one. The lack of supplies, however, would require immediate action. John Burgoyne was faced with a stark reality now that September was near, and preparations would need to begin if a winter encampment was to be possible. While it was a common practice, wintering in North America was never part of an army's original plan. Although the cold months were still likely eight weeks away Burgoyne knew that he was faced with two options. The first and much safer was to settle south of Lake George and continue his campaign in 1778, and the other was to press ahead and capture Albany outright. The conservative officer would have typically begun to settle in for the winter, but Burgoyne had been guided by a grandiose sense of purpose for over a year, and halting for the winter would be a blow to his ego that he could not accept. The decision to press on toward his objective was not without its costs, and the biggest still involved his lack of steady supplies. Burgoyne calculated that to move toward Albany would certainly sap his resources, but if he were to relinquish the multitude of forts to the north that connected him to Canada he could satisfy his army with little unrest. By vacating those posts he would not need to feed and maintain them, and both the men and supplies could be used to support his forces as a whole. Therefore in late August Burgoyne made it known that he would press onward, keeping to himself the fact that the result of such a bold decision was to be all or nothing.

John Burgoyne saw himself as a modern Caesar, and the Hudson would be his Rubicon, but to execute such a maneuver would require a clear and rapid communication along a line that was over three hundred miles long. By the first week of September his army had sat idle for almost a month, and mobilizing these men demanded a sense of urgency; the officer in command of the entire rear of the army was Baron von Riedesel. From his tiny makeshift command post at the Red House, Friedrich received his marching orders and broke the news to Frederika that he once again had to leave, and that this time matters were far more pressing. By the numbers the baron had to mobilize hundreds of Brunswickers, Hanauers, and Canadians for miles around, and Frederika demanded that she join him. Friedrich was genuinely torn, but in many ways the success of the entire British campaign depended on his prompt attention to duty. It was a time of great uncertainty, but days later in a message from the general he received startling news: Burgoyne stated the baron should bring his family along. Now miles away moving from camp to camp, Friedrich sent Captain Willoe to fetch his family so that they could travel with Burgoyne's army on its great march over the Hudson River. Though she did not know it at the time, had Frederika stayed behind or returned to Canada she would not have seen her husband again for another three years.[69]

On September 11 John Burgoyne's army finally reignited its great march toward Albany, and with each step it inched its way closer to what would be a major confrontation with the American rebels. For Frederika it was a time of great action, but also one of tremendous sacrifice. Although she was excited that she would able to travel along with her husband's army, she also knew the potential risks involved, therefore she was content to merely ride behind the marching soldiers in her carriage. She left most of her wardrobe behind, taking only summer clothes. Unlike most of her journey before, however, she was no longer a lone spectacle in a strange and wild country, for now she was joined by a large parade of officers' wives and families. Most of the women that trailed behind Burgoyne's force were English, not German, and in typical fashion Frederika was troubled by the small differences that separated her from the rest of her social circle; in this case it was not language or custom, but a lack of information. She was troubled by the fact that many of her peers seemed to have intimate knowledge of the campaign, and she was largely left in the dark. From her vantage point there was a distinct lack of communication between the British high command and the rest of the army, and from her experience of following her father in the Seven Years' War that was a fatal mistake. While she was rarely critical of strictly military affairs, the baroness claimed that at times she felt as though the American rebels knew more of their plans than even the British allies did.[70]

It must have seemed like a different world. From her prior experience attached to her father's army in Europe, divulging information as crucial as a plan of attack would have been a fatal mistake; yet here in the deeply connected and often surreptitious New

World such intimate knowledge seemed to pass with ease. The free flow of information that so troubled her was indeed a matter of great worry, and the American command was engaging in preparations to meet Burgoyne even before he approached the Hudson River. In the weeks leading up to September 1777 General Horatio Gates had once again been given full command of the Northern Department in the wake of the terrible loss of Fort Ticonderoga. The previous commander, Philip Schuyler, was still troubled by the switch, but unlike the prior occasion now had lost the will to argue his demotion. To bolster Gates's army, General George Washington sent two of his finest officers to aid in the defense of the colony, as well as seven hundred and fifty soldiers. The two officers were Benedict Arnold, now recognized as the Continental Army's most aggressive leader, and a relatively unheralded Massachusetts militia leader named Benjamin Lincoln. Along with these conventional officers Washington also sent the uniquely talented Daniel Morgan and five hundred of his riflemen; by 1777 they had earned a reputation as some of the best shots on the continent thanks in part to their backwoods roots in Pennsylvania, Virginia, and Maryland.

With his new army intact and still growing, Gates began to take advantage of the operational intelligence gathered on his opponent by seeking out advantageous locations to engage. One particular location, known as Bemis Heights, seemed to be the best available position for a defensive stand. Bemis Heights had a number of topographical advantages aside from the fact that it blocked the only road that led to Albany. Situated just south of Saratoga, New York, Bemis Heights sat on a high bluff overlooking a vast stretch of land. To the east was a tiny corridor created by the Hudson River and the mountainous terrain that squeezed into a bottleneck. When, not if, Burgoyne made his march toward Albany, he would seemingly fall directly into the Americans' trap. By the first week in September Gates had already began fortifying the high ground while his British nemesis was headed directly for his waiting rebel army.

Frederika and her family did their best to keep up with the robust pace of Burgoyne's army, but it was a small sacrifice to be so close to her beloved Friedrich. She noted that on September 13 General Burgoyne crossed the Hudson River, the point of no return, and personally reassured the ladies of the camp: "Britons never retreat." From that moment Burgoyne was committed to press on, and however much confidence he actually possessed, he did everything in his power to appear cool and collected in front of his men. The baroness picked up on this and wrote that she was convinced that they would soon reach their destination, and victory was sure to be theirs.[71]

## BEMIS HEIGHTS

*September–October 1777*

There was a certain charm to the American woods, Frederika scribbled in her papers, but by September 19 that quiet and rustic magnificence had been replaced by the drumbeat of war. Since they crossed it a week earlier, the Hudson River had served as the British army's most direct line toward their goal of capturing Albany, and the tiny road that ran alongside its western bank kept the march orderly and predictable. In a cruel irony, the two armies by their very nature had to meet, and that road would funnel John Burgoyne's seven thousand soldiers directly into the waiting arms of Horatio Gates's Continental Army.

The landscape south of Saratoga was by 1777 a familiar patchwork of farms and settlements that were nearing a century old. The rolling country was covered mostly by a thick carpet of impenetrable forest that broke open only for small plots of land that had been cleared by local farming communities. Each tiny pool of meadow then bore the name of the family that originally turned its soil. One such place had been an ordinary patch of grassy meadow planted and harvested year after year, known locally as the Loyalist John Freeman's farm. After September 1777 that piece of ground would be considered hallowed following the collision that was set to occur there. Alongside the Hudson River, approximately eight miles south of Saratoga, was a high piece of ground called Bemis Heights that would become a critical point on the great map of imperial warfare.

Bemis Heights sat only a short distance west of the Hudson River, and the much needed road to Albany ran between. Weeks earlier, General Horatio Gates had called upon his chief engineer to locate and fortify a position where he could face the approaching Burgoyne on almost unconquerable terms; Bemis Heights was determined to be the place where the Continental Army would make its great stand. The man responsible for selecting the site was not an American; in fact, he had been on the continent for less time than some of the men he was preparing to face. The thirty-one-year-old Tadeusz Kosciuszko was born in the Polish-Lithuanian village of Mereczowszczyzna (modern Belarus) and had long studied the art of war; like so many revolutionaries of Enlightenment Europe, the American rebellion was a chance to put into practice the revolutionary theory that he had adhered to his entire life. It was an opportunity he could not pass up.

Kosciuszko studied at the historic Corps of Cadets in Warsaw until the Bar Confederation civil war forced him to flee to France. While there he learned of the brewing American uprising, and in 1776 booked his passage to the New World. After petitioning the seditious Continental Congress in Philadelphia for a commission, Kosciuszko quickly became the finest military engineer in the entire rebel army. His first great achievement was the design and construction of Fort Billingsport in Philadelphia, and after proving his usefulness he was sent north to serve under General Gates along the shores of Lake Champlain. Stationed at Fort Ticonderoga, Kosciuszko insisted that unless Sugar Loaf was fortified it could jeopardize the entire post; time would prove him correct. After the loss of Fort Ticonderoga the Polish revolutionary oversaw the felling of trees along key roadways that so hampered John Burgoyne's supply routes, and as effective as that had been, his great masterpiece was still before him.

Horatio Gates next tasked Kosciuszko with finding the ideal location for his great stand, and Bemis Heights was quickly identified as the single best place to entrap Burgoyne. From the western shore of the Hudson River, Kosciuszko engineered a four-mile-long fortification comprised of tall wooden walls with large quantities of dirt packed up against it. Just below the heights was a *abatis* of felled trees that were sharpened into unforgiving spikes. A large trench was next dug as a secondary failsafe, and finally a three-sided bastion was added and posted with cannons. In short, Kosciuszko had devised a virtually impenetrable fortification atop Bemis Heights that required ten thousand men working almost around the clock; for Burgoyne to advance down the riverside road would be foolhardy.

Thus the great defensive work that kept the New World rebellion alive was entirely conceived by an Old World engineer. And just as Polish revolutionary Tadeusz Kosciuszko worked so diligently to defend his new liberal view of the world, thousands of German soldiers (most pressed into service against their will) fought to deny it. It was unlikely Frederika or her husband ever saw the conflict in North America on these terms, as for them it was merely duty, obligation, and fealty to their duke and their social class that brought

them to such a distant land. In truth it was that same blind igno-
rance that would cause their social and political order to be transformed in the century to come.

By September 18 John Burgoyne was marching almost blind.
After his callous denouncement of his Indian allies, the warriors
deserted his army and deprived him of his single greatest intelli-
gence-gathering force. Still, with the manpower that he had the
general was able to reconnoiter the strong American line at Bemis
Heights and develop a strategy for reaching Albany with minimal
struggle. From what his informants had told him, Burgoyne understood that to march along the river road would be a fatal mistake,
yet in his estimation it was not the only way to surpass Gates. A
frontal assault on Kosciuszko's earthworks would be terribly difficult, and because of the naturally steep edge of the heights' eastern
side Burgoyne knew that his options were limited. Instead of dou-
bling back or attempting a high-risk, low probability frontal assault,
Burgoyne opted to do the one thing that Horatio Gates thought he
would never consider: an attack on the American left.

The left was the weakest point on Kosciuszko's line, and while it
was always a potential target, the rebel commander did not antici-
pate that Burgoyne would ever stray from the river road and venture into the wilderness to perpetrate such a maneuver. While Gates
was ambivalent about Burgoyne's proposed strategy, he was not
without his detractors in his own camp. General Benedict Arnold,
who was perceived as a rising star and undoubtedly threatened
Gates's sense of command, was quite adamant that such an action
was not only possible but highly likely. Along with this dispute,
Arnold had also taken to assigning command posts to officers who
favored the recently demoted General Philip Schuyler, which
insulted Gates on a personal level. For this reason, among others,
the egos of these men obstructed their better judgment, and an
intense rivalry developed. All animosity aside, there was still a great
deal riding on Kosciuszko's line holding up, and while Gates took
effective command of the American right he assigned Benedict
Arnold to the disputed left flank.

For the British commander, the great assault on the far left edge
of the American line was to be a repeat of his earlier conquest of
Fort Ticonderoga. As before, he would rely on General Simon
Fraser to lead the charge against the American left. Since leaving
Canada weeks months earlier, Fraser had defined himself clearly to
Burgoyne as a no-nonsense commander who was respected by his
men and produced dramatic results; the taking of Bemis Heights

was almost tailor-made for him. The center of the British army would be led by General James Hamilton with eleven hundred men in tow, and they would support Fraser by drawing fire and further weakening Gates's flank. Finally the entire left of Burgoyne's force would be commanded again by Baron von Riedesel, and it would be this contingent that hugged the Hudson River. If everything went as scripted, Fraser's column would overtake the American left with the assistance of Hamilton's men. After collapsing the vulnerable point in the rebel line they would force Gates's army to collapse on itself and pin it against the Hudson River; at that point Riedesel would charge down the river road and finish off the Continental Army. The overall plan was ambitious, but in his mind "Gentleman Johnny" saw nothing but success.[72]

On September 19 the two opposing forces drew closer, and by that morning it seemed like a confrontation was not far off. From atop Bemis Heights, Benedict Arnold was infatuated with the weakness that he perceived all around him. He had argued his point with his commanding officer before, and he remained adamant that it must be defended. Finally that morning Horatio Gates gave in to the insistence of Arnold, and allowed for a reconnaissance force to move forward from the high ground and survey the area. The force that was selected for this mission was that of Daniel Morgan and his infamous backwoods riflemen; Arnold believed that they would be best suited to maneuver through the thickets of forest undetected by their enemy. As Morgan's men moved stealthily through the trees, they ultimately emerged on the open field of noted Loyalist John Freeman, and were stunned to have run headlong into an advance group of General John Hamilton's center-positioned column. Although the Freeman farm should have technically been the area covered by General Simon Fraser and his right column, his men were delayed, giving the impression that Hamilton's men were clumsily moving ahead prematurely.

The firing began instantly, and the Battle of Freeman's Farm had unwittingly begun. Although the regulars were better trained, Morgan's men were crack shots and they immediately began to inflict casualties on the British. Showing their eagerness to fight, they charged their enemies, but unknowingly ran directly into General Fraser's men who had freshly arrived to the clearing. The fighting was intense, and the American riflemen wreaked havoc with their sniping. By one o'clock in the afternoon, however, both sides had dramatically reduced their fire to regroup and reload.

After the informal cessation of hostilities, both the rebel and British forces gathered reinforcements and attempted to organize into some kind of practical formation. The fighting soon picked up again and within minutes the tiny clearing of Freeman's farm was transformed into a smoky field of chaos and shouting. If there was to be a pattern to the fighting, it was waves of shifting momentum back and forth between the two armies. As Morgan's men gained the upper hand, superior artillery and range of the British units would quickly take it away. The breaking of the bloody and terrible stalemate came when Baron von Riedesel received communications from General Burgoyne to leave a minimum presence along the Hudson River and bring his left column into the fray. He rushed his men to the farmstead and entered the battle in earnest at three o'clock. The boost that the baron's men gave to the British at that moment was likely only temporary, for combat continued for another three hours. In the end, the falling darkness drove the rebels from the battlefield back to the safety of Bemis Heights, and it seemed that Burgoyne had won the day.

From her position behind the army, Frederika and her children were able to watch the entire battle. Seeing her beloved Friedrich in the midst of the melee was almost more than she could take. Although she was at a location designated to shield her from as much of the battle as possible, it seemed that there was no safe distance. Her daughters remained inside the house that they were using for shelter, but were abruptly thrust into the harsh realities of war when wounded soldiers from the battlefield were ushered into their parlor by their panicking comrades. One by one more young troops, German, British, Canadian, and Loyalist alike, were carried through the door to their temporary home and deposited wherever there was space.[73]

Like Frederika, most of the women that followed Burgoyne's army were the wives of officers from all walks of life and of varying rank. Each time that a wounded soldier was carried back, they all rushed to see if it was their husband; most of the time it was not, and the women would abandon the wounded man just as quickly as they hurried to his side. One such casualty was Major Henry Harnage, whose wife resided in the room next to Frederika, who had grown to know her quite well. The major was shot through the stomach, an especially grievous wound that was often fatal due to the inability of contemporary medicine to treat infection. His wife was filled with sorrow; fortunately, not only would the major survive his injury, he would eventually be promoted as well. For Frederika and her daughters, the Battle of Freeman's Farm was a terrible introduction to the destructive nature of the American insurrection, and happily soon after the battle faded they received word that the baron was among the survivors.

But even in light of Friedrich emerging unscathed, Frederika soon learned that her wartime experience would not be without its own ironic brand of personal tragedy. One of the men who had been carried into her chambers following the battle was a nineteen-year-old named Young; she recalled that she had quite a pleasant acquaintance with a Mr. Young in Portsmouth the year prior. The teenage officer had been shot in the leg, and in the days immediately after the battle the baroness made his recovery her personal project. As the two foreigners conversed, it was determined that the hobbled young soldier was actually the nephew of the Mr. Young that had been so hospitable to Frederika in 1776, and he himself was the only son in his family. She spent hours at his bedside and brought him food and water; it was the least that she could do to honor her former hosts. As the hours passed, the bedridden trooper jokingly referred to Frederika as his "benefactress," and while it did little to mask his terrible pain it certainly lifted his spirits.

One of the most touching aspects of working with Young, the baroness wrote, was that his entire focus was on his parents, knowing how news of such a terrible injury would affect them; in spite of these cares, though, Young was adamant that his mangled leg should not be amputated. The loss of a limb was a near certainty when struck with a musket ball in the eighteenth century, and it seemed that pride overcame Young's sensibility. Before long the stubborn youth's leg became gangrenous, and the infection began to course through his body. Upon his distinct turn for the worse Frederika doubled her efforts, but they were to no avail. The soldier initially protested but the British surgeons eventually decided to amputate his leg. It was too late and the illness had taken hold. Frederika had never considered before that had she not been delayed in the city of Portsmouth in 1776, this desperate youngster that she had cared for so deeply would just have been another faceless casualty. Since she spent such a fond time with his family in England his suffering was now affecting her on a deeply personal level. Frederika wrote emotionally that as he lay dying in the next room she could hear everything through the thin walls, and she agonized with his every groan until he eventually passed.[74]

All told, the Battle of Freeman's Farm was a triumph for Burgoyne, but it was the embodiment of a Pyrrhic victory. He certainly achieved immediate success by capturing the hotly contested open clearing, but there was no operational value in the space. Though the Americans lost approximately three hundred men, they still controlled the strategic high ground of Bemis Heights. For his account Burgoyne suffered far more casualties, around six hundred, wiping out the equivalent of 10 percent of his entire army with almost no meaningful reward for his efforts. Compounding his losses was the fact that the marksmanship of the rebel riflemen had decimated his artillery forces, and the entire 62nd Regiment that held the British center was whittled down to just a single company.[75]

On September 20, while the dead and wounded were still being cleared from the field, John Burgoyne sat in a council of war with his field commanders to discuss their next move. For the British general the most prudent maneuver was to capitalize on their victory by once again storming Bemis Heights, and while he had thoroughly convinced himself, his subordinates were less than certain. General Simon Fraser spoke up at the meeting expressing worries that his light infantry and irregular soldiers had been up the entire night before and were in desperate need of rest; Baron von Riedesel soon expressed his opinion that his men were scattered for miles between the Hudson and Freeman's farm and could not be effectively repositioned in such a short time. Taking these legitimate concerns into account, Burgoyne agreed to postpone his second strike until the following day.

Arrangements were being made on the morning of September 21, and the remainder of Burgoyne's six-thousand-man army was prepared to reinstate their attack. By all accounts the general was ready for any force that the rebels could present, but it was a single clandestine runner carrying a message that ultimately stifled the attack. In a correspondence from General Henry Clinton in New York City, Burgoyne soon discovered that his luck might be changing. In the letter Clinton wrote that in ten days he might be able to reinforce Burgoyne with another two thousand men if desired, but if New York itself came under attack he would have to keep them. He finished the note by writing: "Let me know what you wish."[76] For Burgoyne the memo offered an unexpected and very welcome boost; an additional two thousand men coming from behind Gates's army could surround the rebel position at Bemis Heights and turn the tide of the stalemate. He responded to Clinton in short order, and announced that the army would hold firmly in place until their reinforcements arrived.

While they did not know it at the time, Clinton's army would never arrive due to the uncertain situation of the northern army. The resulting miscommunication left Burgoyne's invasion force in a month-long lurch. For Frederika, however, who only wanted to be near her husband, this time was a gift. Although they were not technically engaging Gates on Bemis Heights, Friedrich was required to stay with his men as the American rebels under Daniel Morgan instigated small, fleeting skirmishes at regular intervals. There was not fighting every day, but there was enough that the British and German troops needed to stay on guard at all times. The baroness, however, made do; while she was approximately one hour's ride away from her husband, she made the trip every morning to have breakfast, and at night Friedrich would take the same trip in reverse to have dinner with this family.

By the time October arrived the air was noticeably cooler and the early morning and late evening rides were beginning to take their toll on the Riedesels. Noticing this exchange, and always seeking a quick profit, an artillery commander named Major Griffith Williams offered to build Frederika and her family a small cabin much closer to the Brunswickers' camp. The home that he built was rough, only about twenty square feet, but it had a chimney and was a short distance from Friedrich's headquarters. The cabin cost her only five guineas to build, and its convenience was worth so much more. The children rejoiced in having their father so close, but Frederika grew worried about Friedrich's mental state due to the grind of waiting and uncertainty. She wrote that in their brief time together her husband could not find one minute of sleep, and never had the chance to remove his boots.[77]

With the month of September gone and still no word from General Clinton's southern force in New York, on October 2 John Burgoyne called a council of war. The previous day he had officially placed his idle army on short rations due to the dwindling supplies and overall shortage of goods. As a direct result of his crossing of the Hudson and disconnect from Canada, the British commander was now feeling the effects of a prolonged stalemate that he had never considered; with still no word from Clinton he believed that his counterstrike would have to occur without him. During the war council on October 4 his subordinates tried their best to dissuade "Gentleman Johnny," to no avail, for both General Fraser and Baron von Riedesel advocated retreat. For Burgoyne, to call for a retreat by that point was simply not an option; he had staked his entire career and political future on leaving America victorious. In his mind, there was no way that London would accept him fleeing the battlefield in the wake of a victory at Freeman's farm, not even scarred by defeat. Instead Burgoyne took offense to the recommendation and returned to his earlier agenda. He claimed that the most prudent action would be another attack on the American left, this time by a force of two thousand. His supporting officers agreed, and prepared their men for the attack.

But despite Burgoyne's lone optimism, he had seen that necessary steps were taken during the month-long lag in activity. Near the former battlefield of Freeman's farm, Burgoyne had constructed two massive wooden walls known as Breymann's redoubt and Balcarres's redoubt; each named after the particular commander that garrisoned them. They were tall and hastily made of dirt and timber, but they gave the British a potential permanent foothold on the rather inconsequential field that they had fought so hard to capture.

Even while Burgoyne grappled with monumental decisions, his mistakes of the past kept him at a severe disadvantage. His men felt the pains of limited supplies, and his strategic capabilities were limited even more because of his lack of actionable intelligence. Due to the desertion of the majority of his Indian scouts, the general was almost completely blind to his enemy's situation. Had he known the strength of Gates atop Bemis Heights it may have drastically changed his plans. As the British steadily went without, the rebel army was stronger than it had ever been before, and news of the Patriot stronghold soon spread throughout the surrounding countryside. With talk of another major engagement on the horizon and enthusiasm at an all-time high over the recent rebuff of Barry St. Leger's force in the Mohawk River valley, rebel militia from across New York and New England flocked excitedly to Bemis Heights. Gates was strongly supported by this recruitment drive, and he was even more strengthened by a trickle of deserters leaving Burgoyne's army; they not only added to his manpower, but also informed the rebel command of just how desperate the British invasion force was.

By October 7 Burgoyne was already positioning himself for a second attack on the fortified American high ground; at the same time he was entirely unaware that his six thousand men would be facing an enlarged and fresh rebel army of over twelve thousand. That morning, the British army began to stir. Led by light infantry, approximately one thousand seven hundred British, Canadian, Loyalist, and German troops were designated as a reconnaissance force to flesh out the precise arrangement of Horatio Gates's left flank. After crossing over the Marshall farm next-door to John Freeman's property, the British force encountered at an unexplored clearing a small American picket stationed in a nearby farmhouse; the picket was quickly sent running back toward the larger body at Bemis Heights. With the space known as Barber's wheat field now clear, the army called upon a foraging party to rush to the area and harvest as much foodstuff as possible.

The opening shots were sporadic, and although persistent they did not constitute a major engagement; the British reconnaissance force waited while the camp followers threshed down the fall wheat crop. By the time the information regarding Burgoyne's where-abouts first reached Horatio Gates, nearly two hours had passed. When he was told of the new ranging of his enemy, Gates decided quickly to send troops led by Daniel Morgan, Enoch Poor, and Ebenezer Learned to force the British off their newly acquired field. Soon after, the riflemen were racing toward the light infantry of the imperial army. The scene that the frontiersmen stumbled onto was one of great complaisance as the Germans and Canadians wandered idly around the open space conversing. The rebels, however, stalked in the tree line, studying their enemy. All was quiet.

At approximately two o'clock in the afternoon the American riflemen were given the order to fire.

That morning Frederika, her daughters, and Friedrich were all but ready to sit down for breakfast. As usual they avoided discussing military affairs, but in this case the baron would have been notice-ably distracted, as he knew that Burgoyne's great maneuver was to begin that morning. With the table set, Frederika wrote that she suddenly noticed a great commotion outside of her cabin window; her husband sprinted outside to investigate. In a hurry the baron called to his staff to assemble, kissed his daughters, and embraced his wife. But unlike the routine exercises, the morning of October 7 was clearly going to be different. Her husband dashed off in a car-riage, and before Frederika could lead her children back inside she was confronted by a party of allied Indian warriors. While it is not clear whether they represented the Iroquois, Abenaki, Huron, or Ottawa, they left the baroness stricken. She described them as "savages" armed and painted for battle, and when she inquired as to where they were headed they only shouted "War! War!" By the time Frederika closed her front door she already heard the guns roaring in the distance.[78]

Bemis Heights had turned into a full-scale engagement. Still occupying the wheat field that they had so speedily harvested hours earlier, British forces were now surrounded on three sides by rebel forces. On the British left was General Enoch Poor and in command of the 1st, 2nd, and 3rd Massachusetts Regiments as well as the 2nd and 4th New York. Firing into the center of the line which was mostly comprised of German soldiers was Ebenezer Learned's 1st New York, 2nd, 8th, and 9th Massachusetts, and 1st Canadian Regiments. Finally on the British right were Daniel Morgan's sharpshooting riflemen.

Poor's contingent on the British left found success early after capturing a significant portion of enemy artillery, and soon the British right was being engulfed by fire as well. Morgan's backwoodsmen decimated the Canadians and Loyalists that they initially engaged, and they soon broke through that initial line and began exchanging volleys with General Simon Fraser's well-trained infantrymen. In the chaos Fraser himself was a ferocious actor and in trademark style led his troops from the front; on this day, however, that virtue would seal his fate. In the melee an American rifleman, speculated by some sources to be a Pennsylvanian named Timothy Murphy, took careful aim at Fraser and fired four shots, the last piercing the general's midsection. It was a crushing loss for the British in the wheat field, and precipitated the total collapse of their already weakened line.

Back at her cabin, Frederika attempted to calm her children but to no avail. Outside, men rushed toward the fighting and others were carried away from the firefight screaming in agony; soon the reality of combat would again land on her doorstep. The baroness had naively believed that the engagement would be over quickly and she had already set her dinner table in anticipation of Friedrich's return. At about three o'clock, however, her door burst open and her entire table setting was tossed to the cabin floor, and in place of the china and cutlery now lay the dying General Simon Fraser. Burgoyne's chief second was brought in on a stretcher and was bleeding profusely, shouting, "Don't conceal anything from me!

Must I die?!" Frederika was simply overwhelmed, and remained fixed to her corner of the tiny room.[79]

In front of her children the surgeon explained to the general that his intestines had been ruptured by the shot and it was unlikely that he would survive. The blood stained Frederika's family table as she attempted to shield her daughters from the sight; all the while the fading General Fraser moaned, "Oh, the fatal ambition!" and "Poor Mrs. Fraser!" The baroness noted that if a commander the level of Simon Fraser could die, her husband could just as easily be on the table next. The baroness showed remarkable calm and awareness in recording the dying man's wishes, noting that he asked to be buried the following day at six o'clock in the evening. In many ways she would always be a soldier's daughter.[80]

Back in the field, the loss of General Fraser was only one of many problems that the tenuous line of British, German, and Canadian soldiers faced. While the left side of their line engaged hotly with Enoch Poor's brigade of rebels, the entire light infantry force on the British right had collapsed. At the center, German soldiers tried their best to fend off Learned's men with their six-pound cannons, but they too began to crumble and break. Although the Germans were renowned for their discipline and resolution it seemed that the Battle of Bemis Heights, or what would become known as the Second Battle of Saratoga, was turning in the Americans' favor. When the right and center finally did give way, it was with little care for their comrades on the left flank. Holding firm they continued to exchange volleys with Poor's brigade, but the rebels chased the other right and center wings so far back that they found themselves behind them. As the last British soldiers on the field, the men of the left flank were soon taking fire into their backs as well. It was a catastrophe.

Compounding matters for Burgoyne's army was the fact that during the fighting the already enthusiastic Americans received a great boost when one of their most revered commanders joined them on the battlefield. Unlike General Gates, General Burgoyne and Baron von Riedesel operated among their men and each of them narrowly avoided being shot numerous times. The rebel commanders, though, tended to stay well out of harm's way. Midway through the fighting, however, General Benedict Arnold attached himself to a group of reinforcements after a heated argument with the higher-ranked Gates and led these troops directly into the heart of the retreating British forces. By all accounts Arnold was incensed, and from horseback he charged Burgoyne's crumbling army. His men cheered and huzzahed as Arnold burst through enemy lines and their morale soared to new heights.

With the wheat field now abandoned and the British army falling backward, the Americans next stormed toward two massive redoubts to the east that had remained far away from the action to this point. The sun was setting, and the German soldiers within the earthworks prepared for the charge they knew was to come; in truth it was almost impossible to miss as their comrades stormed out of the trees past them. The initial shock of the Patriot charge was absorbed by the Balcarres redoubt, and despite their lack of preparation the earthworks repulsed the blow. Yet its survival was to be short-lived. The force that attacked it only grew, and suddenly more and more rebels appeared from the tree line. From behind the structure the commander, Heinrich von Breymann, warned his countrymen that, in spite of the odds, if a German was seen retreating he would be shot on sight for cowardice. Like a great wave the Patriots crashed into the dual redoubts with Benedict Arnold leading the charge. He waved his sword ferociously at his enemy from the back of his horse, and from that day he would be called "the American Hannibal." Colorful nicknames aside, Arnold had placed himself in an almost inescapable situation, and after his horse was struck by a musket ball it fell, crushing the general's leg.

By the time that both of the earthworks had fallen, the entire British force had retreated in a chaotic frenzy, and the German officer von Breymann was found among the dead, shot by his own men, as the archaic ways of the Old World no longer held on this New World battlefield. The capture of the Balcarres and von Breymann redoubts was the crowning achievement of the American army, and the greatest single loss of Burgoyne's entire campaign. Of all the Germans inside the positions, not a single man had escaped; all were either killed or captured. Night had fallen and the results were staggering: Burgoyne's army had suffered over nine hundred casualties and the rebels only one hundred and fifty. Although Gates was in command that day, in the minds of the soldiers that fought there the night belonged to General Benedict Arnold, toasted as the "Hero of Saratoga."

Frederika remained awake into the small hours of the night following the battle. With her daughters wrapped in blankets and still no word from her husband, she did her best to comfort them despite the unfortunate company that now shared their cabin. All around her were wounded men, and throughout the day and night General Fraser's cries and moans had transformed their makeshift home into a sad and desperate place. Aside from the obvious stresses of the dying man beside her, Frederika kept a watchful eye on her sleeping children for fear that they would awake and witness the horrible affair. In this, her darkest hour, she saw the silhouette of her beloved Friedrich in the doorway. The baron was ragged from the battle, his clothes, face and hands were dirty, and his eyes gave away his exhaustion. He embraced his family, but made it clear that he might have to leave hastily, given the terrible situation of the British forces.

That evening Friedrich and his family, along with essential staffers, shared a hasty dinner behind the cabin-turned-field hospital. While the baron was distracted and distraught, Frederika attempted to draw out some conversation by asking about the army's current status. Though it was not likely to be the topic that Friedrich wanted to discuss, it was all that his wife could muster. He explained that they had gained an advantage over the enemy, but it was merely a pleasantry to put his family's minds at ease; his face told a very different story. Before returning to the encampment, Friedrich took his wife aside and spoke to her in confidence, and informed her that things actually had taken a very bad turn for the worse. He instructed her to pack their things in case they had to flee unexpectedly, and above all else to not tell any of the other wives nearby. She took her husband's words to heart and sadly watched the baron gallop away into the distance, back toward the fire and smoke that awaited him.[81]

At three o'clock in the morning a surgeon entered the room to ask the baroness if she would remove her daughters; General Fraser, he explained, was about to breathe his last. They soon removed his body, washed it, wrapped it in a clean blanket and placed it in her bed. The surgeon finally instructed Frederika to take her family inside and remain there until it was deemed to be safe. There, at sunrise, the baroness and her daughters sat uncomfortably alongside the wrapped corpse of the dead general. When morning finally came, it was clear to Frederika that the Second Battle of Saratoga was over, and once again she was alone.[82]

SARATOGA

*October 1777*

The day after the terrible bloodletting of Bemis Heights, Frederika numbly watched the defeated army of John Burgoyne solemnly prepare for retreat. The battle was lost, and all night the five thousand remaining soldiers packed their gear and loaded their supplies. Although the Continental Army was not far away, there was no urgency among these downtrodden men, and they readied their wagons and packs with a distinct sense of resignation; wherever they would be going, their spirits were unlikely to recover. At six o'clock in the evening she watched a tiny ceremony being held atop a nearby hill, and while it was largely unnoticed by the men around her she could not take her eyes away. The men who gathered on that unnamed hilltop were a who's who of the imperial high command that orchestrated the now doomed campaign of 1777. John Burgoyne was present, and though he tried to appear resolved, his look was clearly of utter defeat. The occasion that brought them together was a solemn one; they were burying General Simon Fraser. A military chaplain eulogized the commander, and the officers saluted their fallen comrade. All the while, Horatio Gates was closing the distance between the two armies. From far below Frederika watched intently as the cannon fire and mortars exploded all around this makeshift funeral, and though some of the munitions landed nearby, she was mostly unfazed. Among the men mourning before her was her husband, who was standing in the midst of the enemy fire.[83]

From where she stood her husband seemed so close, yet his martial obligations made the distance irrelevant. Behind her she saw her tiny provincial log cabin now engulfed in flames and burning alongside the other wives' quarters; they had been set ablaze by the advancing rebel army. The small funeral held that day was the dying wish of General Fraser, and "Gentleman Johnny" would not have lived up to his name if he had not honored it. At the close of the ceremony Burgoyne immediately issued full orders of retreat. The withdrawal command was official at that point. His subordinate officers had made sure that their troops were well in motion beforehand, and late in the evening many were already moving back north. Frederika noted that the majority of them had left their tents up and their campfires burning to confuse the rebels who watched them and buy them some extra time.

But Frederika herself was not prepared to leave, not with Friedrich so close by. She was soon approached by the wounded Major Harnage, who persuaded her to flee, and as strong as her protests were she soon realized she had little choice. She delayed as much as possible, until the insistent major pressed her, saying, "All right, then your children must go without you." With that ultimatum she got into her carriage. Along the road she was told by numerous parties that she would be with the baron again soon, but in the meantime she must remain silent so as not to give away the retreat to any rebel spies in the nearby forests. She obeyed, although Gates knew full well it was happening. She took the threat of discovery so seriously that she even went so far as to hold a handkerchief over her middle child's mouth to silence her fearful whimpers.[84]

Frederika's cautious steps were helpful, but probably not appreciated. The task ahead of General John Burgoyne was a herculean one, and as difficult as moving an army toward battle could be, it was even more difficult to move one away. Taking account of his losses, it was calculated that Burgoyne lost six hundred men in the fighting, British and German alike; they were killed, wounded, or captured. Of those now absent his command, approximately two hundred and fifty were in enemy hands along with six heavy cannons and countless amounts of small arms. To complicate the casualty figures even further, the grand total did not take into account the native allies, Loyalists, and irregular Canadian units that also joined in the battle. Whatever the precise numbers, Burgoyne had to move an army of over five thousand men, healthy and wounded alike, back from whence they came. The arrangement of his troops was designed for speed and was led by irregulars under the command of Captain Alexander Fraser, the nephew of the deceased general. Behind him were the Germans led by Baron von Riedesel, followed by the large contingent of British regulars headed by Burgoyne himself. Finally bringing up the rear was a contingent of skirmishers led by General William Phillips; it was this unfortunate crew that would absorb any fire from their pursuers and that would have to drag the cannons along behind them. His army had begun its march after dark on October 8, and by dawn of October 9 after hours of marching General Burgoyne suddenly brought the entire force to a halt.[85]

For Frederika, the command to stop was perplexing. She claimed at six o'clock General Burgoyne ordered all of his cannon lined up in rows and counted. In her (incorrect) estimation, if they had not stopped to tally their true numbers, the whole army could have escaped the pursuing rebel army. But nevertheless she welcomed the break because it allowed Friedrich to momentarily abandon his post and trek back to her calèche for a brief visit. Reunited again, the baron and his family huddled closely together during the idle time. Frederika was content as Friedrich slept for nearly three hours with his head on her shoulder.[86]

October 9 was a hellish day for General Burgoyne's army. Earlier that morning they had restarted their trek north toward the small town of Saratoga, where they would rest on their way back toward Canada, all the while being pursued at a distance by Gates from behind, as well as across the Hudson River on its eastern shore. As if the march itself was not difficult enough, the new day had brought with it a terrible rainstorm. The road was now a swampy mess, and the horses and wagons sank into the muck; the soldiers who still had shoes on their feet found them to be loaded down with water and mud. The men of the British force had to push through, but others with less tangible ties were not so dedicated.

Riding behind the army, Frederika noted that the Indian warriors that accompanied Burgoyne were growing increasingly impatient with the entire venture, and the rainstorm two days after the battle seemed to push them to a breaking point. She explained that she saw the retreating warriors as cowards and without honor as they seemed only interested in plunder. In the observation the baroness was not incorrect, though not fully interpreting the scene before her. One of the great cultural differences between native and European peoples had always been their perception of war. As much as the contrasting peoples shared there remained some stark disagreements, most notably the collecting of spoils after a battle. For the European, to strip an enemy of supplies was largely done for practical or celebratory reasons, for the native warrior such an action was a virtual requirement, and the opportunity to spoil was often a prerequisite for any combative alliance.

The general's insistence on progress along with the terrible conditions likely pushed away the Indian warriors who remained with the British, and with each passing mile Burgoyne's army shrunk ever so slightly. Always diligent, the British command had decided that any Patriot or rebel homestead that they encountered on their march toward Saratoga should be destroyed, and despite the rain the army left a burning countryside in its wake. For General

William Phillips at the rear of the column, the trek was especially cumbersome; it was the responsibility of his men to burn, raze, and dismantle any bridge that could assist Gates in his pursuit, as well as chop down trees across the road to slow them.

The day was taxing for all parties involved, and it even began to unravel Frederika's tiny entourage as well. Her chief lady's maid who had traveled with her party from Germany began to sob uncontrollably during the storm, and ever protective of her image the baroness reminded the emotional servant that she must maintain good form. In a heated moment the maid tore off her cap and let her rain-soaked hair fall into her face, firing back at her mistress that she had nothing to gain by being drawn into the terrible quagmire of war. The outburst drew the attention of the other women nearby, and the embarrassed Frederika soon took on a much more conciliatory tone. She promised the frantic woman that all of her hardships would be rewarded with extra pay, and that she needed to regain her composure or risk being taken for a "savage." The baroness noted that Lena, her second maid, was also afraid but remained silent.[87]

All the time that Frederika traveled she kept a careful account of the people she encountered, and paid special attention to General Burgoyne himself. Over the course of the campaign she had studied his personal traits and demeanor, and had decided that he was not fit to hold his current office. In Wolfenbüttel a military commander was expected to be a true gentleman and only come from the finest family stock; in contrast, Burgoyne only represented himself as a gentleman. One of the unsavory habits that especially offended her was the general's sly womanizing, and she noted that throughout the campaign he had an ongoing affair with the wife of one of his commissaries. Like him, she wrote, his mistress loved champagne, and the pair had danced and drank even during some of the most critical moments of the previous month.[88]

After hours in the storm, the baroness and her rain-soaked children finally saw a place to lay their heads. Saratoga was a tiny village along a bend in the Hudson River that until that day was entirely ordinary in nearly every facet of life, and for Burgoyne's army it would be a place where they could momentarily rest on their way north. There had been an earlier fortification in the area with the same name that was destroyed in the Seven Years' War, and until October 1777 the region had remained relatively peaceful. Frederika took little time to study the new location as she and her

family were thoroughly drenched, but did write a scathing critique
of General Burgoyne's slow-moving progress toward the site. By
her estimate the place that Burgoyne had halted the army for so
long in the midst of the downpour was a mere thirty-minute ride
from the village of Saratoga; with her children now compromised
by the weather she fumed at his hesitation. All the time that the
Riedesels sat exposed to the elements in the middle of the wilderness, she had no idea that warmth and shelter were only a short distance away. In addition to her personal qualms, the baroness was
equally perturbed that the general repeatedly brought the entire
army to a halt for seemingly inexplicable reasons. These new dis-
coveries only compounded her low opinion of John Burgoyne, and
she was determined to voice her concerns.

After putting her daughters to rest at a nearby campfire outside
the village, Frederika was able to draw the attention of General
William Phillips, the commander who struggled so mightily to protect the rear of Burgoyne's army. He knew her husband well, and
while Friedrich was still with his men, Frederika felt that she could
speak candidly to the general. She asked him why Burgoyne insisted on delaying the retreat, and then voiced her own opinion that if
only they kept a more steady pace then they might outrun Gates's
army altogether. Phillips responded, "Poor woman, I admire you!
Thoroughly drenched as you are, you still have the courage to go on
in this weather." The baroness was flattered, and Phillips continued,
"If only you were our commanding general! He thinks himself too
tired and wants to spend the night here and give us a supper." With
his final statement it was clear that John Burgoyne was now losing
the confidence of his fellow officers, and after a rainy day's march
they did not hesitate to say so.

The following morning the men of Burgoyne's army had the
chance to dry out, and after the storm the true measure of the
botched retreat was beginning to emerge. All around Frederika soldiers were starving, and it seemed that the general's decision to
sever ties and supply lines to Canada was finally exacting its terrible
toll. Burgoyne had hoped to feed off of the land as he marched, but
there was far less food available than he had anticipated due to the
lateness of the season. Adding to the distress was the fact that the
rebel army was still in pursuit, less than a day's march behind them.
During this miserable stretch, Friedrich remained with his army but
made sure that his family was well taken care of; on the baron's
orders Frederika's tiny caravan was always fully stocked with food.

For this reason on the afternoon of October 10, while Frederika and her daughters were sharing a tea, she was approached by a humble and desperate officer who began to beg her for food. She obliged the unnamed man, but before long there were over thirty others standing in his place. By the end of the day she had exhausted her modest bundle of supplies, but took pleasure in the small amount of relief it brought the troops. As she had done quite often before, the baroness often busied herself with small side projects such as this one, and soon found herself demanding an audience with General Burgoyne to express her displeasure. She subsequently took out her frustrations on the general's aide, claiming that the poor troops had sacrificed everything, yet received almost no material support. Within thirty minutes of her spirited address General John Burgoyne arrived at her carriage with hat in hand, and Frederika noted that he thanked her "most pathetically" for having reminded him of his duty.[89]

That same afternoon the women attached to the army began their preparations to march on, and word had spread that General Burgoyne was rallying his troops for an extended trek to the safety of the fort to their north. To Frederika it seemed that the difficult journey was well worth the hardship if it could move her family to safety, but there outside Saratoga, New York, it was all about to change. Until that moment Gates's army had only been a distant threat, but that afternoon the danger became all too real. At approximately two o'clock the silence of the countryside was broken by a series of musket volley fire and cannon blasts; before long the women of the camp were scrambling for cover.

It was there along the Hudson River that the first members of General Gates's rebel army had caught up with the retreating British, and though they were only skirmishers, their attack placed the entire camp in serious jeopardy. Frederika was panicked, but an aide of the baron's soon arrived on the scene with a message from her husband directing her to find shelter in the village of Saratoga itself. She next rushed to her carriage with her children, and a wounded English veteran that she had tended to days earlier helped them into the buggy; once loaded though she was rocked by a great explosion nearby, and instinctively threw herself over her daughters. They escaped the blast unscathed, but the very soldier that had assisted them only seconds earlier now lay dead next to their carriage. Bumping down the winding road into the nearby village, the calèche was vulnerable to the rebel attack, which seemed to be going on all around them. Once they arrived in Saratoga, Frederika and the other women of the party ran into the first home they could find, and, as though planned, soon many more camp followers trailed after her. The home was modest, but the baroness spent no time appreciating its design; she ran directly for the basement. Soon there were crying families all around her, and wounded soldiers were filing into the confined space as well. The American rebel forces were attacking them from the opposite shore of the Hudson River, and upon noticing the unusual volume of people at the house began to fire at it. In the confusion the rebels believed that the house contained some high-value targets and honed in on the small cottage. Frederika recalled that only women, children, and the infirm were within its walls, and the frightened civilians cursed the approaching rebel army for firing on them.[90]

In the midst of the firefight the tiny stone Saratoga basement became a last resort for the people inside, and the scene overwhelmed the baroness. "My children laid down on the earth with their heads upon my lap, and in this manner we passed the entire night."[91]

The dramatic scene that was playing out around the quiet village of Saratoga was the beginning of the end for John Burgoyne's now infamous campaign. From its original strength of eight thousand, his forces had been whittled away to less than six, and his supplies were entirely cut off. Since arriving in the village Burgoyne had commandeered a home belonging to the American general Phillip Schuyler and made it into an impromptu headquarters, and it was from this point that he wrestled with decisions that would seal the fate of his army. For the general, Saratoga was meant to be a stopover point to plan his next move, since it was the first real bit of civilization that he encountered since leaving Bemis Heights. The retreat order that had come only days earlier was a broad one, but from its conception Burgoyne had planned on utilizing the myriad forts and posts that connected the Hudson River valley with Canada. Whether it would be a full escape or simply a rearrangement of forces was yet to be seen, but no matter where they would finally settle, the retreat hinged on reaching the next vital post, Fort Edward.

To remove himself to Fort Edward just south of Lake George and Lake Champlain, Burgoyne would need to cross the Hudson River from its southern bank, and he dispatched troops and engineers to reconnoiter a location for a possible bridge. Little did he know though that Gates's rebels were well ahead of him. Since the Second Battle of Saratoga, Gates had wisely decided to simply shadow Burgoyne's army rather than attack it outright, and his reasoning largely depended on his wily foe. Gates understood that if he simply engaged Burgoyne during his retreat he could reignite another pitched battle, and though he was confident, Gates much preferred to trap the British army under his own terms. For this reason he sent a probing party far north ahead of Burgoyne's army to the vicinity of Fort Edward, and when the British advanced engineering force was seeking out a potential bridge crossing they were unaware that Patriot agents were waiting for them across the Hudson. With those troops in place blocking any northbound escape, Gates next deployed forces to the east that would contain Burgoyne from the opposite side of the river. He further strengthened his plan by sending troops from the west that were rapidly closing in on Saratoga. Finally, Gates himself would bring up the remainder of the army trapping the British once and for all; in total there were six thousand men in place ready to bombard the village; the fire now directed at Frederika and her family was the result of these movements by Gates's forces.[92]

All these new developments understandably troubled John Burgoyne, and during a time when decisive action was necessary to save his army the general appeared to waffle. One of the strongest voices among his immediate officer corps that pressed him on his indecision was Baron von Riedesel, who was adamant that if this retreat was to escape surrender the entire army would need to move out immediately; adding to his urgency was the fact that he knew that his wife and three children were hidden somewhere in the village amidst the raining shot. Finally Burgoyne gave his orders, and they were minimal and ineffective. He commanded his staff to fall back into the rear of the army, and then out of frustration ordered Phillip Schuyler's farm and home to be burnt to the ground. The indecision at this critical time did irremediable damage to the British war effort, and while Gates's rebels were preparing to engulf Saratoga, it is likely that Burgoyne had never even considered such an unthinkable outcome.

The day after the bombardment began, the baroness found herself in the most wretched situation of her life. As a member of elite German society she had scarcely seen the horror that war could bring to a population of civilians, but now crammed into a musty stone basement she felt like she had seen it all. Growing up as a child attached to her father's camp she had witnessed many campaigns, but always from a comfortable distance far behind the front lines; now as a woman with a family of her own she viewed the entire affair differently. All night the American bombardment shook the foundations of the small Saratoga home, and the women, children, and wounded feared for their lives. One of the most troubling aspects of Frederika's days-long stay in the tight space was how quickly the relatively refined and cultured people who joined her had to abandon propriety and were reduced to relieving themselves on the floor rather than risk facing the rebel army outside. This new development combined with the smell of putrefying flesh from the wounded soldiers stirred Frederika to take charge.

After convincing her fellow refugees of the potential risks of their situation, she enlisted the help of many of the women to clean out the basement. While they all recognized the hazards of remaining stationary amidst the refuse, a sudden lull in the American cannonade convinced them that such a venture was now possible. Using casks of vinegar that they found in the basement, Frederika and a few ambitious helpers scrubbed the walls and floor while their children and most of the others remained upstairs. All the time that she had spent in the dark, damp cellar had not afforded her the chance to examine it, and upon a very basic inspection she found that there were actually three separate rooms. With its occupants upstairs, she organized a basic plan to separate the wounded men from the healthy, and place the other women and children in their own area.

It was during this time that Frederika received a bundle of messages from her husband now only a short distance away. In typical fashion, most of them were redundant statements that he was safe and made multiple inquiries into his family's well-being; others though revealed just how the stress of combat was affecting the baron. In one instance he wrote to his wife that he had decided to hand her over to the rebels only to ensure her safety. He believed that so long as there were shots being fired she was in danger, but if he could guarantee her safety by trading her and his three daughters to the enemy as prisoners it would be the lesser of two evils. She replied, "to be with people whom I would be obliged to treat with courtesy, while my husband was being killed by them, would be even yet more painful than all I was now forced to suffer."[93] In other words, she was not going to give in until the end.[94]

The sight at Saratoga was one to behold, and the full totality of the American rebellion was in some respects revealed there. If the baroness walked into the open she could see her husband's camp fires burning brightly in the distance, and she wrote that as dusk approached it was the only way that she knew he was still there. Still, she had her own small battle to wage as the *de facto* leader of her basement dwellers, and she returned inside to inform them of her newly formed arrangement. Because of the scarcity of shelter, a party of army surgeons had begun using the first floor of the house to perform medical procedures, and upon reentry she saw a man lying on the dinner table with a badly mangled leg preparing to be amputated. When she saw this gruesome spectacle she told her daughters to head into the cellar, as it was newly cleaned, and to spare them the image; this may have saved their lives. Shortly after Frederika called the refugees back into the house, the American cannonade started again with shocking swiftness, and the peaceful silence of the countryside was now filled by the sounds of incoming artillery. In a panic the terrified mob stormed toward the cellar, and seeing that her children were seated on the stairs Frederika raced to the door. From her position she blocked the entranceway to the staircase with both of her arms extended, and it took all of her might to keep the surging crowd from stampeding over her daughters. "My children were already under the cellar steps," she wrote, "and we would all have been crushed, if God had not given me the strength to place myself before the door."[95]

Eventually she could hold them back no longer and she and the others poured down the stairs; by then her daughters were safely away from the mob. The cannon fire was intense, and unlike the night before it seemed to be coming from both east and west as Gates's army was finally in position. From beneath the floor-boards Frederika counted no less than eleven cannon balls that blasted through the side of the house and that she distinctly heard "rolling about above our heads." It seemed that there was no more shelter to be had, and this fact was only magnified when one of the balls crashed directly onto the table where the amputee was recovering from his procedure; the shot tore off his remaining leg. The noose was now tightening around John Burgoyne's army, and Baroness von Riedesel was as much a part of the war as ever before.

The next morning as the sun began to rise over the hills the firing subsided, and once again it was safe to move about the house and inspect the damage. Unlike the previous day, when the firing was done at a great distance, the small home was now raked with damage and it was clear that Gates's army was much closer.

Frederika busied herself that morning by cleaning up the blasted pieces of wreckage strewn about the parlor, as was quickly becoming her routine, but it was only to pass the time until Friedrich's aide arrived with his daily bundle of letters and notes. Minutes turned to hours, and by afternoon there was still no word from her husband; instinctively she was overcome by a terrible fear.

By afternoon there was still nothing from Friedrich, and the baroness became visibly shaken. She had spent days cloistered in a dank cellar, but she was never alone, and in those fearful hours had grown close to many women, each in a very similar situation to her own. There was the wife of Major Harnage, who saw her husband wounded at Freeman's farm; Mrs. Reynell, who had already lost her husband at Bemis Heights; and a much younger lieutenant's wife that was grateful to Frederika for feeding her husband days earlier during the retreat. These women were all from different stations in life, and each had suffered in her own way; they did their best that day to console Frederika and put her mind at ease. In her own words Frederika said that she and her new confidantes were commiserating together when there was a soft rasp at the front door. To hear such a knock was unusual for the women, as most of their fellow refugees simply walked in and out of the house with no care for privacy, and it told them that whoever was outside was ignorant of this casual protocol. Before any of them could stand, the door opened and a small party of somber officers stepped through.[96]

Their faces said what their mouths did not have to. Each of the women with the exception of the widowed Mrs. Reynell instantly froze; as the men's glances scoured the room they each quietly prayed that the terrible news would not find them; "I noticed … that they cast silent glances toward me," Frederika wrote. As the men somberly approached her the baroness grew weak, and then broke down. "This awakened in my mind the dreadful thought that my husband had been killed. I shrieked aloud." For a few moments, Frederika was overcome with grief and tragic images flashed through her mind, each worse than the previous. That all changed in a split second, however, as the officers bypassed her and delivered the fateful message to the lieutenant's wife, the youngest lady of the group. Barely twenty years old, the woman became irate, and suddenly the horrible anguish that had stricken Frederika melted away at the sight of the young bride realizing that her future was altered forever. The baroness explained that in the bombardment the English lieutenant had his arm blown away by cannon shot and he would not survive the night; only days earlier he was one of the men that Frederika so graciously fed with her own stock of goods. It was a heartbreaking loss all across the camp, and after hearing of the terrible trauma that Frederika suffered (even only briefly), Friedrich left his headquarters and traveled to the village. The rebels were tightening their grasp and he could not stay long, but the baron and his family stole a few moments together in the wake of the tragedy.[97]

For the next five days Friedrich returned to his wife daily, but he bore the emotional scars of a prolonged campaign. When he was with his family he was distant, and he often rejected eating dinner in favor of drinking wine, which according to Frederika was the only beverage Friedrich would take. His outward appearance began to deteriorate, and his morale became so low that the family servant Röckel even admitted to the baroness: "I fear that the General drinks all this wine because he dreads falling into captivity, and is therefore weary of life." Despite his dwindling spirits, Frederika was lucky that Friedrich remained physically unscathed for the entire campaign, a claim that almost no other wife could make. She wrote plainly, "Should I be the only fortunate one?"[98]

After five long days of hiding in the tiny provincial basement the baroness received a message that was both comforting and terrible. On October 16 General John Burgoyne would surrender his sword and almost six thousand troops to the rebel commander Horatio Gates. The small hamlet of Saratoga was only meant to have been a temporary point of respite for the beleaguered British army, but in his decision to remain it seemed that Burgoyne had sown the seeds of his own last stand. In his mind he played out a number of scenarios to escape the clutches of the rebel army that had surrounded him, including a plan to remain in place with a forlorn hope that Henry Clinton's army would save him, but in the end he came to terms with the fact that it was all for naught. He soon agreed to a tentative surrender with Gates, and after frantically questioning his fellow officers to discover if there was any potential to back out, he finally acquiesced.

The character of "Gentleman Johnny" Burgoyne in many ways defined his great invasion of 1777. It was a bold undertaking with lofty goals, sprinkled with just enough hubris to make it seem plausible but perhaps too much to actually make it possible. He had underestimated his foe and placed too much stock in his own capabilities. In short, he did not respect his enemy nor the rugged terrain of North America and he now faced the consequences. In typical fashion Burgoyne viewed the entire affair as a reflection of his own merits, and because he still maintained plans for a bright future he would not agree to the traditional "surrender" that had disgraced so many English commanders before him. Instead, he and Gates agreed to refer to the act not as a capitulation, but specifically as a "convention." Gates understood the massive ego of his foe and also knew that regardless of the semantics, he had won the greatest victory of the entire war.

On October 17 John Burgoyne met with General Horatio Gates at a place known as the Field of Grounded Arms, followed by Baron von Riedesel among the rest of his officer corps. The men greeted each other coldly and Burgoyne famously uttered, "The fortune of war, General Gates, has made me your prisoner." Just prior to the meeting Burgoyne told his staffers and officers to return to their men, thank them for their service, and prepare for the inevitable. While he was likely aware of the gravity of the moment, he most likely did not realize that it was the last order he would ever give in North America. In the end John Burgoyne handed himself and approximately five thousand eight hundred British and German soldiers over to the American rebels, not counting the Indian allies and Loyalists that had been taken along the way.[99]

Soon after, Friedrich sent word to his wife that they were finally safe and that the campaign had officially ended. Even more hopeful was the promise that wherever they found themselves in the coming days, they would be together. For Frederika Charlotte Louise von Massow, Baroness von Riedesel, the details did not matter; wherever her American story would now take them, they would go forth as a family.

In June 1778, nine months after the great "convention" of John Burgoyne's infamous surrender, Frederika and her family had grown closer than ever before. Since the previous fall they had been marched as a "Convention Army" to Boston as prisoners of war, and unlike the thousands of troops encamped in their tents, her family had been given the luxury of a townhome in neighboring Cambridge. While life was not what she was used to in Wolfenbüttel, she was quite fond of the busy port of Boston. Her home was a simple one, but filled with the charm of a provincial city when compared with the busy hub of London, but much more refined than Quebec and Montreal. The people, however, were a different story.

During her months in Boston she was treated as an enemy on the street, and while she usually kept to herself, people never let her or her family pass without expressing their disdain. "The city, throughout, is pretty, but inhabited by vile patriots, and full of wicked people. The women, especially, were so shameless, that they regarded me with repugnance and even spit at me when I passed by them."[100]

She understood the animosity of Bostonians, whose city had been occupied by the British army and singled out as a seditious colony of insurgents. The worst of her recollections centered on noted Loyalist Captain Fenton, whose wife and fifteen-year-old daughter were pulled from him by a mob of Patriots, stripped naked, and smeared with boiling tar. The ravenous crowd of partisans proceeded to parade the violated mother and teenager through the streets. It was an appalling sight.

Politics aside, life for the Riedesels was peaceful in Boston, and her worst fears of being held captive were never realized. The American General Phillip Schuyler had been very cordial with the baron and baroness, even dining with the couple in Albany after the convention, and that same hospitality was maintained among the American upper class during their stay in Cambridge. Along with the rebel command, Frederika naturally stayed in close contact with the former officer corps of John Burgoyne and hosted a myriad of dinner guests every week. On the evening of June 3 Frederika had become such a social presence in the city that she arranged to host a birthday gala ball for her husband. It was a great way to celebrate their good fortune of health and safety during the war.

The event was a major draw, and all of the officers and generals of the now captive army attended in their finest formal wear. As in Wolfenbüttel, the baroness relished her position as the evening's hostess. "We danced considerably," she wrote, "and our cook prepared us a magnificent supper of more than eighty covers. Moreover, our court and garden were illuminated." They partied gaily throughout the night, yet one chair remained conspicuously absent. As the commander-in-chief even under the pretenses of captivity, General John Burgoyne was invited as a guest of honor. Frederika maintained that the true festivities should not begin until his arrival, but despite her best intentions he never came. The consummate socialite, Frederika made sure that the soiree continued as merrily as ever despite his absence.[101]

As midnight approached one of the officers in attendance reminded the party that King George's birthday was the next day, June 4, now only minutes away. They agreed to carry on the engagement until the clock struck twelve, when they would toast their distant sovereign. At midnight they drank to his health, and Frederika made sure to wake her young daughters so that they could witness the scene. She wrote: "All eyes were full of tears; and it seemed as if everyone present was proud to have the spirit to venture to do this in the midst of our enemies. . . . Never, I believe, has 'God Save the King' been sung with more enthusiasm or genuine goodwill."[102]

# III

## Philipp Waldeck

*Field Chaplain, 3rd Regiment
Waldeck*

1778–1781

CARIBBEAN SEA

*November 1778*

Chaplain Philipp Waldeck was a practical man. His personal diary was filled with details about his two years in America thus far, and it covered all aspects of provincial life from customs to cuisine. On this day, though, his entry was sorely unimaginative, as all he could muster was a short note on wind and water. For the last three weeks he had been at sea cruising on the *Britannia* toward the Caribbean Sea with his regiment, and not even halfway through the voyage his spirits were already growing weak. But he would not be deterred; as a man of God, Philipp often challenged himself to find the intrinsic beauty of nature, and he took solace in discerning the spark of the Divine Creation all around him.

The Atlantic Ocean was both beautiful and menacing, and for the chaplain it represented the true paradox of leading a Christian life in a dangerous world. His many months already spent in North America only strengthened that belief. Now at sea, there was little he could do to amuse himself or even keep his sanity, so he spent his restless days reflecting on and reconsidering his experiences thus far. While his time in America had been rewarding, it was also very dangerous, and no matter the outcome it was much more eventful than his life at home in Germany ever could hope to be.[1]

He was born in the German principality of Waldeck in 1750 and his given name was Johann Philipp Franz Elisaus Waldeck; he was raised in the tiny city of Hernfurth. As the son of a minister, Philipp Waldeck had a familial attachment to serving the faithful, and like many boys growing up in Europe in the eighteenth century his commitment to God would be his pathway to worldly success. He was not a privileged person, but a boy of the lower classes, with few opportunities; like many of his fellow Germans he faced joining the military or dying a poor man. But despite the heavy weight of Waldeck's class system, in religion there was salvation. Because he was destined for clerical service he was able to attend a city school in Nieder-Wildungen until 1769, when at the age of nineteen he graduated and entered the University of Jena. At university he learned of the eternal struggle of man and read the great theologians of the past. He studied and received a degree in religion, and upon graduation was instantly among the rare 1 percent of Germans who had obtained an honor almost exclusively reserved for the privileged upper class.

As a graduate the ambitious Philipp was determined to be a renowned theologian, but he soon found that there was money to be made as a philosopher. Therefore from 1772 to 1775 he served the city of Thalitter as a private tutor, a holy man for hire. Yet with all that he had achieved, "upward mobility," let alone a middle class, was unknown in his world and he found himself toiling away in the same German streets that he found so tiresome as a young man. In the meantime he had learned that the Prince Friedrich Karl August had signed a treaty with the empire of Great Britain to quell a rebellion in their American colonies, and for him it was a moment of decision. In 1776 after three years of scraping by, Philipp decided that some adventure was better than none. He joined the military and his collegiate credentials separated him instantly. After taking a routine examination he was commissioned as the chaplain for the 3rd Waldeck Regiment.

The Principality of Waldeck had existed within the borders of the Holy Roman Empire since the thirteenth century, but it was never considered to be a major polity among its powerful brethren. Situated in central Germany next to its much wealthier neighbor Hesse-Cassel, the long-time county had only recently been elevated to a full-fledged principality by the Holy Roman Emperor Charles VI, and its rulers did everything possible to maintain its status. Like many of its German counterparts, the prince of Waldeck had used its martial resources to climb the political ranks of Europe, and by 1776 Waldeck was now almost wholly reliant on its ability to sell the services of its army to the highest bidder. While it was considered to be a lower German polity, it had developed an unsavory reputation as a principality that would sell its army to the highest bidder no matter the circumstances. Building an army of fortune was no easy task, however, and as its popularity grew Prince Friedrich Karl August took drastic measures to expand his military strength by calling upon feudal obligations that were quickly dying elsewhere in the enlightened world. Starting off with a single battalion, its service became in such high demand that it was expanded and divided into four by 1776. The men of this small army had paid dearly for their service in the name of Holland already, and when the American rebellion began these same exhausted troops were called upon to cross the Atlantic in the name of King George, all the while their prince profited immensely. According to their contract each man who served in the rented army would receive a direct stipend of thirty crowns; their prince would be paid over twenty thousand.[2]

For Philipp it was a chance to separate himself from his humble roots and see the world, and unlike most of people he would serve with, he was there by choice. Of all the German armies that were commissioned for battle as auxiliaries in Britain's attempt to squash the Patriot rebellion, the Waldeckers were the smallest. When compared to their Hessian neighbors who sent nearly thirteen thousand troops to the New World, the principality of Waldeck only sent a single regiment of six hundred and seventy men. They were labeled as the 3rd Regiment, and they quickly became notable amongst their other German brethren as they were the sole representatives of their country. It was an incredibly small number considering the immensity of the war to come, but it revealed just how precious a client like George III could be to such a small geopolitical entity.

The 3rd Regiment was a tightly knit group of soldiers, and knowing that they were on their way to a strange new continent to suppress a colonial revolt only strengthened that unity. They were under the command of a fellow Waldecker, Colonel Johann Ludwig Wilhelm von Hanxleden, and their transatlantic crossing was only one of many ferrying German soldiers to North America. Onboard the *Adamant* bound for New York, Philipp noted that their ship was one in a fleet of sixty-six, and while sailing the chaplain was already living up to his sacred duties; he held daily church services and administered Communion to over a hundred people in one day while sailing the high seas. By October 20, 1776, the Waldeckers arrived at their destination, and they soon assimilated into the strange new land with their fellow Germans.

Philipp had seen his Waldeckers battle George Washington's army in New York and New Jersey through the cold winter, and he had been in place for the campaigns of New Jersey. He had interacted with the rebels and experienced the hospitality of the Loyalists; his own interest even led to a slight obsession with Indian culture and politics. America was so different than Germany, and so unrestricted by the artificial social system that dominated his life. He wrote of the average colonist that their land was vast, and that they often purchased a hundred acres for no more than thirty shillings. But for all the good that he saw in that distant land, he saw the terrible consequences of the partisan war. From White Plains to Fort Lee, the battles seemed so wasteful; human life was valued so callously by each side that it tested his faith and resolve. This was his first experience with the emotional trauma of a military campaign, and now sailing in November 1778 under the constant threat of an Atlantic storm he was not certain which peril he would prefer.

THEIR MISSION NOW WAS OF THE GREATEST IMPORTANCE FOR THE Crown and illustrates the global nature of both European politics and the ripple effect of the American rebellion. Following the battles of Saratoga and surrender of General John Burgoyne's army in October 1777, the centuries-old rivalry between the empires of Great Britain and France were reignited when Louis XVI officially recognized the American nation in February 1778. Incensed by this declaration, Great Britain in turn declared war on France a month later. While the French government flooded the understocked American rebels with weapons, money, and manpower, it also began to systematically avenge their terrible losses suffered at Britain's hands fifteen years earlier at the close of the Seven Years' War. Along with all of Canada, France was effectively stripped of many of its most profitable sugar-producing islands in the Caribbean; they were only returned once ransomed in an exchange for the British island of Minorca in the Mediterranean. To Louis XVI the American rebellion was simply a means to achieving their two looming goals. The first was to deal a crippling blow to their British enemies that would allow global French influence to resurge after a decade's absence, and the second, more practical, vision was to protect and expand their sugar-producing empire by capturing British holdings in the West Indies.

French policy makers treated the American rebellion as a proxy war, an analog to the great struggle for influence and colonial control that was the defining theme of European conflict of the eighteenth century. With that commencement of hostility the war that began as a colonial uprising transformed into a global affair. Fueled by Old World rivalries and longstanding animosity over decades-gone wars, the planet was divided into theaters of combat that extended far beyond the initial shots at Lexington Green. The still smoldering kindling of over six centuries of periodic conflict between Great Britain and France reignited in a blaze ranging from the Caribbean Sea and Central America to the subcontinent of India. The two world powers had each lain in wait with long-standing strategic objectives and contingencies in place for capturing high-value possessions of the other, and with the formal declaration of war it did not take long for them to go into motion. Already by the time that the Waldeckers sailed from New York in November, the British East India Company had successfully orchestrated a ten-week siege to capture the highly profitable French-controlled port of Pondicherry on India's eastern coastline.

War had come, and the Caribbean was equally on notice. It did not take long for action to get under way, and for the French it began almost immediately. Situated in the heart of the Lesser Antilles the island of Dominica was a long-standing reminder of the lingering animosity of the Seven Years' War. Originally a French colony, Dominica was captured in 1761, and by 1778 remained firmly in British hands; the fact that it was nestled between the French islands of Martinique to the south and Guadeloupe to the north made this especially insulting. Although it was a painful memento of their past defeat, for the French high command it was now serving as a practical thorn in their side as well. It was no secret that privateers often used the island's ports as launching points to raid enemy shipping, and if Dominica could be captured it would take away Britain's vital toehold in the area. Along with disabling Britain's overall effectiveness, French policy makers believed that reclaiming the island would greatly improve communication between the two island colonies that it separated.

For the British an attack on Dominica was almost a certainty. When the American rebellion began in 1775, former Massachusetts governor Thomas Shirley was the acting executive of the island. He believed that the lone British holding in the immediate area was under a direct threat should the French declare on the side of the rebels; he left office in June 1778, only months before he would be proven correct. The man who replaced him as governor was William Stuart, and while he continued Shirley's defensive buildup, he was not as focused on the effort. On August 17 news reached the governor of Martinique François Claude Amour, marquis de Bouillé, that France had officially recognized the Americans. That same vessel that ferried the message also indicated that he should recapture Dominica as soon as possible. Only three weeks later the governor ordered two thousand men on three frigates to assault the British; by September 7 the island capitulated. The fall of Dominica was a major blow to the Crown in the young war, and all sides understood that it was just the first of many.

The respective empires of Great Britain, France, and Spain each possessed an extraordinary investment in Caribbean island colonies, and because of their close proximity to one another proved to be very attractive during a time of war. When the official declaration of war was announced, the tropical paradise became ground zero for naval squadrons of all three world superpowers. For the terribly weakened Spanish their primary revenue sources and most covetous holdings were Cuba, Hispaniola, Puerto Rico, and the various colonies of Central America. France placed its greatest impetus on protecting Martinique and Guadeloupe, and for the British, strategy revolved entirely around the island of Jamaica.

Since it was initially taken from the Spanish in the seventeenth century, Jamaica had been the heart of the British Caribbean. Although the empire had significant possessions in the Leeward and Windward Islands that produced vast wealth, these tiny sugar islands were largely dependent on the protection of an ever-present British navy. Because of its large landmass and temperate climate the island of Jamaica had become a base of operations for the entire theater, and the key to maintaining stability in the basin.

While each island in the Caribbean had its own unique flair and flavor, administering these individual entities proved to be impractical in the age of limited communication. Typically, London informally considered the British West Indies to be three distinct regions. The first was the Leeward Islands, including St. Kitts, Barbuda, Nevis, Anguilla, Antigua, and Montserrat. The second was the Windward Islands made up of Barbados, the Grenadines, St. Vincent, and Tobago. Third and most essential from a military sense was Jamaica. This four-thousand-square-mile island itself, Jamaica proper acted like a regional satellite power to the smaller colonies to its north, south, east, and west. Because of its close proximity to Central America, settlers in modern Belize depended wholly on British forces from Jamaica to defend them as they were surrounded on all sides by hostile Spanish colonies. Likewise maintaining a sizable force on Jamaica allowed for British policy makers to maintain a position of strength with Cuba, Puerto Rico, Hispaniola, and even New Orleans well within striking distance. The Caribbean basin was filled with enemy colonies that were ripe for the picking in this newly expanded war.

After word of the fall of Dominica spread throughout the rival empires, both sides took immediate action. The French immediately sent the Admiral Comte d'Estaing and his fleet, who were fresh from a failed attempt at Newport, Rhode Island, to the West Indies on November 4. As though on cue, a massive flotilla of British ships disembarked from New York led by Commodore William Hotham on the same day. Among them was the small, unassuming *Britannia,* carrying the chaplain Philipp Waldeck and the 3rd Regiment.

The six hundred and ninety-five Waldeckers that set sail from New York were under the direct command of Brigadier General John Campbell and they sailed with two corps of Loyalist Americans consisting of one hundred and seventy men from Pennsylvania and three hundred and thirteen from Maryland. While Jamaica was first on their list of destinations it was by no means the end of anything. Upon the declaration of war by France, Secretary of State Lord George Germain in London ordered a full-scale deployment of troops to defend all vulnerable colonies in the Caribbean basin. While island colonies in the Windward and Leeward Islands were well protected by the Royal Navy and Jamaica was as defensible as ever, other British holdings nearby were not so fortunate. Only one thousand miles away from Kingston were the loosely held colonies of East and West Florida won originally from the Spanish during the Seven Years' War; although they were con-sidered important, they were never high on the list of imperial pri-orities due to their proximity to the heavily defended Caribbean.[3]

When the formal declaration of war came in 1778, however, these two possessions were considered some of the most vulnerable in the entire Western Hemisphere, and General Campbell was given direct orders from London to protect them. Considered two of the most undermanned posts in the entire empire, the Floridas had an almost entirely centralized military presence in two major posts. In the East it was St. Augustine, and the West Pensacola, and as both were relatively new British holdings, the forts that protect-ed them were uniquely Spanish in design. As early as July 1778 Sir Henry Clinton was given orders to send a body of reinforcements to the Gulf Coast colonies, but he delayed the action until November at which time he elected to send the Waldeckers and Loyalists so as not to weaken his force of regulars at New York. To adequately enforce the king's standard of rule in these places, General Clinton turned to a man that was wholly dedicated to the cause and that had defended the Crown in all corners of the globe; Philipp Waldeck would see this firsthand.

Born in 1727, John Campbell was the seventeenth chief of the Macarthur Campbells of Strachur and a respected member of the Scottish peerage. As a member of Scotland's landed gentry, Campbell had a family name rich with history, and he claimed even

to trace his lineage back to the fabled King Arthur. While the legit-
imacy of his family pedigree was of questionable historic standing,
Campbell's battlefield effectiveness was not. As a young man he
served valiantly against the Jacobite uprising of 1745 and led troops
at the Battle of Culloden. Campbell was next promoted to the rank
of captain after serving in Flanders during the War of the Austrian
Succession, and at the outset of the Seven Years' War fought in the
famed "Black Watch," the 42nd Highland Regiment. While in the
ranks of the Black Watch Campbell was given a whirlwind tour of
the Western Hemisphere; he was wounded at the capture of Fort
Carillon (soon to be renamed Ticonderoga) and next led the 17th
Regiment in offensives against the French island colony of
Martinique and the Spanish stronghold of Havana. In 1775 he
departed for New York to battle the emerging American rebellion
and was a likely choice to command the defense of the British Gulf
Coast at Pensacola in 1778. Before Campbell could take his reinforcements to the old Spanish post, he would need to acquire supplies along the way, and for that purpose Jamaica was considered a
vital stopover en route to West Florida.

The British ships that made their way down the American coastline were an impressive collection, and Philipp noted that on
November 9 the fleet split in half off the coast of Florida. While he
and his 3rd Regiment were on their way to Jamaica, the other group
of vessels was sailing southeast toward the Windward Islands and its
regional powerhouse of Barbados. Philipp offered a lengthy explanation of this place, although it was certainly through hearsay. He
claimed that the island was home to only twenty thousand
Europeans but one hundred thousand slaves who farmed a variety
of goods including pineapples, bananas, cotton, indigo, and most
profitably sugar. He further added his own opinion that few settlers
ever stayed around for long.[4]

Indeed, while his numbers are disputed, his observation about
opportunity was largely correct. From as early as the seventeenth
century, aristocrats seeking prosperous investments poured their
wealth into establishing plantations on the various islands of the
Caribbean. Once their ventures were operational they would typically return to England rather speedily and simply collect their dividends while the lower-class Englishmen stayed behind to ensure
that the enormous enslaved populace continually processed the
crop. An estimated 80 percent of all residents of the Caribbean were
African slaves. The sugar islands were tremendously profitable, and

spending exorbitant amounts of capital to protect them was high on the list of most European bureaucrats.

As the Waldeckers' ship approached the Bahamas on November 13, the chaplain's ship drifted dangerously away from the rest of the fleet, and they soon saw a strange rogue vessel on the horizon. From Philipp's estimation it was not a French warship, as it sailed alone, but as they pushed their way closer, its true identity was revealed. The chaplain described it as a heavily armed privateer, which alarmed the crew greatly. Because the American rebels lacked any navy of a European standard, they often relied on the unique brand of state-sponsored piracy known as privateering to disrupt commerce and harass warships in the Caribbean. The men onboard were technically serving their government, but to most military commanders they were nothing better than pirates. For the British fleet there was strength in numbers, and though Philipp noted that his meager boat had no cannons to speak of, the multitude of warships around them did.

The Waldeckers' tiny transport sped back to the safety of their fleet, and the American bandits sailed directly into the teeth of the British flotilla. The warships expeditiously surrounded their rebel foe and captured the crew; if they had been on their own and not protected by their comrades, the consequences would have been dire. Philipp noted that if the *Britannia* had been captured, the men of the 3rd Regiment would have certainly been taken prisoner, and likely ended up in captivity at the rebel port cities of Boston or Charleston.[5]

For over two weeks he had been at sea, and other than the utter disdain that he had for seafaring, Philipp Waldeck was beginning to see the true beauty of the Caribbean. For most of the time his transport was surrounded by endless dark blue water, but as they passed by the suddenly emerging landmasses, the waters became an aquamarine hue that he had never seen before. For the chaplain it was not the daily grind that most fatigued him, but the monotony of his environment; when these new colorful features appeared, though, it seemed to arouse his interest. He kept immaculate daily records of all things that he found fascinating, and went into great detail describing these new Caribbean surroundings. He made note that earlier they had passed the island of Tortuga, and the Loyalist Americans that sailed with him enchanted him with stories of the island's sordid past as one of the premier pirate havens in the region.

The relationship that the chaplain developed with the Loyalists onboard was unique among German and British soldiers, but the situation necessarily brought them closer. He wrote that as their voyage continued they began to talk among themselves about the possibility of plundering ships that passed by, particularly the Spanish merchant vessels that were untouchable so long as the empire remained out of the conflict.[6] Unlike the men of his prover-bial flock, Philipp was not a soldier. He worked closely with the infantrymen but their typical interactions involved spiritual guid-ance and conversation, not methods of war. During this discussion of sacking and plunder the chaplain saw the Spanish merchant ships not as potential targets, but as fellow travelers on a great expedition. He wrote that he was certain that they were headed to the mysteri-ous capitals of the Orient such as Smyrna, Cairo, and Alexandria.

Philipp Waldeck was a man of the cloth who armed himself with scripture, not weapons, but even he could see that the men of the 3rd Regiment were in dire straits given their current condition. They had been at sea for far too long, and their bodies were mal-nourished and weak; on the inverse the American rebels were now well supplied by the deep spending of the French Empire. Despite the terrible winter of undersupply at Valley Forge and the early lack of any formal training, the chaplain believed that the Americans were vastly more prepared than his own countrymen. He even over-estimated the rebels so much that he questioned whether they could ever be beaten without divine intervention.[7]

With the odds against them more every day, the chaplain and his Waldeckers entertained themselves the way that all soldiers have since the beginning of time—they consumed vast quantities of wine and rum and they chatted about home, future plans, and women. For the Waldeckers as for all soldiers, it was a stark reality that while policy belonged to graying men in hallowed halls, the act of war will eternally be a young man's game. On November 29 Philipp noted a variety of new sights, among them a whale and a startling large landmass. The island that they spotted was the island of Hispaniola, today the Dominican Republic and Haiti. Just as in the twenty-first century, Hispaniola was bisected by two rival powers as the French controlled the western portion and the Spanish the east. It was one of the marvels of the entire Caribbean basin, and since Christopher Columbus first landed there in 1492 the Spanish had made it their operational hub for further explorations into the heart of Central and South America. The Waldeckers were exhausted by the sea voy-age, but as beautiful as Hispaniola appeared to them it was not with-out its dangers. They risked the danger of being engaged if they skirted too close to the island, a primary operating base of operation for the French and Spanish naval forces. Still the chaplain was momentarily taken by the image of the green island appearing from the mist. He wrote that even from the sea he could make out the misty facades of tiny homes, and opined that perhaps in another life he could see himself living there more than in any other Caribbean destination he had yet encountered.[8]

The Caribbean was a veritable stewpot of European geopolitics, and with each mile that they sailed along the Greater Antilles it became more apparent that enemy territory was never more than a few miles in either direction. The fleet's route skirted the eastern side of the Bahamas, south past Turks and Caicos, and west along the shore of Hispaniola. While somewhat hazardous it was the most expeditious route available and one that had been well established by 1778. The British Caribbean holdings played an essential role in the economic development of the New World and proved vital to the empire as a whole. Primarily growing sugar cane but lacking substantial foodstuff agriculture, the people of the Caribbean had a robust trade with the American colonies to their north; they would send sugar and rum northward, while the thirteen colonies sent their more traditional regional produce south. The system ran smoothly and government officials in London reaped the benefits as their colonial machine hummed along. But with the American rebellion all of that changed. No longer did the Britons of the island colonies receive the yields of the rich fisheries of New England or tobacco of the low country. Instead, the self-inflicted wound of trade embargo and provincial boycott virtually crippled Great Britain's entire operation in the Western Hemisphere.

On November 30 the Waldeckers saw a new giant emerge from the horizon as they moved westward: Cuba. The chaplain noted that the Spanish behemoth was not as rocky as Hispaniola and much more flat from his vantage point. The island of Cuba was of particular interest to the explorer and sightseer in Philipp because of its more recent history rather than its topography, and he offered a lengthy discussion of the traditional role that it played as Spain's most impressive revenue-generating colony. Unlike the tiny possessions of the Windward and Leeward Islands, Cuba was by far the largest landmass in the entire Caribbean and was likewise home to one of the single richest cities in the New World. By the year 1778 Havana was already over two hundred and fifty years old. Originally founded by the conquistador Diego Velázquez de Cuéllar in

1514–1515, the city grew from multiple tiny points of settlement into a sprawling urban center. For much of its early existence the Spanish Empire had a complete monopoly over New World commerce, and Havana's population skyrocketed as a result. Even after the French and British had begun to catch up a century later establishing tiny plantations and settlements, Havana still ruled as one of the rare cities on the far side of the world. Its streets were winding and busy, and its architecture expressed the rich history of the Iberian Peninsula featuring both European and Islamic elements.

Just as the Loyalists that he sailed with had informed him of Tortuga's history, they also took the time to explain Britain's past glories in Cuba. A decade earlier during the Seven Years' War the British navy implemented a two-month naval siege of the city of Havana that was remembered as one of their finest triumphs. For the British looking back, the defeat of the Franco-Spanish Alliance made the Seven Years' War a point of national and imperial pride; the fact that both France and Spain were Catholic superpowers and were each guided by Bourbon princes made the victory even sweeter.

From June until August in the year 1762 the British navy surrounded the city of Havana and eventually stormed the island of Cuba itself with infantry to capture the city. It was a maneuver of epic proportions and one of the single largest engagements in the history of the Caribbean basin; in total the empire utilized nearly thirteen thousand soldiers and seventeen thousand sailors and marines to bombard the city, as well as approximately two hundred naval vessels. Havana had traditionally been the single most coveted piece of territory that Spain possessed in the Caribbean, and they could only watch as their fateful decision to declare war against Britain in the aid of their French allies backfired in the worst way possible. Compounding the capture of their greatest colony in the West Indies was that only two months later in October 1762, the Philippines, their most profitable colony in the East Indies, was captured as well. Manila was besieged from September to October by the Royal Navy and also fell into British hands. It seemed that around the globe the Spanish Empire was in decline, and their naval inferiority was finally revealed; it also meant that Great Britain could lay claim to be the undisputed champion of the high seas. The Seven Years' War reshuffled the balance of power in Europe and created festering animosities that would drive French and Spanish policy for years to come.

Havana remained in British hands until the Treaty of Paris ended the global conflict in 1763, but the sting of the loss was not forgotten by either side. For the year that the British Empire controlled Cuba they took specific steps to temporarily integrate the island into their larger regional economy, and the Cubans proved to be the beneficiaries. It seemed that Havana's seventeenth-century prestige had fallen alongside that of imperial Spain, and during the British occupation the island was systematically introduced to a modern, eighteenth-century imperial economy with spectacular results. When the Spanish retook control of the island in 1763 the residents had seen exactly what they had been missing, and Emperor Charles III took proactive steps to ensure a hostile takeover would never happen again. The most visible of these new developments was the construction of the gargantuan stone fortress Fortaleza de San Carlos de la Cabaña that guarded Havana's primary harbor. The Caribbean had proven to be a desperately competitive place, and Spain was faced with either keeping up or falling behind.

When Loyalist Americans spoke of these decade-old victories they glowed with pride, and Philipp wrote the he hoped God would intervene and provide another victory on the scale and with the impact of Havana in the months to come.

DECEMBER 1, 1778, WAS A WELCOMED DAY FOR THE WALDECKERS WHO had now sailed for twenty-seven days straight at a distance of near-ly eighteen hundred nautical miles. As they made their way past the western edge of Hispaniola the *Britannia* made a southward turn into the fabled Windward Passage, a fifty-mile stretch of ocean that separated the landmass from its Cuban neighbor. For the entire journey they had sailed along the outer edge of the Great Antilles, and with the exception of splitting their way between the Bahaman islands they had not made such a sudden change in direction. But regardless of the month behind them, Philipp noted that his men were in high spirits as they expected to land on Jamaica within the next twenty-four hours. In many ways the brief few hours spent in the Windward Passage was the entire campaign in a microcosm. To their east was the French-dominated half of Hispaniola called Saint-Domingue and west was Spanish Cuba; in the middle of the delicate state balancing act were the Britons and their German auxiliaries.

As they made their way south toward Jamaica, the chaplain noted that he felt like a classical European foot traveler. Just as the hiker would rest beneath the shade of a tree, he wrote, the hardships of his prior journey melted away. For Philipp his destination was now in sight and the powerful winds of the Caribbean were propelling them toward it faster than ever. On the way the observant chaplain saw the island of Navassa for the first time, and it taught him a hard lesson about the difficulties of settling in such an unpredictable environment. Since its discovery in 1504 by Christopher Columbus, the tiny two-square-mile island was considered to have potential as a future outpost for the Spanish Empire. It sat ninety nautical miles south of Cuba and forty west of Hispaniola, and given its prime location it could prove to be a vital stopover for those seamen traveling between Santiago (Jamaica) and the previously mentioned northern colonies.

Soon after it was initially explored, however, the island was revealed to be one of the Caribbean's most legendary teases. Unlike some of the other volcanic islands of the basin, Navassa was composed primarily of coral and limestone; for the seasoned explorer that instantly disqualified it because landforms of that nature possessed no natural sources of fresh water. While some coral islands like the administrative center of Barbados shared similar geological compositions, most explorers saw no value in even attempting to settle Navassa and so it sat abandoned in 1778 as it had for the previous two hundred years. To Philipp the location of the island alone made it a naturally attractive place, but its limitations outweighed its potential in the eyes of Europe's great powers.

Navassa only serves to reveal that as precious as Caribbean real estate was in the eighteenth century, Mother Nature still retained ultimate control. The lesson was not lost on the chaplain, but most of the men on board the *Britannia* probably paid no attention. Their exhausting nearly month-long voyage would soon be over, and they were only hours away from their first hot meal in weeks.

JAMAICA

*December 1778*

On December 2 the men onboard the *Britannia* were tired, hungry, and sore, but the approaching image of a lush green island with a bustling port made the entire scene light with joy. They had sailed for one day short of a month, and after they passed around the eastern edge of the island of Jamaica their destination was finally in sight. It would have been a wonderful vision: ships of all varieties— civilian, military, and commercial—trafficked in and out of Jamaica's busy harbors and the unmistakable hum of civilization echoed throughout. Already approaching the bay that separated Port Royal from Kingston the Waldeckers could hear music and chatter breaking up the typically recognizable sounds of a buzzing eighteenth-century seaport. For most people this cacophony of very mundane noises would go unnoticed, but for Philipp Waldeck it was the first true sign of rest and safety that he had enjoyed in weeks.

From their vantage point off the coast, the men of the 3rd Regiment saw Jamaica from a distance and were able to take in the enormity of Britain's most prized colony in one powerful and complicated scene. The chaplain noted that the sugar plantations seemed to take over the island, and he soon understood why that cash crop made the colony so profitable. He surmised that most of the ships heading away from the island were carrying this commodity in abundance and he pondered over the distant reaches of the empire to which the item was set to travel. The particulars of a sugar plantation would have to wait, because for Philipp the single most striking thing about Jamaica at first glance was its topographic profile. Defining the island in a craggy skyline were the enormous rings of mountains at its heart. Philipp wrote that these mountains were lofty and some disappeared into the foggy mist that hung above the colony, and he guessed that they were larger even than the Alps that he had seen so often as a child. The mountains of Jamaica certainly were not the Alps, but Philipp was so thankful to see dry land that he was convinced of that fact. From aboard the *Britannia* the peaks were covered in what he described as a low-lying shrub similar to juniper, and in his estimation the uneven heights of the ranges were a direct result of Jamaica's fabled seismic past. Although the theory of plate tectonics would not be developed for another century and a half, Philipp believed by simple observation that the earthquakes that so plagued Jamaica's history must have deformed the island's mountain ranges; it was not quite exact, but an impressive hypothesis given the information on hand.[9]

Already before landing the Waldeckers had seen the great paradox of Jamaican life, that unnatural dichotomy between the slave and the master. While the white plantation class possessed sprawling coastal plains with lush soil, in the mountains he noticed that there were tiny makeshift farms spread randomly about the slopes. They were small and rough, populated by single families in tiny shacks; a carpenter on board the *Britannia* who had visited once before told Philipp that those were the efforts of free black Jamaicans and the refuge of the runaway slaves. The chaplain joked that as a child his grandmother would admonish him by saying, "I wish you were where the pepper grows," and he penned that he thought he had found that apocryphal place.[10]

At eleven o'clock on December 2 the *Britannia* signaled to shore that it was ready to approach, and as was customary it called for a pilot boat to guide it through the bay. The body of water in front of Kingston was considered perhaps the greatest weapon that the colony had against a French invasion should it ever come. It was vast, and in some cases very deep, but it deceptively washed over a treacherous collection of sand bars and shallow water that could spell doom for an unfamiliar traveler without the help of a local guide. But Mother Nature alone would not be the sole threat to a would-be assailant; the British had equipped the entire bay with over eighty heavy guns and two major fortifications. To enter the harbor one must first pass the town of Port Royal, which sat on a sandy peninsula that jutted far away from the mainland, connected by only a thin piece of ground. Once around Port Royal with its massive stone fort, the approaching enemy would have to weave his way over the unseen natural threats of the harbor and dodge yet another fort, known locally as Apostle because of its twelve guns, before finally honing in on Kingston itself. For Philipp it was a comfort knowing that he was protected by these defenses.

While the Waldeckers awaited their pilot to guide them safely toward Kingston, two smaller vessels coasted toward them from the mainland. Much to their surprise they were filled with a veritable cornucopia of foods and drink courtesy of the Jamaican people, and the men ate ravenously. The fruits and vegetables were ferried toward the *Britannia* by several women from the island whom the chaplain described as slave girls, and he was smitten by their beauty and mystery. He noted that they wore fine white gowns with their breasts exposed and hats laden with exotic bird feathers; he referred to them as his Good Samaritans because of their seemingly genuine concern for the malnourished Germans. By his account they loaded the ship with gifts of the West Indies, including cucumbers, pineapples, oranges, lemons, carrots, and beans, as well as rum and aromatic punch. They had sampled all of these things in Europe, but never in such abundance—and certainly never in the dead of winter.[11]

The Waldeckers gorged themselves on the native feast as they sat idly off the coast awaiting their pilot, and as the men indulged in their new worldly pleasures, Philipp considered the work of the divine. He thought about the terrible journey that they had just undertook and how only hours earlier the men of his regiment were broken and desperate; now they looked as though their spirits had never been higher. It was man's ability to forget and move forward that most inspired the chaplain, he wrote, and it was God's mercy that gave such a simple creature that gift. They supped for hours and enjoyed what they described as royal punch, a mixture of rum and pineapple juice. The rum of Jamaica was considered in Europe to be the finest on earth as a direct byproduct of their legendary sugar-producing plantations, and bobbing steadily in the Caribbean the Waldeckers were hard-pressed to disagree.

By evening the now lighthearted 3rd Regiment saw their pilot vessel arrive and to their surprise it was captained by a black man. The Germans onboard had never seen an enslaved person before coming to America, and few had any idea what to expect. Some believed that they would be treated simply as beasts of burden forced to complete mundane and backbreaking tasks, while others guessed that some would be more specifically trained but far from specialized. The truth of the matter was revealed to them in full force by the time they reached the Caribbean. Guiding the *Britannia* through the harbor was a task of the utmost importance that could not be done by a novice; the sight of a slave shouldering this duty left many of the Waldeckers unsettled. Despite these prejudices the man instructed them and advised them with great confidence, and he glided about the dark waters as though he was acting on instinct alone. This unnamed pilot was simply doing the service he was assigned to for untold months, and Philipp noted that it was done in a manner that no European was likely to replicate.

Under the guidance of their black pilot the Waldeckers passed the obstacles in their way and the ever-curious chaplain began to note the vistas around him. He saw the remains of the old pirate haven of Port Royal that almost a century earlier was swallowed up by the sea after a violent earthquake. He explained the sordid past of the tiny city and referenced it as the modern equivalent of the biblical Sodom, its ancient counterpart, that was washed cleanly away by the wrath of God. After the flood both the city and its ruins remained as a reminder to Philipp of the Day of Judgment that they all must face. By midnight, the city of Kingston was finally within their reach and for the first time since leaving North America a month earlier they heard the church bells ring at the stroke of twelve. The chaplain admitted that after being at sea for so long even the ordinary sound of a ringing steeple was glorious, and the men of the 3rd Waldeck Regiment cheered with delight.[12] By the next morning they would be on dry land.

For the Waldeckers the end of their long journey would bring them a measure of peace, but hundreds of miles away the Leeward Islands were preparing for war. Since the capture of Dominica in September, British officers in the eastern Caribbean pined for retaliation and set in motion a major operation to achieve that goal. The Leeward Islands were under the naval command of Admiral Samuel Barrington, a forty-nine-year-old Berkshireman who had spent his career in the service of the Crown, and by the time that the fleet under Commodore William Hotham had set sail from New York he had devised a plan to take strategic control of the region. The target of their aggression was St. Lucia, a profitable and valuable possession situated in the Windward Islands. Britain had wrestled the striking, mountainous landmass from its adversaries once before during the Seven Years' War, and the French were so determined to have it returned that the Crown used it as leverage in the peace of 1763 to regain some their most valued territory.

The strike on St. Lucia by 1778 was years in the making. Although the British command in the Leeward Islands understood its economic and strategic importance, the absence of any meaningful conflict left them with no justification for taking it. Once Dominica was captured, however, the entire game changed. To take St. Lucia would require an impressive force that Admiral Barrington simply did not have, but the ships that had separated from the Waldeckers a month earlier were exactly the reinforcements necessary for success. While the entire fleet sailed under Commodore Hotham, aboard those ships were approximately five thousand infantrymen under the command of Major General James Grant. With this added infusion of manpower along with the warships that escorted them, St. Lucia would most likely wither in the face of the assault. Making things even more urgent for the admiral was the development that the French fleet under the Comte d'Estaing that recently left New England had been struck by a wicked storm that scattered their efforts and slowed their arrival to the Caribbean basin.

On December 10 the British fleet arrived at Barbados, where Commodore Hotham and Admiral Barrington combined their forces, and by December 12 they were on their way to St. Lucia. On the evening of the 13th Major General Grant's men disembarked and by morning had assumed the strategic heights along the island's coast as well as an unattended gun that overlooked the coast. Slowed by the storm but not deterred, the French fleet arrived on December 14 and a naval battle ensued with a limited British victory. Although Admiral Barrington had done his part, the struggle for the island would take on an entirely new dimension days later. On December 18 four thousand French soldiers stormed the island near the city of Castries on St. Lucia's west coast. Sensing that a pitched battle was ahead, the British commanders quickly moved their men to the Vigie Peninsula where they stood firm along a very narrow strip of land to await the French attack. The redcoats, the majority of whom were veterans of the colonial war against the Continental Army, repulsed three full-scale charges by their enemies before the French finally gave in. Known as the Battle of Vigie, the victory was celebrated throughout the Caribbean. After the Comte d'Estaing's naval defeat and with no hope of reinforcements, the French made the painful decision to flee to the safety of Martinique.

In this single maneuver the British Empire had taken one of King Louis's most precious possessions, and they would keep it for the remainder of the war. For the British and French it seemed that no Caribbean colony was safe, and given its Bourbon alliances the empire of Spain could not remain dormant for long. Although it started as a dispute over taxation without representation, the American rebellion was transforming into a global war.

From the strictest martial perspective, the stopover on the island of Jamaica was a mere matter of logistics, but for Philipp Waldeck it was a chance to satisfy his greater curiosity about the world around him. As the lone chaplain that sailed with the 3rd Regiment, he often served as the voice of reality in the highly organized life of the soldiers around him, and his distinct distaste for combat was no secret. In that regard resting at distant colonies was often viewed as an opportunity to learn and study, rather than simply being a stopover on the way to some other lonesome post in the colonial backcountry. In many journals kept by the Waldeckers who served in the 3rd Regiment, Jamaica was often dismissed as a rallying point, but the chaplain's journals record in rich detail the practical realities of life in the British Caribbean. When the Waldeckers first disembarked from their ship, the typical colonial city of Kingston seemed foreign yet distinctly English. Like a great melting pot the enticing combination stimulated Philipp's senses and revealed the power of imperialism.

Upon their arrival the British General Campbell began immediate preparations to collect supplies and prepare for their embarkation toward Pensacola, a perilously slow task. In the meantime, however, the Germans were able to stretch their legs and explore the veritable tropical paradise that lay before them. The city of Kingston was the heart of a crown colony; the people that strolled down its narrow streets all spoke the language with an accent far more akin to England than anything Philipp had heard in America. While the American provincials had developed a much more unique character about themselves, the Jamaicans were far more traditionally English. Largely due to the fact that very few settlers remained for more than a few years in the Caribbean, the West Indian colonists kept English culture alive more than the Americans, who by 1778 had created an identity of their own.

But as foreign as Kingston seemed to the chaplain, it was not long before a familiar voice was heard; almost as soon as the Waldeckers stepped ashore they were met by a man who, like them, was a German in a distant land. The chaplain never recorded the gentleman's name, but he did leave a strikingly detailed account of how the stranger arrived in the colony. Thirteen years earlier the settler arrived in Jamaica with nothing more than a willingness to work, and as with many travelers, the opportunity of the New World drew him from his homeland. Upon further conversation it was revealed that he was from the German duchy of Holstein and that he was a carpenter. By the time that he met the 3rd Regiment in 1778, he had done so well that he now owned seven homes and found himself in an early retirement. As impressive as his achievements were, they would have been nearly impossible in the still feudalized economy of his homeland. As the men chatted, the carpenter led Philipp through the lightly sand-blown streets of Kingston and gave him a tour of his woodworking shop. According to the chaplain's notes the man had nineteen slaves, each of them highly specialized in making fine mahogany cabinets. The Holsteiner had purchased the slaves shortly after his initial landing and he personally trained them all to be masters of his own craft. In the eyes of the Waldeckers he was a genuine success story, and though he was a German in an English world he had adjusted accordingly. His home was elegant but small, and it was adorned outside by a pair of towering coconut trees.

Unlike many of the slave-owning class in Jamaica, the carpenter was not a planter and therefore was not considered as a member of the elite of the colony; for that reason he was not required to maintain the societal standards of the day and had no wife or children to speak of. Philipp noted that he did however keep a black woman as a "housekeeper" who served as both his maid and mistress, and although it was rather unsavory to perpetuate such a Godless relationship, the chaplain gave him a pass as it was quite normal for a man of his position in the West Indies. The carpenter explained that he began the affair out of necessity, claiming that a European wife was simply too expensive and that there were very few single healthy young women on the island. In this respect he was likely speaking with sincerity, as very few English families raised their children to maturity in such a distant land, and the wealthiest would send their most eligible children back to Europe to find a suitable partner. Regardless of the cultural differences required of living in a far-flung province, Philipp proudly stated that he believed that Germans could be found around the world and that his countrymen were among the most industrious people on earth.

Yet for the chaplain difficult labors did not necessarily tie themselves to financial success, at least not in the West Indies. In the Holsteiner's shop he saw nearly twenty of the finest carpenters he had ever known, yet their servitude precluded them from financial gain. The plight of the African slave was a defining feature of American life, and he had seen its ugly presence in New York as well as Jamaica, and no matter where encountered it was equally appalling to him. While there are stark contrasts between American and German life in the eighteenth century, there was perhaps no greater than the issue of enslaving one's fellow man. From the German point of view, the idea that the American revolt could be justified under the pretenses of freedom, liberty, and natural rights was wholly dismantled by the institutionalized slavery that was so vital to the American economy. To the American, it was the German, not the slave, who was the man of least freedom, as he was still beholden to an antiquated feudal system of monarchial vassalage. It was a stark contrast in values that so defined the Old World from the New, and it was a wide chasm.

In Philipp's estimation his own low social standing at home was not ideal, but he had the ability to earn a wage and feed his family if necessary; more important still was the fact that in return for services to his king he received the benefit of royal protection. But the slave, he wrote, received none of these guarantees and was treated no differently than the cattle he tended. In Jamaica the chaplain saw the worst conditions for the enslaved person that he had ever witnessed. He wrote that in Jamaica, slaves greatly outnumbered owners, and the men in the fields were nearly naked, wearing on a piece of cloth tied around their waist. They were driven to work by a slave driver, a man that the chaplain described as noble simply because he was trying to earn a living, but he reverted to his Christian philosophy when considering the institution as a whole. It was a scathing critique of the Caribbean plantation system that wholly supported the West Indian economy, but the observant chaplain did not leave it without his trademark wit. He noted that in some ways the slave could get the better of his master just based on biology; while the European planter was pale and sickly from the drastic difference in climate, the African was strong and well suited for island life. The observation was made that in West Indian culture a family's wealth was measured by the number of people one enslaved, and that some of the most affluent owned over three hundred persons. He wrote that in the eyes of God all men, both black and white, were created equally; he further disparaged the planters by claiming that their attachment to slavery was an insult to the Divine Creation as well as their fellow man and that they would pay the price on the Day of Judgment.[13]

If punishment awaited the wealthy Jamaicans, they certainly lived life to the fullest during their time on earth. To keep his journal balanced the chaplain wrote an equally detailed sketch of life for the European settler on the island. Opulence was everywhere in Kingston, and the richness of the planters was a testament to the entrepreneurial spirit of the island. Homes were built in such a way that the sea air could breeze effortlessly throughout the rooms, and the locals referred to this occurrence as "the doctor." The English colonists wore clothes made of fine linens and nearly always silken in appearance, and likely to have been imported from the east. Surprisingly though, he wrote, unlike most at the time, the Jamaicans never wore the same shirt for more than a day—an obvious show of wealth.

At an average yearly temperature of eighty degrees the heat was brutal and was by far the worst the Germans had ever experienced, though it did not bother the Jamaicans, as the English colonists were referred to. Because of the intense sun both men and women wore hats made of the highest quality English felt; they never traveled anywhere without a sunshade to prevent unnecessary exposure. They were a proud people. Philipp added that the elite class was welcoming to the Waldeckers, but that they insisted on boasting of their land and its profits while largely disregarding an expected response. These would-be aristocrats spent their days without care, smoking imported tobacco and dining on foods that in other parts of the empire would be considered delicacies.[14]

It was not atypical for a Jamaican planter to live on his plantation, but in order to conduct business to make daily trips to Kingston, where he likely owned a second home. His primary means of travel was typically a two-horse carriage. But in spite of all of the ostentatious trappings that so defined the West Indian planter, the most striking difference between him and the American planter was the origins of their goods. In America nearly everything was made in the colonies, while in the islands even their carriage harnesses were imported from England. The American items were satisfactory, but they retained a provincial quality that most Englishmen considered to be disagreeable; in the British Caribbean, colonists were accustomed to the highest grade and unlike most of their American brethren they could afford to purchase it.

The differences between the American rebels and the contented Jamaican planters were astounding given their shared imperial origins, the chaplain wrote. While only a small percentage of the American population owned slaves or shared in profits from slavery, nearly every settler in Jamaica participated in the slave trade in some form. In the West Indies profit was tied almost entirely to the work of slaves; this was Philipp's greatest critique of the plantation system. As poorly as enslaved human beings were treated by their owners, in his estimation the planters' entire way of life would be impossible without them. No point illustrated this more than an event that occurred within a week of his arrival at Jamaica, which would shape his opinions for the rest of his life.

After spending a week simply adapting to Jamaican life, Philipp Waldeck and his German comrades were sitting along the docks of Kingston finishing a bottle of Madeira wine when a great commotion began. When he rose to investigate the matter he saw a French merchant vessel that had been captured by the Royal Navy only a few days earlier being piloted into the bay, and the excitement over its cargo was palpable on shore. The transport itself was large and imposing, and while its physical dimensions meant little to the inexperienced Germans, the opportunistic Jamaican investors on shore had a clear understanding of what awaited them onboard. It was a slave ship.

The vessel carried nearly six hundred people below its decks, and they were kept in the most dreadful conditions imaginable. Chained at their wrists and ankles, the men, women, and children had sat in cramped quarters for weeks as they were ferried swiftly away from their African homeland until the day they arrived in Jamaica. When they were finally brought into the sunlight from below deck, the chaplain was appalled at the sight. The Africans were chained in a line and paraded off the ship, some were on the verge of death and most were suffering severe malnutrition. He soon learned that this method of transport was to prevent an uprising at sea, and that fifty people had died while making this particular voyage. One man stated that slaves were shipped much in the same way of horses, and that like the beasts of burden the prisoners below deck would necessarily defecate on themselves. Philipp wrote that the poor individuals before him were at no disadvantage other than the color of their skin, and that their current state was an infringement of all holiness, reason, and nature. He next witnessed planters, who he described as tyrants, harshly examine the chained peoples as though they were inspecting cattle and recorded that a mere one hundred pounds could purchase a human life.[15]

When the ship had finally emptied its cargo, a page boy weaved his way through the streets of Kingston with fliers listing exactly how many persons would be for sale that day and reciting the height, weight, and age of the unlucky souls. Later that day the enslaved, stripped of all clothing for full consideration, would be presented with a tag around their neck to be auctioned. After the sale, the chaplain continued, the slaves would be driven to a plantation where they would be rested and fed; it was then that Philipp said their true horror began. They would work the field with no shoes and their feet would be burned raw; if they had to relieve themselves they would often squat where they worked or face the consequences of the slave driver's whip. Some women would receive better treatment and their mistresses would dress them in fine clothing when they went into the city as though they were a mere fashion accessory. The chaplain ended his description by asserting that as wealthy as the Jamaicans were, they seemed improverished when it came to human kindness.[16]

But not all slavery that the Waldeckers had seen was as terrible as the events that transpired in Jamaica. The chaplain observed that the enslaved in America were treated much better than the poor wretches of the West Indies, and that many of them were merely domestic servants whose treatment he likened to his own at home in Germany. From his viewpoint, many American slaves were often incorporated as members of the family and never forced to wear simple loincloths and go barefoot. In point of fact the reality was somewhere in between. The 3rd Waldeck Regiment had spent their entire American tenure in the Northeast at New York and New Jersey. In these cities slavery existed but only in limited domestic roles, as the region lacked the cash crop plantations of the American South. While the chaplain may have seen an enslaved person receive far better treatment in the Northeast, he certainly would have not made such a broad and definitive statement had he witnessed the slave auctions of Savannah or Charleston in the lower colonies.

The regiment's time in Jamaica was supposed to be a brief one, but after three weeks the job of supplying the ships and soldiers for their Gulf Coast odyssey was proving much harder than expected. Because of the state of war in the Caribbean basin, the ships that would have normally brought new English goods had been severely hampered. There were plenty of fruits, vegetables, and livestock for General Campbell, but essential items such as guns and ammunition were strictly imports; that stream had slowed to a trickle. If the commanding officer was going to take his eleven hundred Germans and Provincials to West Florida as planned, he would need more time, so his only option was to leave his ships in the Kingston harbor and wait.[17]

While the stream of supplies was dramatically decreased by this lack of commerce, manufactured goods were not the only precious commodities lost. During these hot December days Jamaica was forced to sit in virtual isolation due to the fact that most news and information traveled onboard these vessels as well. Midway through the month and almost two weeks after their initial arrival in the colony, the chaplain and his Waldeckers rushed to greet a merchant vessel arriving from New York. As the sailors disembarked from their transport they brought with them newspapers from their home port and promptly nailed them on a bulletin board for all to see. That small piece of paper quickly became the talk of the island, for it contained a report that the Comte d'Estaing had sailed with his fleet from New England in early November, and though six weeks had passed the entire colony was abuzz with excitement. Philipp speculated that the French admiral was speeding his way to Jamaica and would arrive any day; others guessed that their orders to proceed to West Florida would be immediately dropped. There were many wild stories flying about, and although many were said with great conviction, none were based on anything more than mere speculation. In truth the French fleet was fully engaged with the

British at St. Lucia, but due to the limitations of communications they would not know that for months.[18]

AFTER SPENDING ALMOST ALL OF DECEMBER IN JAMAICA, THE Waldeckers and Loyalists under the command of General John Campbell finally received word that they would be starting their journey to the Gulf Coast of North America. It had been a strange month for the chaplain that had shown him the many faces of modern imperialism in the West Indies, and whereas he sometimes felt admiration for the planters, he mostly felt disdain. They proved to be gracious hosts, for that he was grateful, but their particular lifestyle was one that he could never grow accustomed to.

As much as he had grown tired of the sandy shores and windy evenings spent on the remote island colony, Philipp was even less enthusiastic about loading onto another ship for a voyage that could take as long as two weeks; in preparation for the sojourn he made his way to a local church to regain the good graces of the Lord before his embarkation. Although Philipp came from a unique sect of German Protestantism, he had no qualms attending the Anglican service that his English hosts practiced despite their dogmatic differences. The chaplain noted that most of the congregation arrived for the midday services in fine carriages and were typically well dressed. When they entered the simple yet tasteful building they opened their ceremony with a hymn and followed by reading the Articles of Faith and reciting the Ten Commandments. But as they rhythmically proceeded, the chaplain was surprised to see just how treacherous West Indian life was and how much the harsh climate had taken out of its residents. He described the women of the congregation as visibly mature beyond their years, and the men as pale with the musculature of a corpse. Of course they were all dressed in their finest attire, but it seemed that the lavish displays were merely a façade to disguise the true hardships that they faced.[19]

After leaving the church Philipp found himself in the middle of the local cemetery just outside and in that place he saw the true nature of Jamaican life. There were many richly carved marble headstones, and by his estimation the consecrated ground was filled to capacity. All around him he witnessed the graves of men and women barely his age, few of whom lived beyond their fiftieth year; in one dramatic example he found the plot of an entire family who died after their arrival in the colony. The father of this unnamed family died at the age of thirty-five, his wife at thirty-seven, and his two sons at seventeen and eleven, respectively. His two daughters also perished, but their ages were unmarked, indicating they passed away as infants. The most startling aspect of this family tragedy, however, were the dates of the burials; all of the six were interred between 1735 and 1739. Standing in the solemn place the chaplain said a prayer for the dead and his mind wandered back to New Jersey where he once passed a headstone of a Mrs. Faehnrichin, who lived to the ripe age of eighty-three. In this recollection he reaffirmed that although Jamaicans tended to be much wealthier than their American neighbors, nothing came without a price.[20]

The chaplain left the cemetery in quiet reflection, but it did not last long as the peace that had soothed his rattled nerves was soon broken by a startling rhythmic beat resonating from the heart of the city. As it was Sunday all of the peoples of the island were practicing their faith, and just as the Anglicans held a solemn service, so did their slaves. In a dramatic showing Philipp stood along the side of the sandy road to watch an African funerary procession pass by and recorded as much of the elaborate ceremony as possible. There were more than three hundred participants, he wrote, and they were led by two men beating with their fists a pair of hand-crafted drums to a steady, pulsing beat; following close behind were two more mourners rattling chains to the same melody. As though the music was the central bonding feature of the ceremony, the drummers were trailed by a man carrying a coconut that was adorned with pearls, and they all performed the same synchronized dance. The casket of the deceased was covered in a dirty white satin sheet and carried by four women, who each carried ritual tobacco smoking pipes, and the parade concluded with a single female who carried a basket of locally harvested fruits effortlessly on her head.

The chaplain timidly tracked the funeral to its final destination, where he witnessed all of the mourners finally place the casket down and dance around it; while he did not stay long he was later told that the dance continued for hours until the sun finally set. The chaplain was not sure how to describe his feelings toward the ritualistic display because of his deep Christian faith, but the slave owners provided their own theories on the matter. They told him that the enslaved celebrated death more than birth and that when the spirit left the body it surely journeyed back to its African home. The planters seemed to have their own narrative for the travel of the slaves' departed soul, and it was astounding how many liberties they took in telling the tale. In the chaplain's mind, he considered all peoples to be children of God, and to him it was only fitting that the Jamaicans would attempt to control the death of the unfortunate slave just as they did his life.[21]

After a few more days in the city of Kingston the Waldeckers had their fill. They had originally intended to only stay a few days in Jamaica until they could resupply and continue on into the Gulf of Mexico, however they had been docked for a full month. Though the experience was a rich one for the chaplain, the empire had ordered their departure for Pensacola almost eight months earlier in New York; delays and disputes had cost them valuable time, and General Campbell insisted that they press on within the week. The Waldeckers observed Christmas Day with dreams of home in their hearts, and were humored by the fact that the winter chill was nowhere to be found; Philipp wrote jokingly that he never believed he would celebrate the birth of Christ while shirtless in the sweltering heat. The men of the 3rd Regiment spent the holy day together sharing stories of their families in Europe and took turns toasting their temporary island home. When a person offered a praise of Germany they drank Rhine wine, and for the West Indies it was rum punch.[22] On December 31 they celebrated the new year by setting sail for the Gulf Coast.[23]

## West Florida

*February 1779*

Few words could describe the British colony of West Florida, but chaplain Philipp Waldeck repeatedly used just one: pitiful. It was a landscape unlike he had ever seen and was easily the most inhospitable area he had yet encountered. There were no arable fields, and no farms or homesteads for miles; there were colonists in the city of Pensacola but for the most part they were surrounded only by sandy desolation. When the Waldeckers under General John Campbell first spotted land days earlier following their departure from Jamaica, they all cheered at the prospect of settling in yet another coastal colony. As they inched closer to shore, however, their enthusiasm melted away entirely when West Florida revealed itself to the weary travelers. Unlike in the West Indies where they saw plantations and settlements even from a distance, in this coastal region all they witnessed were endless dunes of white sand. They knew that there were small pockets of colonists and planters scattered all throughout the region, but the province they saw looked devoid of all settlement. The chaplain's first instinct was to wonder why any major power would invest any of its treasure to fortify such a desolate place, and once he stepped off of his ship his incredulity only grew.[24]

The colony of West Florida was everything that an imperialist hoped to avoid, and the prospect of transforming it into a profitable venture was highly unlikely. Where most colonial investments offered fertile land, rich trade opportunities, and centralized position, West Florida only yielded dry stretches of sand; further inland the prospects were not much better as explorers found a nasty, steamy expanse of mucky swamp. But for all of its shortcomings Britain played an imperial game of global chess, and because of its commanding situation on the Gulf of Mexico the colony had to be developed. Only a short distance from the edge of the colony was the massive expanse of Spanish Louisiana and its beating commercial heart of New Orleans, and while it may not have been pretty, West Florida was essential for British competitiveness on the Gulf Coast. In Philipp Waldeck's opinion, the risk may not have been worth the reward.

He was new to this place to be sure, but the Waldeckers had plenty of time to render a judgment before landing there. The small fleet left Jamaica on December 31 and was told that the short sail into the Gulf of the Mexico should take two weeks, and by January 15 they joyously saw their destination emerge from the fog. But despite their closeness they were given orders to remain onboard. It seemed that a change was afoot. The chaplain wrote that General Campbell had given orders to continue past Pensacola toward the Mississippi River only to change them a day later, and so they waited. He next gave the command to begin their approach into Pensacola Bay but was delayed by a sudden storm that virtually sealed the waiting harbor, and they waited still. In total five miserable days had passed where Philipp and his men just bobbed in the water staring at their waiting port until they finally were piloted toward the city of Pensacola.[25]

There were many natural advantages to the bay that protected Pensacola. Before entering one must navigate a rather unpredictable surf and next sail around an elongated island called Santa Rosa. Once through those barriers, the attacking fleet had to negotiate the treacherously shallow harbor that could ground them in an instant. For these reasons Pensacola was the administrative heart of the colony, and its value was magnified after the French declaration of war. Mother Nature's defenses were unforgiving, but they were also unprejudiced, and even the Britons of Pensacola had to adjust to their challenges. Because of the shallows near the shore, no vessel—friendly or otherwise—could dock directly at the city, and Royal Engineers had constructed eight long piers or wharfs to remedy this hazard. When Philipp took note of these innovations though, he received more bad news; it seemed that the city was woefully unprepared for the eleven hundred reinforcements. General Campbell ordered his men to remain on their vessels for another twelve days until quarters could be constructed. The Waldeckers first spotted land on January 15 but did not actually step foot on shore until two weeks later.[26]

The city that they clamored for was hardly worth the wait; Pensacola was an old Spanish creation from the sixteenth century, and by 1779 it was in a state of disrepair. By the chaplain's estimation there were approximately two hundred homes that were all relatively new construction. Since the city was taken over by the British nearly every home was reconstructed from local timber, and only the original three remaining Spanish buildings were made of stone. Those three relics of the imperial past were considered the finest in all of Pensacola, but that was not saying much. One was the former home of the colonial governor, the second that of the chief royal Indian agent, and the last a powder magazine. It seemed that the city had been so neglected by its former occupants that almost the entire place had to be reconstructed quite literally from the ground up. The Pensacola that the Waldeckers first saw was designed and built in great haste, and that urgency was evident all around. The streets of the city carried the names of modern British gentry like Harcourt, Cumberland, Granby, and Bute, but they were so quickly established that they were made wholly of sand. Philipp regarded this as especially terrible as he compared it to walking barefoot in the German snow with the white powder severely burning the feet and ankles. It was as though Pensacola shoddily attempted to provide all the necessities of any major city but in a very rough and unsatisfactory way; however the Chaplain was offended most by the absence of the one structure that he valued most. Pensacola had no church.

The city that was ruled first by Catholic Spain and next by a pious King George had only managed to plan for the construction of a house of worship, and when the chaplain sought it out he found an empty sandy lot. He was not necessarily angered by this discovery, only intrigued how such a vital piece of a community could be absent. After some quick investigation he learned that not only was a plot prepared, but one hundred pounds had been set aside to pay for a full-time preacher. With this stirring development he offered his services as a pastor to the entire city, and while there was little fanfare of his pronouncement, there were also no arguments against it.[27]

Philipp Waldeck took great care to note the problems of the colony that he witnessed at first glance, and they were many. The people of the province hugged tightly to the garrison that was stationed in the heart of Pensacola, but they were a motley collection of drunks and vagabonds. Upon the arrival of General Campbell the locals were overjoyed to see actual soldiers taking an interest in their tiny corner of the Gulf Coast. Due to their near complete reliance on trade that had been disrupted by the war, the people of Pensacola were a state of regular starvation. Individually they maintained tiny gardens to grow cabbages, pumpkins, and beans that Philipp claimed were of such bad quality that they would have been fed to the cattle in Germany.

The city had fortifications which the garrison held, but they were in nearly as bad a condition as the troops themselves, and if the British were going to make any kind of a defensive effort they would have to be rebuilt. When the reinforcements landed they were shocked at the condition of the old Spanish forts, and they were perplexed as to where the Spaniards acquired the stone to construct it. All around there were trees, but the white sand gave no indication of any local quarry to build such a post. Almost as soon as their inspection began they found that the previous day's storm had washed away much of what sturdy remnants were left.[28]

By 1779 the French were fully at war with Britain, and the empire of Spain was almost certain to follow; when the Spanish officially declared war West Florida would be the first to feel the effects with Louisiana only miles away. To transform Pensacola into a bastion of royal authority and make it defensible was a tall task, but even the regimental chaplain knew that it had to be done. Like the Israelites of Egypt, he wrote, they would need to work around the clock. It was far from ideal, but still much better than the alternative.

LIKE SO MANY FEATURES OF COLONIAL AMERICAN LIFE IMMEDIATELY
before the events of 1776, the story of West Florida began with the
end of the Seven Years' War. Since the sixteenth century Spain had
held near complete control over Florida, and the stories of Juan
Ponce de Leon's fabled expeditions still ring as a critical part of its
history. However after years of significant exploration and colonization Florida had not proven itself to be a profitable colony in the
eyes of Spain's high command. It certainly had its fair share of fertile land and strategic defensive positions, but next to the immensity of the Central and South American precious metal trade it paled
in comparison. Policy makers in Madrid made it very clear by their
actions that when weighed against the enormous wealth of their
Caribbean holdings, *La Florida* was relegated to a secondary status.

At the outset of the Seven Years' War the Spanish king Ferdinand
VI was deeply hesitant to choose a side in the titanic struggle
between Britain and France; he was effectively watching Europe's
premier powers vying for the status that his own waning empire
once held. The winner would be the supreme imperial force on the
planet, and if Ferdinand remained disciplined there might still be a
place for Spain at the conclusion. Ultimately courted by both sides,
he personally opposed direct action. After Ferdinand died in 1759,
his successor Charles III was much more proactive than his late
brother and by 1760 he witnessed a drastic shift in the Great War
for empire. With France reeling after dramatic losses from 1758 to
1760, Charles believed that Britain was poised to claim victory and
create a radical shift in the centuries-old power dynamic in Europe.
Therefore, as both France and Spain shared dynastic Bourbon
roots, in 1761 Charles invoked what was known as the Family
Compact and joined forces with the tumbling French Empire.

In what would be remembered as a pivotal moment of the war,
the British met their new foes with force and captured their coveted Caribbean prize of Havana in 1762. Spain was never a true threat
to the British in the Western Hemisphere by that point in the war,
but the conflict had transformed into a game of hostage taking
designed to increase leverage during the peace process. As planned
in 1763, all parties came together to sign the Treaty of Paris in
which the rival empires parceled out millions of acres of land
around the globe; while Spain had chosen the losing side they were
faced with the crippling scenario that their most valuable city in the
Western Hemisphere was in the hands of the enemy. To regain their

beloved city of Havana, Spain offered King George the entire colony of Florida at nearly sixty thousand square miles.

Months after the war had ended, Britons the world over were celebrating their great conquests over their old enemies, but few were looking objectively at the logistical realities of maintaining the new territories. With the signing of the Treaty of Paris the British Empire doubled in size overnight, and though it was understandably a time of great triumph, it was also a time to reconsider London's colonial policy. The system utilized by the empire was effective at governing what holdings they possessed prior to the Seven Years' War, but the enormous volume of land that they acquired proved to be too much for the old bureaucratic systems still in place. All across North America problems began to arise, most notably an Indian insurgency that had the potential to spread across the continent, and an inability to defend British settlers in its destructive path. It was also during this troublesome year that *La Florida* was proving itself to be simply too large to govern efficiently.

The empire of Spain had allowed Florida to slip into relative disarray because it was an acknowledged imperial afterthought, but the British had no intention of letting their precious new commodity go to waste. In October 1763 King George issued what was called the Royal Proclamation, or more colloquially as "the Proclamation Act," which drew an artificial boundary between western frontier settlers and Native American lands; it was essentially an attempt to mitigate the emerging conflicts during the Indian insurgency. But along with this controversial act the Royal Proclamation also officially divided Florida into two entirely new colonies. The bulk of the land to the Apalachicola River would be called East Florida, and the remainder of the Gulf Coast to the Mississippi would be West Florida. To make governance more effective the eastern capital would be North America's oldest city, St. Augustine, and its western counterpart the decaying Spanish post of Pensacola. By modern standards West Florida encompassed all of the Florida Panhandle as well as the southern coasts of Mississippi, Alabama, and parts of Louisiana. While the colony would require a great deal of work to develop and settle, at least in principle the British Empire now commanded an enormous portion of the Gulf Coast, finally had a colony west of the Appalachian Mountains, and broke Spanish Louisiana's monopoly over the region.[29]

With the addition of these two new colonies it brought Britain's total acquisition from the Seven Years' War in North America to three, the largest being the complete conquest of Canada known administratively as Quebec. But these new colonies were not readily accepted by the much older neighbors between them, and the thirteen Atlantic colonies retained a deep suspicion of the newly minted numbers fourteen, fifteen, and sixteen. In contrast to the well-settled American colonies, policy makers in London were faced with the challenge of speedily "peopling" their new acquisitions. If they failed, then Britain would only nominally control the province with no assertion of practical control on the ground. In solving this dilemma lay the seeds of the great ideological chasm that would separate old from new, and ultimately prevent East and West Florida from joining the rebel cause as allies a decade later.[30]

The social development that drove this primary difference was one of time; the thirteen American colonies were over a century old by the end of the Seven Years' War and each had steadily developed its own unique character. From the devout religious zeal of New England to the fierce independence of the frontier, colonial America was a place of strong identity. It was the belief of the mild Pennsylvania farmer and the gentrified entitlement of the Virginia planters alike that their system was unique and different that most fed the cause of rebellion. There may not have been much agreement on the why's and the how's, but by 1776 all of the Atlantic colonies consented that their new "American" identity had far surpassed the traditional "British" identity that had guided them for decades before, and that separation was the only course of action to remedy their grievances. The transformation was natural and cohesive; there was simply no way to replicate the cultural and sociological bonds that created the Patriot movement other than time and experience.

But East and West Florida never had the opportunity to develop such a sentiment, because by 1776 the colonies were merely an imperial experiment and their population was far from a unified body. Policy makers in London took drastic steps in 1763 and beyond to flood their new colonies with settlers, and like most new provincial ventures they had to accept that such a measure would involve the relocation and cooperation of colonists from different backgrounds and vastly different socioeconomic circumstances. The state-sponsored public relations campaign that followed varied greatly and many wild stories emerged about the wonders of the Floridian colonies, but the most effective tactic was the promise of true, no-strings-attached free land. Land grants had always been a pull factor for colonists toward the New World, but by the dawn of the American rebellion it was becoming a thing of the past; in East and West Florida, however, it was very much in evidence. The empire offered one hundred acres of free land to anyone who moved there, and added an incentive of fifty additional acres for each member of their families. For a veteran of the Royal Army or Navy the deal was sweeter yet, as officers were offered up to five thousand free acres, with each corresponding lower rank granted slightly less on a graduated scale.[31]

In some respects West Florida was entirely engineered by royal officials, and there is a corresponding monetary trail to further reflect the high hopes for the colony's future. Like many of its British neighbors West Florida was organized with an executive branch led by a governor and lieutenant governor as well as a bicameral legislature featuring an upper and lower house. Unlike other North American colonies, though, was the manner in which it would be funded; most colonies to its north were funded by some imperial treasure but mostly by domestic taxes and tariffs. West Florida, in contrast, was fully supported by imperial funds. Budgets of the 1760s subsidized the Gulf Coast colony until its population could create enough revenue to keep it afloat, and the value ranged as high as an exorbitant seventy two hundred pounds per year.[32]

But as much as the British tried to pitch West Florida as a destination worthy of their efforts, the realities of life in the province soon became apparent. Rumors of illness and disease in the colony reached London swiftly, and the *Gentlemen's Magazine* described it satirically as North America's chief provider of mildew and sand. In truth the firsthand accounts coming out of West Florida did little to mitigate these rumors; in August 1765 the men of the 31st Regiment of Foot landed in Pensacola and less than a month later a quarter of them were dead or dying from any combination of typhus, malaria, dysentery, or yellow fever.[33] But for all of the challenges and dangers that seemed to lurk all about the southern colony, there were some distinct and profitable advantages to moving there. Once discovered the colony soon became a magnet for some of the worst scoundrels the empire had to offer.[34]

In many ways West Florida was the edge of two imperial domains. The primary trading hub of the Spanish Empire was based in New Orleans, and West Florida was an adjacent neighbor; therefore the regular commerce and shipping that flowed from that former French capital was forced to pass directly by a freshly installed

British neighbor. During times of peace this relationship was beneficial for both sides; thanks to this new proximity, the West Floridians traded local supplies to the Spanish in exchange for precious metals. But with that virtually constant shipping came another danger that European powers had been fighting for centuries: piracy. Whether state-sponsored privateers or common buccaneers, some of the worst criminals of Europe, the Caribbean, and North America flocked to West Florida. The colony contained the perfect combination of elements needed for such a venture; it was centrally located to both New Orleans and Pensacola, and was otherwise so wild and unexplored that it was quite easy to strike a passing ship and then disappear into the dark swamps just inland. The Gulf Coast had always carried a reputation as an unchecked safe haven for illicit activity, but unlike years prior it was very much a British concern as the nefarious actors took up residence in British territory. By the year 1766 West Florida was working its way through the growing pains that all new provincial establishments struggled with, and after months of investment the British had established a reasonably successful colony. One record keeper from the time estimated that the province was home to 3,700 Europeans and 1,200 slaves; in the eyes of most royal investors those were figures that needed to grow for any significant return to be collected.[35]

As in all southern colonies, large-scale plantation farming soon took hold in West Florida after the initial rush of settlement, but the extreme climate and landscape greatly hampered its initial successes. By the year 1776 the colony was growing quite rapidly, but it was still considered a rough backwater when compared to the population explosion in other parts of North America. By the time that Philipp Waldeck and his 3rd Regiment arrived in 1779 he did not find a colony in revolt, a pleasant surprise after his time spent in New York, New Jersey, and Pennsylvania. Whereas each of these seditious colonies held a generally mixed population regarding loyalties and partisanship, in the chaplain's initial observations of Pensacola, West Florida seemed impervious to the rebellion. In his mind there was no urgency toward revolt among the residents, and if there was any discussion of the matter it was almost exclusively a fear of invasion from the rebels themselves. While he did not know it at the time, the recent history of West Florida in regards to the American rebellion was directly responsible for their nonpartisan tendencies. In fact, London had taken great measures to ensure that the infectious call for independence never made it to the Gulf Coast.

By modern standards, on a simple map of British North America, there is little to distinguish one separatist colony from another. In most maps and charts of the American Revolutionary War, the Floridas and Quebec are almost never labeled as actual colonies and simply sit blankly as the northern and southern flanks of George Washington's great rebellion. This phenomenon is so prevalent that the vast majority of modern Americans have no idea that these vital colonies were even British possessions; when confronted with that fact one must inevitably ask why they remained Loyalist during the conflict.

The circumstances that kept the spirit of 1776 from reaching West Florida were as murky as the bayou that engulfed the colony, and due to these confusing circumstances few historians have taken on the task of examining it further. Due to the spurious demographic makeup of the province and the efforts of the Crown to artificially inflate the population, there was always a distinct lack of common ground among the people who settled there. Whereas other colonies shared a social cohesion from decades of colonial life, the only cause shared by West Floridians in the 1770s appeared to be a desire to survive. Together they lived in some of the most treacherous climates that North America had to offer, and the constant threat of disease and native incursion brought the colony together in a union based somewhat on shared survival, but mostly on fear. After a decade of settlement, avoiding impending doom was associated directly with the imperial government's ability to protect them. If an Indian raiding party would sweep into a settlement, either British soldiers or local militia had to defend the province; out of this pattern of protection came a dependence on royal protection that only existed in small pockets elsewhere on the continent.

The typical narrative of the American independence movement did not apply to the Floridas. In places like Boston, Philadelphia, and New York, the Stamp Act of 1765 was met with outrage and open dissent in which demonstrators damaged both public and personal property; on the Gulf Coast, there was no such result. The act itself was designed to aid in paying off the tremendous debts of the Seven Years' War to which West Florida owed its very existence. The governor of West Florida, George Johnstone, noted that his constituents were well aware of the act, but met it with ambivalence. It appeared that since the colony itself was a completely subsidized government experiment, there was an unspoken understanding that increased revenue was simply the cost of their version of freedom.

As the rebellion further intensified in the New England colonies, stories of violent partisanship through imprisonment and public humiliation soon spread southward as well. As the lone colony west of the Appalachians, the West Floridians were geographically removed from these events, and they were not sympathetic to the rebel cause. In some respects the notoriously Loyalist qualities of southern colonies like Georgia and South Carolina were magnified to extremes along the Gulf Coast, and these combined with the recent developments of shared dependence kept the Patriot movement from taking hold in the region.

Although the people of West Florida had seemingly little interest in joining in the dissent, rebel policy makers still attempted to win their favor. In October 1774 the First Continental Congress in Philadelphia resolved to invite the colonists to join them since they chose not to send representatives to the now historic meeting. Three delegates were selected by the Congress in the persons of Richard Henry Lee, Thomas Cushing, and John Dickenson to draft a letter to the West Floridians officially inviting them to the proceedings. The congressional correspondence implored: "So rapidly violent and unjust has been the late conduct of the British administration against the colonies, that either a base and slavish submission, under the loss of their ancient, just and constitutional liberty, must quickly take place, or an adequate opposition must be formed."[36]

Though the target of the memo was the people of the colony, it was addressed to the Speaker of the House Assembly, who was a noted Loyalist; he soon passed the letter to the governor who simply hid the letter in secrecy from the audience to which it was intended. While there was some backlash upon the discovery of this cover-up, it largely fizzled out. The following year in 1775 the Continental Congress resolved to punish those colonies who had rebuked their offers by passing a resolution stating that "all exportations to Quebec, Nova Scotia, the Island of St. John's, Newfoundland, Georgia . . . and to East and West Florida immediately cease." West Florida was by no means the lone colony of British North America to opt out of the First Continental Congress, and each had its own reasons. In Canada the Quebec Act had granted sufficient freedoms that settlers there felt that attending was unnecessary, and in Georgia the colony had financially benefitted so much from the empire's mercantile system that most residents dismissed the entire rebellion out of hand.[37]

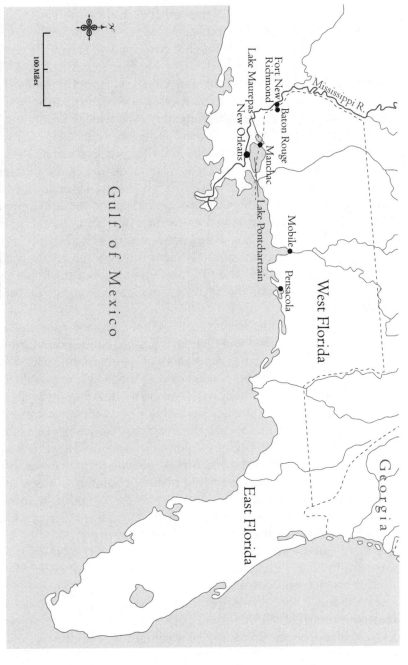

Philipp Waldeck in the American Revolution, 1778–1781.

And thus the hard line was drawn between those provinces that favored opposition and those that resolved to remain firmly under the control of the Crown; although Georgia would eventually enter into the fray, like its neighbors to the south it stood firm as 1774 passed into 1775. The Continental Congress imposed economic sanctions on the Gulf Coast colonies to coerce them to join the Patriot cause, but the results were far from what was intended. Because of their proximity to the Caribbean, the Floridas never truly depended on domestic North American trade to sustain themselves. On the inverse, however, the frontier regions of the thirteen Atlantic colonies relied heavily on the Mississippi River to receive and ship their own manufactured goods. In the end the embargo on Floridian products only served to further squeeze the Americans who were already suffocated by earlier boycotts. Whether intended or not, the aggressive sanctions also sent most Floridians the message that the rebel command in Philadelphia viewed them as enemies rather than allies, and this separated the colonies from one another even more.

By the time that the Second Continental Congress convened in May, the West Floridians and their northern neighbors were further apart than ever. Given the reputation of a hinterland that West Florida held among the far reaches of the empire, Philipp Waldeck was surprised to see as many residents as he did. Pensacola alone had over one hundred families, and while it was the most concentrated settlement in the colony, the quality of life was so far below the West Indies or the Atlantic colonies that he could not fathom why a person would move there. After exploring the city in the days after his arrival, he soon discovered that the community was mainly refugees who came to West Florida from the last place he would have expected. In his mind he envisioned settlers from Europe as he had found all throughout the New World, but many of these peoples were Americans, just the same as the rebels. They came from Georgia, the Carolinas, and the frontiers, and they all chose West Florida for the same reason: safety.

While the Second Continental Congress was meeting to determine the future of the American nation, British secretary of state Lord William Legge, 2nd Earl of Dartmouth, was drafting a policy of his own. In July 1775 the governor of West Florida, Peter Chester, received a transatlantic memo from his superior stating that his colony had been selected as a place of temporary refuge for any Americans still loyal to King George. To make this new burden of settlement less stringent, he also pledged an additional subsidy of one thousand pounds per settler per year. Lord Dartmouth's letter opened with the following statement:

> In the present situation, His Majesty wishes to afford every possible protection to such of his subjects in the colonies in rebellion, as shall be too weak to resist the violences of the times, and too loyal to concur in the measures of those who have avowed and supported that rebellion; and it is hoped that the colony under your government may not only prove a secure asylum to many such, but may also, under a proper encouragement, afford in part at least those supplies to the island in the West Indies, which they cannot now procure from the other provinces.[38]

Unlike its southern neighbor of Georgia, which would eventually send delegates to become full voting members of the Continental Congress, West Florida was forever changed with this influx of migrants seeking to retain their British way of life. These people came primarily from southern colonies, seeking to spare their families from the retribution of radical Patriot militias seeking to squash Loyalist opposition.

If there was to be a moment when the final hopes for a Patriot West Florida were extinguished, it came in the spring of 1778. Since the overtures to join the Congress, a two-headed fear-mongering campaign had swept through the colony; the first half was a general panic that Patriot rebels would lay waste to the countryside, and the second was an overarching fear that the Spanish in New Orleans would invade and occupy the entire Gulf Coast. While the Americans in Philadelphia did not know it at the time, they were about to unleash the dreaded dogs of war that the Loyalist population feared so much, and ruin their chances for alliance once and for all.

An agent named James Willing, a vocal advocate of rebellion, was given an assignment to venture southward down the Mississippi River to New Orleans where he would collect supplies promised to the rebellion by the Spanish governor of Louisiana. Willing had formerly resided near the West Florida settlement of Natchez and was well aware of the region and its potential for a Patriot coalition. Because of his deep local connections, he was soon commissioned by a select committee of the Continental Congress to take thirty men to the Spanish capital where he would be given desperately needed goods and quickly return north. While he was given no express orders to attack anyone as a primary objective, Willing was told to capture any enemy shipping if practicable. After sailing in January from Fort Pitt on the Ohio River aboard the vessel *Rattletrap*, Willing and his men soon saw their campaign break down into an unruly exercise of diplomatic disaster; by mid-February the Willing expedition landed on the eastern bank of the Mississippi River and began their invasion of West Florida. As they made their way toward the small but growing settlement of Natchez, his command disintegrated into a frenzy of pillage and plunder and if there were any remaining colonists still open to revolt, they were soon driven away in disgust.

The rebels confiscated Loyalist property of all types, collected slaves as the spoils of war, and by March had rampaged through the colony to such a degree that the damage tallied tens of thousands of dollars. With over one hundred confiscated enslaved men and women in tow, the rowdy Americans made their way to the safety of Spanish New Orleans, where they sought to finally complete the actual objective of their mission. By April the news of the raid had spread throughout the colony and the West Floridians were aghast and terrified by the results. Whereas the mission was undertaken in the hopes of winning the hearts and minds of some settlers in the fringes of the province along the Mississippi River valley, the actions of the disobedient and defiant Americans had the opposite effect. The rebels had revealed themselves to the Floridians as the disorganized rabble that British officials had so adeptly portrayed them, and even more alarming was the fact that it was done with the very public addition of Spanish resources.[39]

In response to the Willing raid, British policy makers put the entire colony on high alert and made the Gulf Coast one of their top priorities; the British navy soon filled the mouth of the Mississippi with warships and closed it off entirely. Along with this radical venture that would almost certainly precipitate Spain's entry into the conflict, orders were given from London to send reinforcements to the colony, and it was that very command that brought General Campbell, Philipp Waldeck, and the 3rd Waldeck Regiment to Pensacola. The Willing expedition, as it came to be known across the colonies, was nothing short of catastrophic for the Patriot government in Philadelphia and virtually ensured the loss of West Florida for the remainder of the war.

AFTER HIS FIRST TWO WEEKS IN PENSACOLA, PHILIPP WALDECK WAS searching for a miracle. His days were long and tedious, and his fellow countrymen were growing tired, often confiding that they longed for their families in Europe; each day was a struggle, but he maintained form. He had become a well-known face in the community and often spent his evenings dining with a local German family that had settled there months earlier. For all of his distant travels, the chaplain had never felt more secluded and alone than in West Florida, for as isolated as Jamaica was the familiar Englishness of imperial control remained all around him. Pensacola was different; although it was still a crown colony it retained the same provincialism that defined the other regions of North America and that was conspicuously absent in the West Indies. He wrote in his journal that word was beginning to spread throughout the colony that Holland and Russia, two imperial giants that he was terribly familiar with as a native German, were contemplating joining the war on the side of the British against a common French enemy. Though he did not know it at the time the reports were entirely baseless, but such was the precarious nature of intelligence gathering in such a distant and lonesome backwater.[40]

On February 15, just days after his arrival in West Florida, Philipp fulfilled his first duties as pastor. As the city had not had a church for a decade and not seen a clergyman for months, he hoped that the residents would be as hungry to receive divine scripture as he was to deliver it. That day the great religious melting pot of Pensacola turned out in droves to hear his sermon, and they prayed solemnly as a single community. In an age defined by dogmatic differences, the ceremony ended as peacefully as it began. The chaplain had found his miracle.

## PENSACOLA

*Spring 1779*

The Waldeckers had served through harsh northeastern Januarys and a breezy Caribbean December, but they were not prepared for a humid and sticky springtime on the Gulf of Mexico. It rained almost every day in Pensacola.. In the morning the men of the 3rd Regiment would focus on rebuilding the crumbled fortifications of Pensacola, and at midday almost like clockwork a rain swell would bring their work to a slippery halt. When the storm passed they would often find that whatever improvements they had made were washed away along with their patience.

For all of its faults West Florida was a growing colony, and although he was initially dismayed by its shortcomings, Chaplain Waldeck was beginning to grow fond of the people. It was now March and he had been in the city for almost two months, and as with the regiment he served, his work never ceased. Whereas his fellow Germans were working fruitlessly to attempt to salvage the dilapidated fortifications of Pensacola, Philipp was busy saving the souls of its citizens. In his first month alone he speculated that he held dozens of church services for anxious and fearful residents, and he boasted that he performed ten baptisms in his first week alone. It was part of his personal war against the evils of temptation and worldliness that kept the chaplain fixed on the colony's welfare, and he believed that his presence was giving the outpost a spiritual outlet for the first time in over a decade.

As the city grew confident with the arrival of General Campbell's reinforcements, Philipp Waldeck believed that he grew in his own ministry. Until his arrival in West Florida he had almost exclusively served the men of his regiment, and he enjoyed offering guidance and peace to civilians along the way. During his quiet evenings in Pensacola the chaplain would let his mind drift back to his time spent in New York and New Jersey, where he regularly offered communion to the local German populations. He recalled one of his first interactions in New York when he was fresh off a transatlantic crossing, and a local widow invited him into her long-empty home. He wrote humorously after departing that until she filled his belly with her finest cooking he was thoroughly convinced that she was a witch.

In Germany he never had a church or a congregation to call his own, and over the previous weeks he had unofficially adopted Pensacola. Philipp genuinely loved his vocation and he owed his life to his faith, and until washing up on the sterile white shores of West Florida he had nearly forgotten how strong his devotion was.

By 1779 West Florida was a colony of renewed spirit. When General John Campbell first arrived he was not encountering a population of stragglers and castaways as he initially believed, but a population fueled by opportunity. While most West Floridians came from poverty and low social status, North America's newest colony was a democratic promised land compared to their previous life. Like many of the colonial neighbors in the New World, the Floridians were granted a legislature of their choosing that would both express their grievances and defend their rights; it was limited when compared to the proposed self-governance of the American rebels, but far greater than anything else they had ever experienced. Their elected officials in the colonial Assembly stood as a cross-section of the colony itself and for all of its diversity was firmly on the side of the Crown.

All through the lead-up to the American rebellion, royal officials had to juggle the unenviable task of implementing imperial policy and pleasing the population; for every inch gained on one front, miles were lost on the other. If a governor or administrator failed to employ the standards and practices of the Crown he risked losing his position, and if he pressed too hard he almost certainly would incite the vocal opposition of the mob. General Campbell had a host of issues to contend with and each day brought its new administrative challenges, but he took solace in the fact that a rebellious populace was not one of his problems.

With the entrance of France into the war and the presumption of coming Spanish intervention, officials in London made the security of the Gulf Coast a new focus of the emerging global war. By sending General Campbell from New York to Jamaica and ultimately to Pensacola they hoped to transform West Florida into a formidable imperial bastion. When General Campbell arrived with his Loyalists and Waldeckers he learned that such a venture was easier said than done, and he took careful notes to express his concern. In a letter written to Sir Henry Clinton, his commanding officer, Campbell described the scene stating "all the province of West Florida seems hitherto to have been attended to only by starts, after which every thing was again permitted to fall to ruin and decay." Campbell was correct in this assumption which Chaplain Philipp Waldeck also observed; after the Seven Years' War there was a sense of imperial euphoria in North America which led to a general inattention to its colonies. That creeping temptation had rendered London ill-prepared to manage such a vast new empire and West Florida was its dilemma in a microcosm.[41]

It was one thing for politicians in Whitehall to recommend improvements to colonial defense, but for Campbell in Pensacola it was another altogether. He was tasked with meeting a number of very specific objectives, and while there was no deadline, the Spanish menace across the Mississippi taunted the British. Before he could accomplish anything, the British commander needed to assess his resources on hand, and he soon found his prospects to be grim. When he first landed in Pensacola with his eleven hundred reinforcements, he saw the deplorable condition of the soldiers garrisoned there. The forces were entirely inadequate. Serving the entire colony of West Florida were only a handful of overused troops including seven companies of the 16th Regiment and eight companies of the 60th; they were all veterans of former battles and had little more to offer the Crown without significant aid. These weary men were not ideal for the task, but they were all that Campbell had to work with. He wrote that he did not see them fit for duty in their current state, and that he feared that they would desert at the first chance. These worries were not unreasonable, as the Spanish governor of Louisiana had already offered free land to any British soldiers who fled across the Mississippi into their waiting arms. The general described these men as "condemned criminals" and added that they were "almost worn out in the service."[42]

Along with commanding his new uncertain army, the primary mission of Campbell's military tenure in West Florida would be to construct a new collection of forts that met the standards set by London. When he first arrived in the colony Campbell was met by a letter from the secretary of state asking him to build them wherever he pleased, but to pay careful attention to the location where the Iberville River and Mississippi joined; after some exploration he found the spot completely impractical. The waterway was unpredictably shallow, the ground was too unstable, and like everywhere else in West Florida there were few usable resources, stifling his initial planning. When looking at a map of the colony Campbell had to focus on two matters of practical engineering that all commanders faced: where to build, and how?

West Florida was a very large colony with many different localities that could be strategically advantageous for a new outpost, but the terrible quality of the land made many attractive places untenable. From the air the colony appeared as a large rectangle; the entire southern coast faced the Gulf of Mexico and the eastern and western borders were defined clearly by rivers. On the east side the Apalachicola River separated the colony benignly from East Florida, and on the west the great Mississippi defined a hostile boundary with Spanish Louisiana. With great distances spanning between the two, the administrative heart of the colony was ideally located at its center, with Pensacola being the capital, and the old French town of Mobile only fifty miles away. With the bulk of the population in this central region, Campbell elected to build his most durable fortifications on its sturdy ground, but still wrestled with the fact that he needed some kind of new post in the west to keep Louisiana at bay.

Lord Germain's instructions for his supposed fort in the west were very detailed and though his specified site would not work, the other demands were quite clear. With New Orleans so close by, the secretary of state wished Campbell to build a fort that could garrison at least three hundred men. He also demanded that the post be sturdy and permanent, aware that the other existing structures in West Florida were not. This fort would protect British trading interests, fend off any unseen Patriot incursions, and of course ward off the threat of Spanish river crossings. The place that Campbell scouted was called Manchac, just south of modern Baton Rouge in the heart of the dark bayou. Described by Campbell as "extremely sickly," the location was far from ideal but one of the only places that seemed a compromise between the secretary of state's and his own sensibilities. With stagnant water covered in green scum all around them, Campbell's workers began to resurrect a forgotten post from the Seven Years' War dubbed "Bute"; it would prove to be an effort they were wholly unprepared for. After weeks of construction Campbell selected Lieutenant Colonel Alexander Dickson to not only head the Manchac site, but also the entire Mississippi River valley. He was based in the struggling town of Baton Rouge and commanded what came to be called the Baton Rouge district. While Fort Bute was far from imposing, Dickson eventually added control of Fort New Richmond in Baton Rouge itself and Fort Panmure in Natchez. Each tiny outpost had its own garrison and though they were relatively weak their presence spoke volumes in the face of a Spanish regional opponent.

Any number of issues plagued the construction of the swampy outpost, and they all pushed Campbell to the brink of resignation. First the colony lacked skilled engineers to build such a structure and as a result most of the men working on site had little or no experience. Second, the primary request of his supervisor to make the fort "considerable" was almost impossible given the lack of good timber and absence of any mineable stone in the region. Third and most pressing to Campbell was that as important as a western fort was to defending the border, there was still a glaring weakness in the colony's integrity. With his construction efforts focused on taming the wild bayou, he was deeply troubled by the fact that both Mobile and Pensacola were defended only by rotten old fortifications that he believed should have been improved before any new ground was broken. All of these seemingly inoperable factors combined with his utter disdain for many of his forces led General John Campbell to finally submit a letter of resignation to Henry Clinton on March 10, 1779:

> My spirits are almost exhausted with the difficulties and troubles that I have had since my arrival at this place. I must own there is nothing I wish for so much as a relief from my present command, finding myself unable to undergo the fatigue and trouble of it, and indeed I must say (with great *truth*) insufficient for the variety of important business attending it . . . you cannot bestow a greater favor upon me, than to recall me from West Florida.[43]

Twelve days later, to further his now desperate cause, he wrote to Lord Germain in London, "In short, my Lord, I find myself in the most disagreeable, the most irksome, the most distressing of all situations to a soldier and a man of spirit; unable implicitly to fulfill the mandates of my sovereign, the duties of my station, or perform any immediate service to my country."[44]

If the crumbling psyche of their commander on the Gulf Coast was troubling to the British, it was welcome news to the administration of Louisiana. Since 1777 the Spanish Empire had been secretly funneling goods, ammunition, and weapons into the American colonies via the Mississippi River. While there was no outward draw to supporting the revolt for most Spaniards at the time, Emperor Charles III believed that in the event of an American separation his now-weakened domain would be rewarded handsomely for their efforts; their demands came in the form of Britain's Floridian colonies. Out of his base at New Orleans the interim governor of Louisiana oversaw the actions, and by 1779 the contraband flowed smoothly up the river valley into Illinois and the Ohio country with the British largely powerless to stop it.

But for all the importance of the clandestine American-Spanish agreement, the history of Louisiana and its jewel of New Orleans offer a much needed context into the negotiations that preceded it. Founded in 1718 by Jean-Baptiste Le Moyne de Bienville as Nouvelle-Orléans, the site was initially selected because it was a crossroads of natural waterways along the Gulf Coast. It sat ideally between Lake Pontchartrain and the Mississippi River and was well placed to command not only contemporary commerce but all future economic shipping to come.

As time passed New Orleans grew in importance for France's overall plans of expanding its imperial influence; in 1722 it was named the capital of Louisiana. The city grew at an astonishing rate, making it nearly impossible to control its population until in September of that same year a hurricane virtually wiped New Orleans off the map. In the months before the natural disaster, Bienville believed that tightly knit grid pattern of settlement was the safest way to maintain the city. While the settlers resisted his early overtures of reform, the necessaity of rebuilding after the hurricane made the process much easier, and Bienville's plan went into effect. Seen today in the French Quarter, the newly constructed design of the city would remain intact for the next three centuries.

Under French control New Orleans became the single busiest port in the Western Hemisphere and was an international bastion of trade. Its position at the mouth of the Mississsippi River meant that the capital of New France instantly became a vital stop for any imports or exports going into North America or out to sea. New Orleans was a legendary city even by 1750 and it served as a great melting pot of the world, but it was dramatically changed by the Seven Years' War. As the conflict was nearing its conclusion, Spain's Bourbon alliance with France seemed to be a diplomatic disaster; not only did they side with the losing party but they stood to suffer vast territorial losses as a result. In anticipation of losing Florida to the victorious British, King Louis of France offered Charles III all of Louisiana as compensation for their anticipated losses in the 1762 Treaty of Fontainebleau. In many ways this arrangement benefited the Spanish on the continent itself, but it was only a small bright spot in a failed overall war effort.

By 1763 Spain was an empire on the verge of collapse. Its American gold and silver reserves had been depleted and as a world power it was growing increasingly obsolete. Louisiana gave Spain a new opportunity to redefine itself in the New World, and the Spanish were anxious to make the most of it. Although they nominally controlled Louisiana by 1762, they did not dispatch a colonial governor to New Orleans until 1766. Once there the imperial administrator was met with violent backlash by embittered French colonists who had settled the regions for decades. In 1768 the gov-

ernor had to flee Louisiana altogether. From the safe haven of nearby Havana the Spanish authorities quickly apprehended the seditious ringleaders and gained control of the colony, fully aware that
Great Britain was just across the Mississippi in West Florida. There
was an undeniable tension between the two powers following the
Seven Years' War, but the British and Spanish maintained a healthy
commercial relationship for almost a decade.

The American rebellion ended that.

Opportunity was knocking for the Spanish in the form of East
and West Florida. While the Spanish were pleased to hold the busy
hub of New Orleans as their own, snatching back the Floridas was
critical to resurrecting their grip on the Caribbean Sea. Along with
Louisiana, Charles III still controlled the entire Mexican coast as
well as most of Central and South America; if he was able to reac-
quire Florida, the entire basin would be virtually surrounded by
Spanish mainland colonies. It was a lofty goal to be sure, and one
that history would prove to be fruitless, but for the small price of
funneling illegal goods to a group of North American rebels it was
well worth the risk.

Aid to the Patriots was a directive from the imperial capital, but
the one individual most singularly responsible for its implantation
was the interim governor of Louisiana. Born in 1746 at the quiet
mountain village of Macharaviaya in the Iberian province of
Málaga, Spain, the thirty-three-year-old Don Bernardo de Gálvez
was a dashing young man, hopeful of climbing the ladder of success
in the Spanish world. He was everything that an aristocratic
Spaniard was expected to be; finely dressed, battle tested, and ambitious to a fault. From his base in New Orleans the army captain
oversaw much of the illegal commerce that flowed into the
American colonies, and he often skirted the fine line between
ambassador and assailant that so reflected the spirit of his city.

The journey of Bernardo de Gálvez from a relatively unknown
quantity to colonial governor reveals the opportunity that military
service and personal pedigree could deliver in the eighteenth century. During his teenage years Gálvez studied the science of military
combat at the Acadamia de Ávila, and at sixteen gained his first taste
of combat. Like so many men of his time, Gálvez was baptized in
the fires of the Seven Years' War. He participated in the 1762
Spanish invasion of Portugal and was promptly promoted to lieutenant. While he first saw action in Europe he was soon transferred
to the dangerous frontier of Spanish Mexico at the end of the war.

During his first tenuous years in New Spain, as the enormous Central and South American provinces were known, Gálvez earned his stripes. He battled hostile tribes, was wounded on numerous occasions, and ultimately developed a reputation as a soldier who could match the legendary ferocity of the Apache warriors of the frontier. He appeared to be a man born to tame the distant corners of the empire and soon rose to commandant of arms for all of northern Mexico. In 1772 the twenty-six-year-old hopeful was making considerable waves in the Spanish military and was recalled to Europe to take a station in Bourbon France. During his time in France the enterprising Gálvez became a master of the French language, which would become immeasurably valuable over the next decade. In 1775 Gálvez joined the Irish-turned-Spanish naval commander Alexander O'Reilly in a misguided invasion of the Arab Sultan Muhammad III's stronghold of Algeria; the entire venture was a failure and badly damaged Charles III's reputation around the globe.

Finally in 1777 Gálvez was sent to New Orleans at the rank of colonel to become the interim governor of Louisiana; for the thirty-one-year-old it was a great honor. Soon after, he was promoted to brigadier general, and he became determined to make his mark on the gargantuan province. He used his language skills to win over the French inhabitants, married a Creole woman of mixed ethnic heritage. They had three children: a son Miguel, and two daughters Matilde and Guadalupe. Bernardo de Gálvez was determined to enhance the reputation of Spain which, given recent geopolitical developments, had diminished considerably. One of his first measures was to expand Spanish colonization into areas of the Gulf that had not seen them before, and the other was to reverse the empire's official policy regarding native Indian populations. Until his tenure the Spanish had been very guarded when approaching Indian diplomacy in Louisiana, and the relationship could typically be defined as hostile. But given the emergence of the American rebellion and the British residing in West Florida, Gálvez believed that he could never have enough allies, and he began openly trading weapons and goods to the local Indians. His logic was simple enough: if he did not provide opportunities for trade, the British Floridians would.

The brash and debonair Gálvez quickly became one of the single most influential figures in all of the Gulf Coast, unafraid to make waves. In 1778 he was an open advocate of Willing's raid that so alienated the Loyalists of West Florida, and he was the primary point of contact between the Continental Congress and the Spanish

Empire. Although he was still carrying out the royal policies of Charles III, by 1779 Governor Bernardo de Gálvez made it very clear that any Spanish efforts of war, peace, or diplomacy in North America belonged to him alone.

DURING THOSE DAYS OF MARCH 1779 PHILIPP WALDECK WAS A MAN in demand, but never too busy to fill his journal with details about provincial life. Since taking over as the city's primary clergyman he had began to familiarize himself with many local families, yet he was determined to maintain his primary focus on the men of the 3rd Waldeck Regiment. In such a desolate place the Waldeckers all grew closer as a unit and depended on one another for support when confronting the unknown obstacles West Florida presented them; on one evening in particular they were met by a surprise that none of them had ever anticipated. At midday the city of Pensacola came to a halt when a dozen Indians, a delegation of the Creek Nation, appeared in the city center demanding an audience with the ranking officer.

Philipp had read about the Indian warriors of the southern frontier but he had never seen them in person, and when the proposed meeting took place he was certain to involve himself. He was by no means a thrill seeker, but such a rare and uniquely American experience as a native council was something he could never experience in Germany. He and a few of the officers looked on the delegation from a distance, taking note of their dress and weapons, and he was struck by just how familiar they all looked. From the German viewpoint the American Indian was the proverbial "savage," and the chaplain used this term throughout his journal to describe the men he observed. He did not use it disrespectfully, in fact he wrote candidly of his admiration for them. These warriors were not the ravenous, cannibalistic caricatures that he had read about as a child in Waldeck, in fact they were quite *European*. They carried muskets that had clearly been manufactured in England bearing the bold "GR" insignia of King George, for *George Rex*, and they wore some European garments. Their outward appearance retained a wild quality, but they had more similarities to than differences with some of the more distant American frontiersmen. For chaplain Philipp Waldeck the events of this day would be nothing short of transformative.

The council began soon after the arrival of the Indian elders, or sachems, but General Campbell made it clear that he was not interested in taking part. Instead he ordered his subordinate and direct commander of the 3rd Waldeck Regiment Colonel von Hanxleden to sit in his place. By the time that Philipp finished his sacred duties the proceedings had already begun and he rushed to take part. The meeting itself was held in one of the large open halls of the city, and as the tardy chaplain entered the room a member of the Creek delegate was already speaking. In a moment of embarrassment the native speaker stood silent as though acknowledging Philipp's lateness, and sensing the tension the chaplain quickly was seated next to his comrades. The scene before him occurred countless times in the annals of America's colonial past and was an integral part of native power and politics. As the Creek sachem spoke he did so in short bursts so that a translator could relay the message to the other party; Philipp noted that this particular translator was very talented.[45]

The agenda of the day seemed mundane, which was why General Campbell chose to occupy himself elsewhere, but for Philipp the spectacle was enthralling. The unnamed Creek delegate came to Pensacola to demand food from the British commander stationed there, and his justification was legitimate. Unlike the European settlers who were regularly supplied with goods from overseas, the great Indian nations of the South still depended on their own ingenuity to feed their families. While there were small pockets of subsistence agriculture in the colonies, most still relied on hunting. Since the outset of the American rebellion, though, the British had placed a great emphasis on wooing the natives to their side with offers of gifts in exchange for alliance; as the warriors were now operating in accord with the Crown they had very little time to attend to their own needs.

Philipp largely tuned out the proceedings and directed all of his attention to recording the visual details all around him. He wrote that most of the chieftains present were elders of the tribe and they all sat on the floor, he also noted that they each smoked a ceremonial tobacco pipe throughout the negotiations. The speaking was done by one person, and the man did so while waving a large red feather in his hand. All the while the sachem spoke he did not look at the German officer but only the interpreter so as to ensure that his exact meaning was expressed.[46]

While the faces of these men were stern, they were also terribly scarred. To become an elder, a great sacrifice earlier in life was expected. That tally was only collected by proving oneself in battle, and Philipp saw that many of the men present carried tremendous battle scars across their bodies. As he studied their mannerisms and reactions the chaplain soon noticed one of the sachems was different than the others . . . he was white. Although the mysterious stranger dressed as a Creek headman and decorated his body similarly, he was certainly not of Indian blood. After asking around, Philipp discovered to his amazement that the man was a fellow German, formerly named Johann Konrad Brandenstein. Years earlier the forty-nine-year-old Brandenstein migrated from Germany to the New World and married a Creek woman. After his adoption into the community the expatriate proved to be a valuable asset to his communal brethren and there he sat in 1779 not as a German but a full member of the Creek Nation. While they sat in council Philipp was astounded by the fact that even though he was surrounded by his countrymen, Brandenstein never behaved as anything but a member of the Creek delegation.[47]

The chaplain wrote that the sachems and warriors before him were physically strong and well built, and although they had varying interests they were fully behind King George. In reality the proceedings he witnessed were much more nuanced and the result of months of negotiations. From the beginning of the war the British Empire had sought to gain the favor of the native populations of North America, and though the diplomacy was complex it was essential for the war effort. In the northern colonies and southern colonies chief superintendents were put in place for the sole purpose of gathering favor among the Indian nations of their respective regions. While the northern tribes used the Mohawk River valley and Great Lakes as their primary locus of Anglo-Indian negotiations, in the South it centered almost entirely on Pensacola.

The Superintendent of Indian Affairs for the Southern Department was John Stuart, a trusted and vocal advocate of the major tribes of the region. Stuart worked tirelessly to develop good relations with the native populations of Georgia, the Carolinas, and the Floridas and succeeded in personifying royal authority with sincerity and humility. The great nations of the American South included the Cherokee, Choctaw, Creek, Chickasaw, and Seminole, each with its own priorities as well as deeply stratified history. For Stuart the most pressing challenge was to meet their collective tribal needs while respecting their rivalries and alliances; it was a difficult assignment, but Stuart handled it exceptionally well. For the native tribes of the South an alliance with Britain would need to be profitable for their own members, and as the entire American Indian economy of the eighteenth century was trade-based they would need guarantees. If they were to join the war against the Patriot rebels it would not be because of some ideological disagreement, but because King George could provide them the material support on which they depended. By 1779 Stuart's efforts were beginning to pay spectacular dividends. Using Pensacola as a base of trade, members of the Cherokee and Creek nations poured into the city to engage with the supply vessels that sailed regularly into the bay. Unlike its counterparts in Savannah and Charleston, this port city was as yet untouched by rebel assaults and a natural point of connection for the two cultures. By drawing the southern tribes into the war on the side of the Crown, Stuart had provided a nearly untenable situation for the rebel armies in the South. It provided a two-front war.

Since the British army made its fateful decision to move the conflict into the southern colonies under the command of Lord Charles Cornwallis, the American rebels were struggling to fight them off. Now, however, with the threat of royal assault from the sea and Indian attacks on the frontier, the Patriots would almost certainly be overwhelmed. This two-front war was a worst-case scenario for American policy makers and was almost completely the work of Indian Superintendent John Stuart. He was recognizable to nearly every warrior and headman in the southern colonies and the agreements that he formed with the tribes relied on him and not enough on the Crown itself; in March 1779 Stuart suddenly died, leaving the entire precarious Anglo-Indian coalition on the verge of collapse.

When Philipp Waldeck saw the Creek delegation enter Pensacola it was likely the first time they had done so since Stuart's passing, and many questions still needed to be answered. For the Creeks, they needed assurance that the British still understood the terms of their earlier agreement and that the new liaison would honor previously discussed terms. The Creeks were adamant throughout their negotiations that their own concerns needed to be met before any combat was to take place; Stuart had understood this and took steps to insure it. Like most tribal nations of the age the Creeks had signed numerous land concessions to the empire under the impression that no further settlement would occur, yet with each new treaty it seemed they received less and less in return.

Settlers poured into the protected Indian lands and forced many native families to become refugees, and the Creeks had allied with the British under the express agreement that this flood of migration would cease. With Stuart now removed from the equation, though, there was great uncertainty whether any worthy figure would be able to replace him, and as General Campbell had already written the delegation off as a bother by refusing to participate, it seemed that the alliance was doomed.

As the unnamed sachem spoke, the Waldeckers looked on with growing interest. Although they were all strangers the American war brought them together, and despite skin color or ethnic history they all confronted the same enemy. At the conclusion of his speech the Creek headman reiterated his peoples' support for the British, whom he called his "brothers across the water," and he once again pledged his support. He claimed that in the days that followed he would lead a party into the colony of Georgia to attack the rebel militia who resided there and he would need fresh weapons and ammunition to do it; with this request Colonel von Hanxleden suddenly saw the urgency and benefit to his petitions. In what was considered a physical display of brotherhood the Creeks left the city of Pensacola with new rifles in hand and made for their camp only miles outside of the city. By Philipp's estimation the guns that they were provided were the most aged and worn that the garrison had to offer, but to the Creeks they were essential. There were clearly differing motivations that brought the unlikely allies together, and like most of the warriors Philipp understood that he had no personal attachment to King George either. In the effort to suppress the American rebellion the British had employed tens of thousands of his German comrades. They killed their fellow man in a war in which they would not benefit, in a land that was not their own, and in the name of an empire to which they did not belong. In that way they were not unlike the "savages."

SIX MONTHS LATER, ON SEPTEMBER 8, 1779, PHILIPP WALDECK MADE his way down to the shore to greet a newly arrived supply vessel from the West Indies. He wrote that the winter was desolate and the summer was filled with terrible storms, but he was pleasantly surprised by the mildness that fall ushered into the province. That evening he and his fellow Waldeckers were dining in the commissary when a runner brought news that a three-masted supply ship had just arrived. In such an isolated place the people of Pensacola relied almost completely on imported goods brought by ships that only came a few times each season. Typically their holds were filled with the necessities of war, but that was not munitions alone; armies need clothing, tools, shoes, and hats, but also rum and flour. It was not a common sight but after several months the chaplain knew that being at the front of the line meant first dibs at the best cargo. Some soldiers made right for the liquor while others sought out newer firearms, but Philipp was anxious for only one thing—information.

As the men of the 3rd Regiment all took turns staking their claim to the goods being unloaded, Philipp caught wind of the news that he so restlessly sought. He may have been hoping for stories of British victory or potential peace negotiations, but received nothing of the sort. Reports were spotty, but believed to be true, that weeks earlier the empire of Spain had declared war on Great Britain. With Louisiana only a river away the colony of West Florida would be the front line. Philipp knew his quiet city on the Gulf would never be the same. For the next week the garrison buzzed with activity under the belief that an impending Spanish attack was due to strike the colony, and paranoia triumphed over rational thought. On September 12 the chaplain entered into his diary that for the first time since his arrival not a single soul attended mass. Pensacola had transformed into a city at war.

## LOWER MISSISSIPPI RIVER VALLEY

*Fall 1779–Spring 1780*

The mild and peaceful fall weather in Pensacola turned to winter almost overnight, and with the news of war against Spain Philipp Waldeck took it as divine intervention. By September 17 the wind roared throughout the day and thick fog blanketed the bay that protected the city; the chaplain wrote that never in his life did he sweat through the day and nearly freeze at night. The rainstorms were continual though not as heavy as in the summer and the mist condensed so thickly that the Gulf of Mexico virtually disappeared from sight. Philipp prayed that these terrible conditions would stifle whatever Spanish attack was brewing in Louisiana; most of Pensacola's residents, however, feared that a hostile armada would emerge from the sea at any moment.[48]

The city was as lonesome as ever in September 1779, and wild rumors only furthered the growing panic within the colony.

Information seemed to come from all stretches of the province from Natchez in the north to Manchac in the west, but no one knew for certain what was factual or merely hearsay. Within a week of learning news of the Spanish declaration, small warships and packet boats patrolled the misty harbor, and four Indian sachems and two hundred warriors of the mighty Choctaw Nation arrived to pledge their support to the general. In many ways the colony of West Florida had been readying itself for months. Philipp wrote that almost immediately after the arrival of the packet boat that delivered the fateful news the men of his regiment were discussing a preemptive invasion of New Orleans, and the chaplain knew that as so often was the case in garrison life there was a distinct kernel of truth behind the story.

Within days of Spain's declaration of renewed hostilities, Secretary of State Lord George Germain wrote to General Campbell that an anticipatory strike on New Orleans should be undertaken immediately, and after the city was captured British forces should immediately begin to fortify it. It was a lofty goal and General Campbell knew that his weak army could not possibly be successful, but he made preparations regardless. To stress his sincerity even further Germain wrote Lord Cornwallis in the east that capturing Louisiana's capital was essential and that he should "if possible to lay hold of New Orleans which would give us the Mississippi and all the southern Indians." In short, the secretary of state writing from London was now entirely committed to making New Orleans a top priority for the American war effort. In spite of the terrible conditions on the ground in West Florida, General Campbell wrote to the governor of the colony to prepare for war. These events stirred the rumor mill of the 3rd Waldeck Regiment and prompted Philipp to write a letter to his loved ones in Germany in the event of his demise; his attitude toward Pensacola changed so much that he began to describe it as a penal colony unfit for even the worst of the criminal world.

Amid the confusion all of Pensacola's preparations were undertaken to cripple Spanish Louisiana before it could cross the Mississippi River and mount an invasion of its own.[49] Though all seemed clear in Pensacola, information traveled slowly. Two hundred miles away Don Bernardo de Gálvez already had done precisely that.

UNTIL THE MID-NINETEENTH CENTURY, BATTLEFIELD COMMUNICATION was largely unchanged since the age of Alexander the Great. While word-of-mouth transmission posed challenges to many great armies of the past, the outbreak of combat on the Gulf Coast during the American rebellion powerfully illustrates its consequences.

Chaplain Philipp Waldeck's journal gives the specific timing of events as they occurred in Pensacola, and multiple sources have verified that General Campbell and his garrison learned of Spain's wartime declaration on September 8, 1779. Because the news was delayed for months (the Treaty of Aranjuez in April marked Spain's decision), the British could not have possibly planned any meaningful attack on New Orleans that was not guided by speculation. Therefore when word finally reached Pensacola they had some contingencies but these were entirely reactive. In contrast, the Spanish Empire was well aware that it would declare war on Britain for some time and could prepare, giving them a distinct advantage in the Mississippi River valley. As a case in point, Don Bernardo de Gálvez received warning of an imminent declaration of war as early as August, a full one month before his foes in Pensacola. Four months earlier Spanish officials sent a communication to Gálvez dated May 18, 1779, that war was on the horizon and that he should make every effort to secure both Pensacola and Mobile for Charles III. By the time that Philipp Waldeck and his regiment found out that war had even been declared, Don Gálvez was already marching troops through the swamps of the Mississippi River valley.[50]

Their ultimate target were the two major cities at the heart of the colony, but Don Gálvez needed to conquer the western half of the colony before moving farther inland. By capturing the major sites of Baton Rouge and Natchez, Gálvez believed he could easily capture the eastern bank of the Mississippi River and therefore completely control the most vital waterway on the continent. The advantages would be tremendous both militarily and commercially, and it would only lend more credence to Spain retaking West Florida at the end of the war. The invasion of West Florida was set to begin August 22, but four days earlier a tremendous storm tore through New Orleans and damaged many of the army's supplies. Finally on August 27, 1779, Don Gálvez left New Orleans with seven hundred men in preparation for an assault on the decrepit Fort Bute at Manchac. Fort Bute had been somewhat reinforced months earlier by General Campbell, but its poor condition and tiny garrison were

no match for the Spaniards marching from Louisiana. As Don
Gálvez trekked through the bayou he gathered more support from
the countryside and by the time he reached West Florida he had
over fourteen hundred men. His army was a motley assortment that
embodied the entire Spanish colonial experience. It included five
hundred regulars, six hundred and sixty local militia, eighty free
black soldiers, and one hundred and sixty allied Indian warriors.
Tagging along the march which lasted eleven days were seven
American rebels led by Oliver Pollock, a wealthy trader based in
New Orleans. Pollock was considered one of the most vocal propo-
nents of revolt in the region and these connections made him an
effective aide-de-camp to Don Gálvez. [51]

For Don Gálvez the invasion of West Florida was less daunting
than most of his contemporaries believed. Although the province
was vast, the Spanish general felt that by accomplishing a handful of
small victories in highly specific places the entire colony would be
at his disposal. From the beginning Gálvez understood that success
on the Gulf Coast meant first controlling waterways deemed essential by the enemy, and as they would soon be cut off from supplies
his foe would naturally start to weaken. Furthermore Gálvez calculated that this strategy would also dissolve the communication lines
of the British in West Florida. The dashing young officer was no
stranger to managing the risks associated with ruling the Mississippi
River valley, and he knew well how precarious the whole system
could be.

After the end of the Seven Years' War the British Royal Navy
cemented its place as the unquestionable master of the seas, and
Gálvez had no intentions of allowing that dominating force to affect
his campaign. Once Gálvez crossed the Mississippi he would be in
enemy territory, but that river was not the sole waterway that the
Royal Navy could command when war actually broke out. High on
Don Gálvez's list of essential targets were the other bodies that separated the two rival colonies: Lake Maurepas and the much larger
Lake Pontchartrain. Since the beginning of the American rebellion
Lake Pontchartrain was patrolled meekly by the British warship
*West Florida*, and though it was only one vessel it had effectively
controlled the lake. Just before Gálvez's march a group of Creole
inhabitants from Louisiana captured three supply ships sailing
across the lakes, and one of them was a transport carrying fifty-five
Waldeckers from the 3rd Regiment; they were meant to be reinforcements to Fort Bute but became prisoners of war. Both lakes

would eventually fall into Spanish hands, but Gálvez was determined to push on without them in August 1779. Other recent naval victories strengthened his overall invasion plans as well. At the city of Galveztown Spanish forces had captured four British supply vessels meant for the post at Manchac; it only weakened Fort Bute further. Word of the naval losses spread to Fort Bute, and Colonel Alexander Dickson took swift action. He ordered a shipload of provisions that had escaped the wrath of the Lousiana Creoles to be burned and destroyed so it would not fall into enemy hands when Gálvez's army closed in on his post.

Galveztown was constructed in 1776 by a collection of Loyalist refugees fleeing the American colonies at the advent of the Patriot revolt. Because it was so early in the conflict, the Spanish governor allowed these people to settle and they named their new town after him accordingly. But as time passed the administration in New Orleans grew more hostile to the supporters of King George, and the paranoia of war that so gripped Pensacola began to drift across the Mississippi. When the British began to increase their presence on the eastern bank of the river, it was done under the pretense that it was only designed to fend off a rebel attack. Gálvez, however, believed that it was all done in preparation for an Anglo-Spanish conflict. In essence fear gripped both sides, and escalation was the natural result.

On the morning of September 7, 1779, the solitary Fort Bute was only garrisoned by twenty Waldeckers, and they were woefully unprepared. Days earlier Colonel Alexander Dickson learned that Gálvez's sizable Spanish force was headed in his direction and wisely chose to move the bulk of his four-hundred-and-fifty-man army northward to safety at Baton Rouge. Despite his unfortunate position in the middle of the dark swamp Dickson was no fool; he was highly critical of the posts he commanded and wrote often that even a minor attack could sever the entire Lower Mississippi River valley from its capital at Pensacola. When Gálvez's army sloshed its way toward the aged Fort Bute it had been all but abandoned by its commandant. The Waldeckers who stayed behind were only recent arrivals from Pensacola under the command of a Captain von Haacke, and being foreigners Dickson considered them to be the most dispensable.

In the immediate days before his attack Gálvez had lost almost half of his men to the myriad of diseases that plagued the colony, but still retained more than enough troops to overtake the position. All around Fort Bute the Germans grumbled and complained of the mosquitoes and snakes that inhabited the bayou, and none expected to hear the silence of the swamps shattered by the crack of a musket. In a flash the darkness was lit by the flashing of barrels, and before long the Louisianans had the weak position completely surrounded. It was just after dawn and almost as fast as it began the vital fort at Manchac was overrun by Don Gálvez's patchwork force. In the firefight twenty Germans including Captain von Haacke were taken prisoner. For six more days the Spanish general allowed his men some deserved rest at the captured site before moving on to continue his conquest at Baton Rouge.

In Pensacola news of the fall of Manchac took a full nine days to arrive, and the Waldeckers were crestfallen. The intelligence was incomplete, and the atmosphere of half-truths and flat-out lies made the Germans distrustful of any information that they gathered. As the day passed more details trickled in, including the erroneous story that Colonel Dickson had burned Fort Bute in anticipation of an attack; it was only later that the chaplain learned that his countrymen suffered the worst of the engagement. His last entry for September 16 read "O was kostet uns der Mississippi manchen braven Mann" (Oh, how many brave men the Mississippi has cost).[52] His grief was well placed, and though he acknowledged that the river was vital he was beginning to question whether the sacrifice was just. That night he looked out over the fog-covered bay and wrote that he prayed to God asking what would become of them; he finished his entry by adding that Pensacola was no place for a human being, and if the Spanish did not finish them he feared West Florida certainly would.[53]

Only fifteen miles away sat the emerging village of Baton Rouge and the feeble earthen redoubt called Fort New Richmond. The post itself was inherently weak, but Colonel Dickson understood that its central location made it his obvious base of operations. For all of its shortcomings, Fort New Richmond sat on high ground that gave him a clear view of the Mississippi River for miles around, and it was surrounded by an eighteen-foot-wide ditch that was a serviceable nine feet deep. He still had some men posted to his north at Natchez, but with only four hundred and fifty men at his disposal he had to be selective with his resources. During the collapse of Manchac, Dickson was gratified to hear that six men slipped away during the melee and the escapees informed him of Don Gálvez's total strength; he was grateful for the information given the disastrous circumstances. No military commanders whether British,

Spanish, German, or American, was entirely comfortable making critical decisions with only partial facts, but Dickson had almost no intelligence whatsoever. He was in the unenviable position of having the responsibility for defending the over one hundred miles of shoreline near the continent's most vital river with fewer than five hundred men. Compounding Colonel Dickson's dilemma was the fact that he had almost no way of effectively communicating with his commanding officer two hundred and fifty miles away in Pensacola. The situation was dire for the British commander, and the news that seven hundred hostile enemies were bearing down on his position only made things worse.

Since the end of the Seven Years' War the city of Baton Rouge held a special significance to many colonists across the continent. Given its prominent location along the Mississippi River, it was the southwesternmost city in all of British North America. As it was quite distant from the major cities of the east, even by the standards of West Florida it was a desolate place. When the early French first came to the region they found a grisly sight: red cyprus trees fashioned into poles and adorned with severed bears' heads. While they did not know it at the time, these gruesome spectacles were used by local tribes as boundary markers between rival hunting grounds. The terrible spectacle became the defining feature of the area, and the French adopted the name Baton Rouge, or "red stick." The small city blossomed under French control for another six decades until the Seven Years' War thrust the continent into tumultuous disarray. In 1755 the Acadian settlers of eastern Canada were forcibly removed by the British during their conquest of Canada, and as a result the refugees moved into the friendly French confines of the Lower Mississippi River valley and became the "Cajuns."

Just like their French neighbors, the Cajuns took defeat in the Seven Years' War personally and resented the new boundaries of British West Florida carved out in 1763. When Don Bernardo de Gálvez took control of the colony as interim governor he fostered these ill feelings against the British by allowing the Cajuns to retain their language, customs, and continue to practice their own Roman Catholic faith. By the dawn of the American rebellion the Cajuns in and around Baton Rouge were enthusiastic partners of Don Gálvez in his prospective war against their old nemesis. History, it seemed, was a powerful motivator and Bernardo de Gálvez was more than willing to enlist their services.

Colonel Alexander Dickson was preparing for the worst. His position behind the redoubt of Fort New Richmond was defensible, but not enough to withstand a frontal assault from the Spaniards. He had thirteen heavy guns on hand and approximately three hundred soldiers, but even from high ground they were still unlikely to fend off Gálvez's seven-hundred-man army; he could not change many of the factors that worked against him, but Dickson made every attempt to level the playing field. All around the hill on which sat Fort New Richmond were the tiny, ramshackle homes of the people of Baton Rouge, and the colonel ordered them to be razed instantly. He believed that when the Spanish arrived they could use the private residences for cover, and by tearing them down he could buy his cannons precious time to deliver their shot. He knew that the enemy would be upon them shortly, and with the nearest reinforcements over two hundred and fifty miles west there was little room for error. The British were outgunned to be sure, but when compared to the Spanish force the odds were not terrible. Dickson still commanded the advantageous high ground and retained over one hundred men just north at the city of Natchez. If he were to be surrounded he theoretically could have rationed out the supplies and munitions that he had on hand until a relief force arrived, but the military cunning of Don Gálvez virtually nullified any scenario of British victory.

On September 20 Gálvez was within a mile of Fort New Richmond and was able to safely observe how Dickson had arranged his men for the coming battle. The city of Baton Rouge was empty and thanks to the earlier tactics of the British commander had nearly disappeared altogether. At the top of the hill sat the British fort with Dickson's entire garrison inside; Gálvez calculated that to take it with a frontal assault would cause considerable casualties and decided on another tactic: to blast it apart with his own artillery. Though the Spanish were close to their target they were not close enough to strike it with any accuracy, and Gálvez immediately sought to move his guns closer without taking any fire in the process. It was then that he initiated a masterful stroke that both shortened the distance and forced the enemy to waste their own precious resources. In one of the great feints of the entire war, Gálvez sent a party of black soldiers, Indians, and militiamen into a heavily forested area directly adjacent to Fort New Richmond. Once there the men began to chop down trees as though they were attempting to fortify the location, knowing full well that they were within range of the British guns. Gálvez was fully committed to the diversion, even posting sentries to initiate fire on the fort as though they were protecting the workers. His gamble paid off. Just as he anticipated they would, the Britons inside Fort New Richmond began to pour fire into the deceptive scene and with no new supplies on the way, each ball fired was one that they would never replenish.

As the farcical display continued on one side of the fort, Gálvez used the cover of nightfall to entrench the opposite side. With the British distracted by what they thought was the forward column of the Spanish army, Don Gálvez was able to entrench his own guns within lethal range of the tenuous redoubt. When the sun rose on September 21, 1779, Colonel Dickson saw the Spaniards' new battle position and realized that he had been fooled. The great guns from New Orleans opened fire at 5:45 A.M. and Fort New Richmond was no match; the surrender of the entire garrison came at 3:30 in the afternoon. For Don Gálvez the victory was merely a result of sound strategy implemented correctly, and the loyalty of the men that followed him grew exponentially. The diversion of the previous day was an example of flawless execution, and when it was discovered that every man returned unscathed, the mixed force of Spaniards, Creoles, blacks, Cajuns, Americans, and Indians celebrated Louisiana's greatest victory as one unified army. Spanish Louisianan culture was fueled by ethnic and racial diversity, and on September 21 at Baton Rouge the forces revealed what a valuable asset that could be.

Gálvez's terms of surrender were severe, in line with the actions of a man who was determined to take over an entire colony. Colonel Dickson asked initially for only a truce rather than full surrender, but the calculating Gálvez would accept nothing less than total submission. The Spanish governor wanted his vanquished enemy to give up not only the city of Baton Rouge, but Natchez as well. Now, quite literally under the gun, Dickson signed the articles of capitulation, handing over what was considered the entire Baton Rouge district, and therefore all of West Florida's crucial new defenses on the Mississippi River. Gálvez knew his enemy well and understood that Fort Panmure at Natchez was easily the strongest of the three forts in the district; if he could acquire that post without a battle it would save him a great deal of hardship and likely spare him dozens of casualties.

Given a twenty-four-hour grace period the following day, Colonel Alexander Dickson, the men of the 16th Regiment of Foot, and a handful of Waldeckers exited the defeated Fort New Richmond under the colors of the Union Jack. They beat their drums and ceremonially handed over their weapons; on that day over three hundred and fifty British and German soldiers were taken captive as prisoners of war. As for the settlers, militiamen, and black soldiers who participated, Gálvez set them free under the pretense that when the war was over he would be viewed as a fair and just ruler. He sent a party of fifty men northward on a ninety-mile march to read the surrender terms to the garrison at Natchez, and they were astounded by the proclamation. Fort Panmure was the most structurally sound fort in the Mississippi River valley, and its population was strongly in favor of King George. The idea that it would be captured without a single shot being fired left its residents crestfallen. The commander of Fort Panmure and Colonel Dickson's subordinate was Captain Anthony Forster, and upon his orders the British soldiers on hand peacefully laid down their arms. Natchez was universally recognized in the Gulf colonies as the finest land on the Mississippi, and its plantations produced legendary harvests year after year. It was valuable real estate, and to keep up his reputation of fairness Don Gálvez soon announced to the residents there that they had eight months to sell their land and vacate the city. If they chose not to leave they could surely stay so long as they would continue their farming operations under the Bourbon flag of Spain.[54]

In Pensacola the news of the capitulation of Baton Rouge was met with widespread panic and a crushing sense of defeat. On September 20 Philipp Waldecker wrote in his journal that they received news that Colonel Dickson had been captured by the Spanish, which he added that he did not believe in the slightest. In this regard the chaplain's instincts were correct as the Battle of Baton Rouge would not occur for another twenty-four hours. But as the days passed it became more and more clear that something of terrible consequence had befallen their posts on the Mississippi. The following day, more news trickled in of a potential surrender, and because the previous story was so widely disputed most of the British in Pensacola treated all new developments as falsehoods. This systematic disregard of potentially vital intelligence especially perturbed the even-handed Philipp, who saw a grave danger in the practice. He repeatedly derided his "English" cohorts as fools and dunces considering the nature of some of these discounted reports. Finally on September 24 the complete details of the capitulation emerged, and the conspiracy theorists were forced to accept the fact that General Campbell's army had lost its entire western half.[55]

In the following days General Campbell grappled with the decision to attack New Orleans as proposed by Secretary of State Lord Germain or scrap it altogether. For him the most pressing concern was not capturing Spanish territory but fortifying and defending Pensacola and Mobile, the heart of West Florida. For Philipp, however, the general's decision did not come soon enough, and he details in his journal a farcical scene that he witnessed, with scathing criticism of his commanding officer. On September 25 the supply vessel *Thomas* was ordered to be loaded with supplies for what the chaplain interpreted to be the beginning of a mass exodus of the city. Once it was loaded another order came from General Campbell to unload the ship in preparation to remain where they were. Amazingly, once the *Thomas* was emptied Campbell requested that all the supplies be reloaded a second time. Finally, Peter Chester, the governor of the colony, who also resided in Pensacola, held a council with General Campbell; by 8 P.M. after twelve hours it was finally decided that they would in fact stand pat and reinforce Pensacola. Philipp wondered rhetorically to his journal if he had ever seen anything more foolish than the *Thomas* affair.[56]

If the confusion at the British capital was unsettling for the chaplain, his distress might have been mitigated if he knew of the disarray experienced by the Spanish command at Baton Rouge. Since capturing the city Don Gálvez felt very strongly that the entire colony of West Florida was finally within reach, but he needed major support. The seven hundred men that he used to capture Manchac and Baton Rouge sufficed for the western invasion, but were not formidable enough to lead a frontal assault against the heavily fortified Mobile and ultimately Pensacola. If he was to lead an expedition two hundred and fifty miles westward he would need more manpower, ships, and supplies, and that meant he would require the cooperation of his fellow commanders in Spanish America. The person that most held the fortunes of Gálvez's West Florida campaign was Diego José Navarro, the captain-general of Cuba and a rival of the Louisiana governor. Like all empires of the age there was a clear path to personal glory through military service, and both Gálvez and Navarro proved to be masters of climbing the bureaucratic ladder. Because of their seemingly parallel upward mobility, the two men often squabbled over resources and strategies; now in a full-scale war with Britain that professional competition was only magnified.

Gálvez and Navarro both believed that Spain was primed to strike at the heart of West Florida, but their intended targets were vastly different. Gálvez believed that moving on Mobile first was the key to the entire campaign, and he wrote to his colleague in Havana that "Mobile does not need Pensacola, but Pensacola could hardly exist without Mobile, for from there must come the means of provisions." Yet Navarro took the opposite stance, that an amphibious assault of Pensacola was the best course of action, and that the timing had never been better. The administrative quarrel frustrated Gálvez for several weeks until Navarro finally said that unless his Pensacola plan was adopted he would send no help to the Louisiana governor. With the situation seemingly at an impasse, Gálvez left a small Spanish garrison at Baton Rouge and returned home to New Orleans; he decided that if there was going to be an assault on Pensacola it would be on his terms alone.[57]

Six months later, in March 1780, Philipp Waldeck was in high spirits. At the heart of Pensacola now stood General John Campbell's great response to the loss of the Mississippi River valley, and it was impressive in its scale. Since word of Gálvez's conquest and subsequent return to New Orleans, the British commander had ordered his men to work around the clock building an entirely new fortification at the heart of Pensacola. It sat high atop a formerly unoccupied piece of ground renamed Gage Hill after the famed British officer Thomas Gage, and it offered a commanding view of the bay as well as the vast wilderness beyond. The post, called Fort George after their monarch, was an example of the strength of eighteenth-century military engineering. While he felt safer with the new fort, Philipp's spirits were also raised by brighter news coming out of the east. In the fall of the previous year, at the exact same time as Gálvez's capture of Baton Rouge, the British-held city of Savannah, Georgia, successfully fended off a joint Franco-American attack. Though it was slow in coming, when word of the victory did arrive the garrison at Pensacola threw a wild party on that same night, and the usually mild-mannered Philipp was filled with German patriotism. He wrote that this repulsion of the much stronger French force mirrored the victory of Prussia's Frederick the Great at Rossbach in the Seven Years' War, and the Waldeckers all thumped their chests proudly. He believed that retaining the city of Savannah would surely win Georgia's residents to their side, and they drunkenly toasted to the hope that Charleston would be next to fall.[58]

While the British at Pensacola were celebrating, Don Bernardo de Gálvez was amassing troops at New Orleans. Since the previous year he had received promises of reinforcements from Cuba, and with the personal hostilities between himself and Havana's Navarro subsided, the two men proved to be a formidable team. On January 11 Don Gálvez left the city of New Orleans with over seven hundred soldiers; they sailed on twelve vessels and set their sights squarely on the city of Mobile. To land at their destination the Spaniards faced a daunting task. They first had to navigate the Mississippi River delta toward the Gulf of Mexico, and once on the open sea they then needed to sail due east to Mobile Bay. Thirty miles long and six miles wide, the bay that protected the formerly French city of Mobile had a narrow entry point between an elongated peninsula called Mobile Point and a jagged expanse known as Dauphin Island. Once in the bay Gálvez would need to sail his ships its full length to the city of Mobile tucked away in its far northwestern corner. Along the shores of the cove there were a variety of inward-flowing rivers and streams in which he could dock his fleet if he chose to strike Mobile by land rather than by sea. By January 20 Gálvez's fleet was safely at the mouth of the Mississippi, and by February 9 they were at the opening of Mobile Bay.[59]

Storms constantly plagued the Spanish invasion fleet and they were scattered on a few occasions, but the much-needed reinforcements out of Havana arrived on February 20, bringing the Governor's forces to a total of more than fourteen hundred. While the city of Mobile was their overall objective, the greatest challenge they would face was the post that defended it called Fort Charlotte. The post itself was built originally in 1717 by the French prior to the Seven Years' War, and like so much of West Florida it was a purely local construction. It was four-sided, four–bastioned, built entirely of handmade brick and oyster shells; when the British took command of the colony it, like most of Mobile, was in a state of decline. The man who commanded Fort Charlotte and oversaw its resurrection was Elias Durnford, an ambitious former lieutenant governor and experienced soldier. He had served throughout the Seven Years' War in the Caribbean and was present at the British siege of Havana; in short he was well aware of Don Gálvez's intentions and capabilities. For all of his knowledge of his opponent, though, Durnford was even more troubled by his own weaknesses. Fort Charlotte remained in a ragged state, and he only had approximately three hundred men under his command to fend off an approaching Spanish enemy that was more than four times his own strength.

Don Gálvez's fleet entered Mobile Bay with some difficulty, and after losing a vessel after it ran aground in shallow water he elected to proceed by land. Gálvez disembarked his troops at the Dog River just ten miles south of their target on February 25 and proceeded to march for four days until he could see Mobile. With Fort Charlotte now within reach, Don Gálvez drafted a letter of surrender on March 1 to his British counterpart which Durnford refused; it was an interesting exercise between two men who were both military and political figures. Both of them wore the dual hats of battlefield commander and colonial executive, and their respect for one another came through in their polite correspondence. With the Englishman's refusal the Spaniard moved his cannons into position and on March 2 the bombardment began. The scene was familiar to Don Gálvez; he had his British enemy surrounded and completely outmatched. Unlike his previous targets of Forts Bute and New Richmond, the post at Mobile was much stronger, and Gálvez initiated the order to dig trenches. Rather than rushing in and capturing the fort outright, the Louisiana governor retained his previous strategy of exploiting his advantages while allowing as little damage as possible. From inside Fort Charlotte, Elias Durnford witnessed the beginnings of a siege.

Durnford wrote to Pensacola for aid but none would come, and though his men posted a spirited defense the weight of inevitability began to crumple his spirits. After twelve long days of slow bombardment the British commander inside Fort Charlotte raised the proverbial white flag; for Gálvez the capture of Mobile was his most satisfying victory yet. The penultimate piece of the puzzle for reclaiming the colony for the empire of Spain was now in his hands. In 1763 the acquisition of Florida signaled a new beginning for Great Britain in North America, and now just seventeen years later all that remained of their legendary conquest was a tiny city on Pensacola Bay.

In the wake of the fall of Mobile, the city of Pensacola was more vulnerable than it had been the entire war. Although it was much more heavily fortified in the spring of 1780, the Spanish army was now bearing down at what seemed like an unstoppable pace. To remedy the threat coming out of Louisiana, British policy makers sent fresh recruits from Jamaica to West Florida; it seemed that the often disrespected Gulf Coast colony now had the full attention of its administrators in London. On the morning of March 22, 1780, Philipp Waldeck awoke to the sound of distant cannon emanating from the Gulf of Mexico and he instantly sprang from his bed; his first instinct was sheer panic that the Spanish had finally come. He soon learned that the shots were not hostile, but friendly, and they were merely to signal the arrival of new recruits from across the Caribbean. He penned happily in his journal that Pensacola's fate was in their hands, and the soldiers from Jamaica could not have chosen a better time to come ashore. He added finally in Latin verse:

> Teach that which may be beautiful, brave, great and virile. The remaining may willingly rest in conquering the enemy and pursuing the evil. That which is contrary to our lives, is unknown to us.[60]

## Gulf Coast

*Spring 1780–Spring 1781*

Philipp Waldeck offered communion to his congregation on March 31, 1780, under the direct pretenses of war. Since the fall of Mobile weeks earlier the men and women of Pensacola sought comfort and spiritual guidance with the chaplain, and for many of the English and American settlers it was the first time that they ever had a personal relationship with a German. Such were the powers of fear and anxiety to bring typically separate ethnic peoples together, and the city of Pensacola was rife with both. Although the word of God subdued many panicked hearts that spring, relief did not only come from the divine; many Floridians took great comfort in the new fort that dominated their city. Like a great citadel the newly finished Fort George commanded Pensacola and offered a reassuring and bold statement to its residents: the British Empire was the most potent military force in the world, and Pensacola was safely under its wing.[61]

The construction of Fort George was far different than anything that British policy makers in West Florida had undertaken since 1779. While the original plan was to merely resurrect the broken-down relics of the Seven Years' War like Fort Bute at Manchac and Fort Charlotte at Mobile, General John Campbell felt that Pensacola was too important to the empire to simply reinforce the existing garrison post; it needed to be rebuilt entirely, bigger and better. The original post the garrison had been living in until 1779 was laughably inadequate—a simple wooden stockade located in the city's central plaza directly in front of a large, empty hill known locally as Gage Hill, crowded on all sides by the rough-hewn homes and public buildings of Pensacola. In that regard the unnamed military outpost essentially used the residents it was assigned to protect as a shield to defend itself. Worse still than its cowardly design was its horribly flawed physical placement as it was. When Campbell surveyed the place to construct his new fort he could not help but notice that if an invading Spanish army were to capture that vacant high ground and place guns there, the city could be laid waste with minimal effort. The original post was falling into terrible disrepair and had to go.

Gage Hill, in contrast, was a formidable site. It sat approximately twelve hundred yards north of the city center and offered a commanding view of the bay as well as the road that connected Mobile to Pensacola. The hill itself was three hundred yards wide and offered a full, three hundred and sixty degree perspective on any major route that the Spanish could possibly use to attack the city. The design of Fort George was impressive in both its scope and scale, and Campbell used the existing topography of the city to rank it amongst the best defended posts in North America. The primary construction of Fort George was a four-walled, four-bastioned wooden stronghold at the top of Gage Hill, but the true strength of the post lay in its supplementary supports. At the northwestern end of the hill Campbell constructed a hearty, dual stockade he called the Queen's redoubt. This addition would stop any advancing Spanish attack from the Mobile-Pensacola road, and it was further bolstered by another smaller redoubt three hundred yards south. Called the Prince of Wales redoubt this lesser construction became the third point in a triangular design that allowed for maximum protection and uninterrupted interior communication on Gage Hill. For all the peace of mind that the new Fort George brought, the true defender of Pensacola remained the British Royal Navy.

One of the great strategic advantages that London gained by moving the war to the American South was the ability to apply its superior naval strength against the rebels and their allies; West Florida was no exception. Due to the outstanding number of available vessels, Pensacola was given more than enough protection to fend off an errant Spanish attack. The primary naval defense came in the form of two sloops, the *Hound* and *Port Royal*, and the man-of-war *Mentor*, which arrived on April 9, 1780. Although these ships were small in number they were heavy in cannons. After the fall of Mobile, British West Florida *was* Pensacola, and Campbell was determined to defend it to the last.[62]

On April 2 Philipp Waldeck emerged from his quarters in the late morning to the sound of gunfire. It was not the organized volley of a European army, but scattered celebratory shots. The muskets were soon followed by the whoops and hollers of an approaching Indian war party, and the chaplain rushed out to meet them. The band of warriors and sachems that entered the city were a contingent of representatives from the Choctaw Nation, and they had arrived to show their continued support for the British Crown. The Choctaw were not a unified people, and by the time of the American Rebellion the community had split their allegiances based on individual need and regional supremacy. While some of the Choctaw had ventured to the side of Don Gálvez at New Orleans, this particular group had never been swayed away from Pensacola's trade-based economy. Philipp noted in detail that the Choctaw were not like the Creek at all, and he was perturbed by his countrymen's insistence that all native peoples were essentially the same. The Choctaw, he wrote, were taller and leaner than the Creeks, and their cultural dissimilarities were most apparent in their dress. The Creek displayed their social prowess through bodily mutilation, most notably in the piercing and stretching of the earlobes; from Philipp's observations the Choctaw did not participate in such a ritual. He further described the visiting warriors through the only lens that he had in this distant world—his own experience. He recalled that as a child he had studied the Roman Empire, and the Choctaw bore a striking resemblance to those ancient peoples. He even wrote in his own humorous style that one particular sachem wearing a coral necklace and deerskin shoes was the spitting image of Julius Caesar himself.[63]

For most of the British in Pensacola the appearance of the Choctaw delegation was a welcome sight. Since the fall of Mobile the Indian presence in the city had been very uneven. When the natives were nearby, many were pleased simply to know that they were not fighting for Gálvez, but when they began to slip out of the city to attend to their families or fight elsewhere, most Floridians feared the worst. After Don Gálvez's successful operations in the western portion of the colony, General Campbell had wavered on his desire for Indian support. When he arrived in West Florida the late Indian Superintendent John Stuart had brokered alliances with most of the major tribes of the South, but in his absence those treaties had become uncertain. Campbell believed that the tribes he encountered were all basically the same; he felt that they only fought on the side of the powers that could supply them with material wealth, with no scruples or principles to guide them. He referred to them as "a mercenary race . . . the slaves of the highest bidder without gratitude or affection."[64]

Guided by those prejudices and pressured by the surging Spanish invasion, General Campbell sent mixed messages to his Indian allies. When Mobile was under attack weeks earlier he sent a six-hundred-man Choctaw war party to defend the city, only to arrive after the battle was already finished. Feeling cheated, approximately two-thirds of the warriors abandoned the British to fulfill their hunting needs or simply relocate elsewhere in the South where there actually was a fight to be had. The natives that returned to Pensacola were received with little fanfare and suffered great mistreatment. Further straining the Anglo-Indian bonds during the time period was Campbell's general indecisiveness so well illustrated by Philipp Waldeck's account of the *Thomas* affair. As part of the general fear that Gálvez would march on Pensacola any day, Campbell ordered members of his diplomatic corps to gather as many allied Choctaw, Chickasaw, Alabama, and Creek warriors as they could. He believed that if Gálvez was to assault Pensacola he would need the additional strength to defend the city, but when an immediate attack failed to materialize he rescinded the order. As a result hundreds of allied warriors flocked to West Florida's capital city only to be unceremoniously turned away. By March 1780 there were approximately eleven hundred native men, women, and children in Pensacola and the number was dropping by the week. Many of General John Campbell's actions that spring were dictated by the great uncertainty that overwhelmed the city after the capture of Mobile, and his decisions were entirely reactionary in the wake of Don Bernardo de Gálvez's recent actions. In the great struggle of empires, a field commander always seeks to force his opponent to adjust to his own actions; in this regard the proactive commander sets the tone for the war and forces his nemesis to abandon his own strategy. When this happens the reactionary officer slowly loses control and eventually unravels in an undisciplined collapse. For Don Gálvez in Mobile, it seemed as though he had the British General John Campbell exactly where he wanted him, but he soon fell into logistical pitfalls of his own.

In the days immediately following the fall of Fort Charlotte and the capture of Mobile the spirits of Bernardo de Gálvez and his men were high. To that point their six-month campaign to recapture West Florida had been nearly flawless, and with Pensacola less than sixty miles away it seemed logical to continue to ride their current wave of momentum. But for all of their recent conquests, Gálvez understood that his army in its current form would not be strong enough to move on the capital in any meaningful way. Manchac, Baton Rouge, and Mobile had fallen with minimal losses, but Pensacola and its new Fort George was an entirely different kind of imperial control. The Louisiana governor had firm control over Mobile, but his close proximity to Pensacola was as much a liability as it was a blessing. For Gálvez to strike the capital with his small force was unlikely to succeed, but to waver for too long could potentially open the window for Campbell to lead his own attack. In short each option had its risks and rewards, and the only option that was not available was to hold still.

As he waited Gálvez became proactive regarding the possibility of a British retaliation out of Pensacola by building a new fortification on the path that connected the two cities. On the opposite side of Mobile Bay along its eastern shore Don Gálvez ordered the construction of a roughly hewn fort to act as a buffer between the two armies; while most of the Spanish force would be in Mobile proper, a small contingent of men would garrison the new fort directly opposite. This place would come to be known as "the village of Mobile," but for the British at Pensacola it would simply be known as "the Spanish Fort."[65]

Complicating matters tremendously for Gálvez was the fact that he knew that there were over two thousand men waiting to aid him in Havana should he need them, but to gain their support would require going there personally. In the days after the fall of Mobile a small Spanish fleet out of Cuba did explore the possibility of attacking Pensacola by skirting along the Gulf Coast, but after receiving word of the new Fort George *and* the recent reinforcements out of Jamaica they turned back. It was a difficult position for a man of action like Gálvez, but by no means unheard of. Like many young commanders attempting bold achievements, the Louisiana governor rushed into West Florida and caused a great stir across North America; also like many others before him, Gálvez achieved so much, so fast that the rest of the Spanish military in the region had not yet caught up with him. The result was essentially a stalemate of inaction in which the young general gave away his greatest strategic asset: the element of surprise.[66]

On April 11 Gálvez held a council of war with his closest officers to discuss the best course of action. On that day a party had returned to Mobile with valuable information regarding British reinforcements and the possibility of marching on Pensacola given their current condition. The party was a scouting unit commissioned by Gálvez to determine if the road connecting the two cities was suitable for an extended march—it wasn't. With his greatest tactical edge now having escaped him, it was glaringly apparent that he had to change strategy. In an ideal world Gálvez would have continued his lightning campaign into Pensacola taking the city by storm, but the new reinforcement of the capital made that impossible. Days later the governor left one Colonel José de Ezpeleta in command of Mobile to hold their precious ground and set sail for Havana.[67]

THE MORNING OF SUNDAY, JANUARY 7, WAS COOL AND DARK. WITH THE sun yet to rise sixty men of the 3rd Waldeck Regiment sloshed through the muck and brush on their way toward the Spanish Fort on the eastern shore of Mobile Bay. They had not seen combat since leaving New York two years earlier, and now they were operating under complete secrecy and marching toward an enemy whose arrival they all feared. They were not alone but a minority in a much larger force; it included one hundred hardened veterans of West Florida from the 60th Regiment of Foot and more than two hundred Loyalist Americans. Most unsettling of all though for the Germans was the notion that fighting alongside them would be four hundred warriors of the Creek and Choctaw nations, the very "savages" that they had speculated so much about. For the Waldeckers in the blue jackets, black tricorn hats, and bright yellow lapels the

Indian warriors were a ghastly sight. They were fully painted in the traditional colors of war, red and black, and anxious for the engagement ahead. The Waldeckers were not unlike most Europeans of the age when it came to their perceptions of Indian warfare; they had heard the stories of hyperaggression and torture, and they shuddered at the complete disregard for the conventions of Western warfare. In truth the warriors understood the psychological edge that their reputation gave them on the battlefield, and their elaborate painted appearance was meant to magnify that fear.

Their intended goal was to strike the newly built "village of Mobile" without warning, and hopefully wrestle Mobile back from the Spanish in the absence of their great leader. As well designed as the plan was, it all hinged on silence, execution, and most essentially timing—none of which was ever certain in a mixed army such as theirs. The officer who led this bold maneuver was Colonel Johann Ludwig Wilhelm von Hanxleden, the regimental commander of the Waldeckers who had personally guided their journeys in America since the day they left Europe. Though the Germans were only a mere fraction of the force, they took great pride in this fact and saw it as a great honor for their beloved colonel.

As capable as the mixed army was, in the mind of von Hanxleden the entire exercise needed to be flawlessly executed for it to be successful, and he developed what he believed to be a foolproof plan of attack. Using the cover of darkness in the early morning hours he would position his men all around the Spanish Fort, knowing how under strength it was. The post was merely a secondary contingency to defending Mobile itself, and therefore required only a small garrison at any given time. By surrounding the structure von Hanxleden believed his British, American, and German troops could actively engage the Spaniards until they wasted the majority of their supplies. At that moment he would signal to the Creek and Choctaw warriors still hiding in the swampy forests to rush onto the scene and overwhelm the already tiring garrison. It would require a steady hand and unwavering discipline in the face of several unknowns, but that was why Colonel von Hanxleden was selected to lead it in the first place.

The events that followed Don Bernardo de Gálvez's departure from Mobile had led precisely to that moment, and when General John Campbell initially conceived a preemptive strike to gain control of the city it was because of those very developments. Almost three months earlier in October 1780 the governor of Louisiana was stationed in Havana planning to strike the city of Pensacola. He had put his personal grievances aside with Diego José Navarro and the two officers pooled their collective resources to deliver what they hoped would be a crushing blow. From the summer to the fall of 1780 the busy ports of Havana were bustling with warships and supply vessels in preparation for their great invasion of West Florida, and when they finally set sail for the capital in October it seemed as though nothing could stop Gálvez. At his disposal were thirty-eight hundred men and three months' worth of supplies on seven massive warships, five frigates, three auxiliary boats, and forty-nine transports. There likely was no naval force that could have cut off their attack or turned away their small armada, but as any soldier stationed in the Caribbean could attest, the greatest threat was often not brought forth by the work of man. As the fleet left Havana on October 16 the Spanish were brimming with pride, but the Gulf of Mexico was quick to humble them. After only two days of sailing a wicked, five-day hurricane struck the fleet and stopped them in their tracks. The damage was not catastrophic, and miraculously Gálvez lost only one ship at sea, but by October 19 the remainder of the fleet had been forced to return to Cuba and Pensacola was given yet another reprieve.[68]

Those developments in the fall of 1780 prompted General Campbell to organize his clandestine assault on the Village of Mobile in January 1781. After receiving word of the fortuitous storm that spared his city once again, Campbell began making careful arrangements for the march. He knew that the Spanish navy was an ever-present threat in and around the Gulf Coast, so before he sent Colonel von Hanxleden he ordered the *Mentor* into action. For the last eight months the man-of-war had been patrolling the mouth of Pensacola Bay, and because of its ability to effectively close off the opening Campbell redirected it to do the same at Mobile. Consequently the Waldeckers, Loyalists, regulars, and warriors had to postpone their counterstrike on the Spanish Fort until the *Mentor* could take its rightful place at the mouth of Mobile Bay to prevent any outside incursions. On December 31, 1780, the men departed on foot, and by January 6, 1781, the vessel had easily sailed the fifty-mile stretch and the army marched steadily toward its destination. The trek that took Colonel von Hanxleden's force from Pensacola to the eastern shore of Mobile Bay lasted almost an entire week, and when the men finally arrived they were exhausted. Throughout their preparations it was stressed to each soldier, with special attention to the Creek and Choctaw warriors, that silence was their most precious asset. As long as it remained practical the men should attack their enemies only with the bayonet, and if possible they should avoid firing their muskets until the walls of the Spanish Fort were breached. The strike force arrived at their destination a day early, but the German colonel decided to quietly encamp through the night to strike at dawn. By waiting, von Hanxleden estimated that the assault could begin in almost total darkness, but come to its dramatic fruition in the light of the early morning.

And so in the black hours of January 7 the army moved into position still five hundred yards from the Spanish Fort at the village of Mobile. As they crept closer there was no indication that their enemies had any idea that the jumbled assembly of men was bearing down on them, and so von Hanxleden ordered his men to stalk even closer to the outer walls of the fort. Finally, when his army approached within two hundred yards, the German colonel gave the order to attack. Like a flash the British charged the enemy post but almost immediately gave away their intentions by shouting and yelling, and as a result the now-alarmed Spaniards opened fire. What was intended to be a subversive action suddenly revealed itself, and the British force was now confronted with the harsh reality of charging through a veritable wall of lead and grapeshot to even attempt to reach the fort's outer wall. One Pennsylvania Loyalist, Benjamin Baynton, recounted the initial push in a letter to his brother, stating:

> The particulars of this action you will I suppose see in the publick papers; but, this I will venture to assert, no action since the rebellion, (for the numbers) was more severe while it lasted, or where more honor has been reflected on the astonishing intrepidity of the British Troops. They pushed on upwards of two hundred yards through an incessant fire of grape & musket shot, from at least twice their number, entrenched up to their teeth. One continual sheet of fire presented itself for ten minutes. You may judge of the gallantry of the Officers, when you read in the papers that out of ten, six were killed and wounded. It was Bunker's hill in miniature.[69]

As expected the encounter was an entirely chaotic affair for all parties involved. While the majority of the Spanish garrison stayed in place inside the fort, some ran for a nearby boat tied off in the bay; these men were targeted by the attacking British and riddled with musket fire during their attempted escape. The assault was not developing as planned, and though it was disorganized it was about to deteriorate even further into madness. As discussed earlier, four hundred Indian warriors had yet to take the field of battle since they were ordered to remain hidden until the German colonel signaled them. Since he was adamant that they hold firm and stressed that the entirety of the mission hinged on their ability to remain disguised, they waited patiently throughout the firefight. Only moments after their initial charge, however, a well-placed shot struck Colonel von Hanxleden and killed him instantly; with this shocking development the signal that the Indians waited for never came, and unsure of the directive the warriors simply sniped at the enemy from within the tree line. Despite the challenges that the Spaniards presented, the British did finally reach the walls of the post, and the roaring gunfire broke down into brutal hand-to-hand combat. The men ferociously swung their rifle butts at one another, but the Spanish Fort held resolute. In the midst of the fighting there were reports that the fallen colonel's son, a infantryman in the 3rd Waldeck Regiment, was so incensed at his father's untimely death that he charged unknowingly into a waiting Spanish bayonet but survived his wounds.[70]

Upon the death of von Hanxleden, command fell to another German, Lieutenant Stierlein, who was also killed. The line of succession next placed the army in the hands of Lieutenant James Gordon of the Sixtieth Regiment of Foot, but he was felled as well. Finally after a period of terrible confusion Captain Phillip B. Key of the Loyalist Americans took charge and ordered a full retreat back to Pensacola. In the aftermath the Spanish suffered approximately thirty-seven casualties, with the British tallying their loss at thirty-eight. Colonel von Hanxleden was buried just off of the field of battle, and his body remains interred in the swamp to this day. Four days later, Pensacola mourned the arrival of the defeated force and the loss of their German commander. The garrison was mired in grief, and almost everyone in the city understood that the failed attempt at the village of Mobile was likely their last chance to fend off a Spanish attack on the capital. For all of its shortcomings General John Campbell stood firmly behind his decision to send the army against the post, and offered his own postmortem of the attack. He believed that the plan was sound, but the loss of the beloved colonel was too much for the operation to withstand. In a conciliatory letter to Secretary of State Lord George Germain he wrote: "This expedition I can now venture to say entirely miscarried from Colonel ... Hanxleden's early fate." He also praised the men who fought valiantly in the assault: "They did everything that zeal and honor could dictate for the success of His Majesty's Arms."[71]

That evening Chaplain Philipp Waldeck held mass in the garrison's mess hall, and the somber loss of their regimental shepherd weighed heavily on the men. Although Philipp had grown accustomed to a certain amount of enthusiasm among his congregation, he understood that the circumstances at the Battle of Mobile loomed too large for the Germans to worship with their usual zeal. At the conclusion of mass he resumed his nightly ritual of returning to quarters to pray and write in his journal. His lone contribution summed up his entire two-year stay in West Florida: it is all for nothing, all is in vain.[72]

TWO MONTHS LATER THE CITY OF PENSACOLA WAS ROCKED BY THE sounds of cannons in the distance. On March 9, 1781, the man-of-war *Mentor* was patrolling the mouth of Pensacola Bay when it spotted a daunting apparition of white sails on the horizon heading directly toward them. These were not the typical reinforcement vessels from Jamaica or a friendly convoy; they flew the Bourbon flag of Spain. The *Mentor* quickly understood this to be the beginnings of the dreaded invasion force, and this time there was no hurricane to stop them. Operating coolly under the pressure of this alarming new development, the ship's captain ordered seven cannons to be fired as a signal to the mainland. When the echoes of these blasts finally reached the capital, every person in the city instantly knew that the moment had come, and Pensacola was about to be invaded.

The fleet first witnessed by the *Mentor* was Don Bernardo de Gálvez's great attempt to finish what he had started two years earlier. With all of the Lower Mississippi River valley and Mobile firmly in Spanish control, Pensacola remained the last British obstacle to the complete reconquest of West Florida. His efforts at sailing the previous fall had been disrupted by a relentless storm, and though it hurt his prestige it did little to deter him from his goal. When Gálvez set out on his earlier expedition he had nearly four thousand men at his disposal, but when the storm stifled his efforts he lost considerable support from the empire's administration. Now, however, in the winter of 1781 he had a force less than half as strong but more than enough to capture Pensacola and complete the task for which he had waited so long.

He had remained in Havana since August of the previous year and spent months preparing to attack the colonial capital, and for his efforts he was given a capable fleet. He commanded thirteen hundred men on thirty ships and knowing the relatively weak naval defenses at his target he felt that his force was up to the task. His fleet was highlighted by the twin thirty-six-gun frigates *Santa Clara* and *Santa Cecelia*, the eighteen-gun *San Pio*, the twenty-gun *Chambequin*, and spearheaded by his personal seventy-four-gun warship *San Ramon*. The *San Ramon* was among the strongest ships that the Spanish Empire had to offer, and before leaving Havana it rocketed a fifteen-gun salute and ceremonially raised a pennant to signal that Gálvez was officially onboard. The fleet left for Pensacola on February 13.[73]

By March 9 Gálvez had witnessed the *Mentor* signal to the capital that his fleet was nearby, but he cared very little for it. His plan was a full-scale siege of Pensacola the likes of which the Gulf Coast had never seen, and with the promise of eventual French assistance he had no doubt it would be successful. Only five days earlier his massive fleet encountered the British vessel known as the *Hound* and successfully drove it away from its assignment; the encounter only strengthened the Louisiana governor's already high hopes for an easy victory. By the time that the *Mentor* had sent its seven-gun signal the Spanish fleet was already approaching the mouth of Pensacola Bay, and once it passed inside Gálvez intended on keeping it there. Rather than immediately shooting for the entrance, the Spanish general elected to capture every fortification that the British had in place nearby so that he could easily turn them to his advantage when royal reinforcements eventually came. By the end of the day he had landed and taken command of Santa Rosa Island, which served as Pensacola's best natural defense.[74]

Gálvez was in command of both the Spanish navy and army, no easy task. Instead of simply using the flotilla to land troops and disembark, the general treated each as its own entity designed to work in concert with the other; it was a juggling act that proved to be far more challenging than he expected. For the next several days the Spaniards remained on Santa Rosa Island developing a strategy for attack, and after hours of planning it was agreed that a successful siege required stable footing somewhere on the mainland of West Florida. On March 18 Gálvez initially crossed into Pensacola Bay for the first time and in doing so met stiff resistance from the British guns at Red Cliffs. A peninsula that jutted out into the bay, Red Cliffs sat just beyond Santa Rosa Island and formed a natural S-curve that would trap any approaching fleet in a bottleneck. For this reason the British established a battery on the sight as the second line of defense for the city of Pensacola, and Gálvez was determined to slip by it unscathed. To take his entire fleet into the narrow passage would have given the guns on Red Cliffs the ability to direct their cannons with a high likelihood of striking one of the many ships; by taking only a few vessels through at a time, Gálvez made the battery take much more careful aim. Just as he calculated, the British at Red Cliffs opened fire but found no success. It seemed that patience and timing would be enough to render the position just a nuisance.[75]

With the capture of Santa Rosa Island, the breach of Pensacola Bay, the Spanish invasion was beginning to harden around West Florida's capital city. After placing guns on the Santa Rosa Island position, Gálvez successfully used the battery to repulse British vessels from following his fleet through the bottleneck. From March 24 onward the Spanish retained complete naval supremacy over Pensacola Bay, and with the urgency of outside attack gone they began to search out a location to establish their first base camp. From there, Gálvez hoped, they could slowly but surely move toward their target and choke out the city once and for all. The area Gálvez selected for his camp was a dry, defensible piece of ground between Moore's Lagoon and Sutton's Lagoon just two miles southwest of Pensacola; he initially met with resistance from British-allied Indians but fought them off with minimal losses. With a permanent foothold now established on the mainland of West Florida, Gálvez could begin his march toward the city. Because the affair was designed to be a siege rather than a brief engagement, the Louisiana governor took every precaution to ensure that the exercise would be successful, and as with any siege warfare it revolved around two prerequisites: being well positioned and easily supplied. His intended location to institute the full force of the maneuver was a large hill just north of Fort George called Pine Hill; a year earlier General Campbell disregarded this high ground overlooking Gage Hill because he believed it was too distant to be a threat. If Gálvez could place guns on the elevated hilltop, he believed that the combined

might of the Spanish navy from the south and battery from the
north would be too much for Pensacola to withstand. Rather than
directly marching at the city, Gálvez took on the long, slow investment of entrenching his men along the way, literally carving his way
toward the high ground that commanded the city. The venture took
weeks, and by April 22 Don Gálvez was reenergized by the news
that his promised French aid had arrived: along with sixteen hundred new Spanish reinforcements the Marquis de St. Simon had
emerged with eight more warships and seven hundred French
troops.[76]

From within Pensacola the British garrison was alarmed at their
inability to stop the progress of the Spanish force bearing down on
them. For the three weeks that Gálvez's army had been digging its
way toward Pine Hill outside the city, General Campbell had
harassed his works with Indian, militia, and Loyalist raids that all
proved to be nothing more than a distraction. Using diplomacy as a
last hope he wrote Don Gálvez regularly, but the terms which he
offered were far from realistic and the daring Governor was confident that he would achieve his goal without a negotiated settlement.
By May 1 the Spanish and their French allies had assumed the high
ground overlooking Fort George; adding insult to injury they
quickly built an earthen redoubt on the site to mock the surrounded British Army's inability to stop them. Upon the discovery of this
new Spanish redoubt opposite Fort George, General Campbell
ordered a full-scale shelling of the post and the warring forts
exchanged heavy artillery for days. As the distance was great and the
guns inaccurate, both entrenchments attempted to gain the upper
hand by sending infantry raids on the other, but neither was able to
gain much success without considerable loss.[77]

Ultimately, on May 8 just before nine o'clock in the morning, the
Spanish struck a fatal blow to their enemy, largely a matter of luck.
The constant shelling had gone on for almost seven days when the
Spaniards launched a shot that landed directly on the powder magazine of the Queen's redoubt. In a flash the outpost erupted in flame
and was completely demolished in the blast. From the reports of
General Campbell it was noted that in that one moment forty-eight
soldiers, twenty-seven sailors, and one slave were killed. In the
aftermath of the explosion, Gálvez ordered his men to charge the
shattered redoubt, and though the British held them off long
enough to remove many of the wounded, it eventually fell completely. With the capture of the Queen's redoubt General Campbell

understood that one-third of his mighty Fort George was now gone. After taking control the Spanish next turned their fire on the remaining Prince of Wales redoubt, and it too proved to be no match for the superior force.[78]

Knowing that his command was almost entirely reliant on out-side supplies that could no longer arrive and that Fort George was almost entirely compromised, General John Campbell signaled to Don Gálvez with the white flag of surrender at three o'clock in the afternoon. At the end of the eight-week siege of Pensacola the British had lost one hundred and thirty-six casualties and eighty-three deserters; the Spanish lost two hundred and ninety-eight. Although the attacking force suffered the worst of the fighting, Gálvez ultimately carried the day, reporting that they took over eleven hundred prisoners (including Chaplain Waldeck) and a veritable fortune in supplies and ammunition. Finally on May 10, 1781, exactly forty-eight hours after the original surrender, Don Bernardo de Gálvez and General John Campbell met to negotiate the official capitulation of Pensacola. Flags flew on both sides and drummers added an air of ceremony to the proceedings, but for the British Empire there was little dignity to be found. From that day the rebellion that began in a tiny corner of New England had proven much more costly than ever anticipated and in a matter of weeks the Bourbon flag of Spain flew proudly over Florida once again.

THE CAPTURE OF PENSACOLA AND SUBSEQUENTLY ALL OF WEST Florida brought to a close one of the most controversial and misunderstood conflicts within the larger revolutionary era. Don Bernardo de Gálvez has been long admired by social organizations that commemorate the American rebellion; the Sons and Daughters of the American Revolution have granted official status to Hispanic descendants of those who battled along the Gulf Coast. But from the historical vantage point there has been a struggle to place Spain's role in the greater conflict and measure accurately how important it was. Some historians claim that Gálvez's invasion of West Florida was entirely separate from the larger American rebellion, going so far as to call it the "Anglo-Spanish War." Still others believe it was so vital that they refer to it as "George Washington's Second Front." As is typically the case in history, the truth is somewhere in-between, but important parallels can be readily drawn that warrant further investigation.

The actions of Don Gálvez along the Gulf Coast were not the sum total of Spain's contribution to the rebel war effort, but merely an active part of it. Spain lent the equivalent of tens of millions of dollars to the would-be American nation, and like France that generosity was largely fueled by a desire for revenge from the Seven Years' War a generation earlier. But regardless of the motivations behind the governor of Louisiana's actions, the results are undeniable. The entrance of both France and Spain into the war drastically changed the way that administrators in London viewed the conflict; rather than it being a separatist rebellion it became a global struggle for imperial supremacy. By the end of the conflict King George's focus was directed so much toward his old European enemies that the ongoing struggle in the colonies was considered by many to be less important and by some as a distracting afterthought. Following the surrender of Pensacola, Don Gálvez also maintained that the greater American struggle must continue, and he offered one hundred thousand pesos to his French allies so that they could head up to Virginia and aid in the siege at Yorktown.[79]

The ultimate reconquest of West Florida would not be complete for the Spanish until the signing of the Peace of Paris in 1783, but Gálvez's victory made immediate waves. Charles III made the young commander "Count of Gálvez" and subsequently promoted him to governor of Louisiana *and* the freshly acquired West Florida. It was a time of great glory for Spain, but ultimately it was only a spark in the darkness for a dying empire. For the people on the ground in Pensacola, however, the defeat was devastating. As part of the agreement, soldiers taken prisoner were not to be held in the legendarily cruel dungeons of Mexico or Central America but paroled back to British control. For Philipp Waldeck, one of the hundreds of Germans taken prisoner on that extraordinary day in May 1781, the future was uncertain. They were told that they would be in friendly hands soon enough, but that time frame was fluid and their immediate future was in doubt.

Within days of the capitulation it was announced that the Waldeckers would be transported as captives to Havana, Cuba, where they would await further information. Philipp and his countrymen were soon loaded onto a transport and sailed into the Gulf of Mexico as prisoners. He said a prayer as West Florida shrank away in the distance, glad to see it go.

# EPILOGUE

O N SEPTEMBER 3, 1783, DIPLOMATS OF THE UNITED STATES OF America and Great Britain met for one final time to officially conclude eight years of war. Representing the emancipated American states were John Jay, Henry Laurens, John Adams, and Benjamin Franklin; standing in place of George III were David Hartley and Richard Oswald. Peace negotiations had begun the previous April, and by the next fall both parties had reached terms to finally bring the contentious age to a close. Although the American rebellion began in Boston and escalated in London, the official peace was being finalized at the landmark Hotel d'York in the heart of Paris. With the signing of the Treaty of Paris the British Empire officially recognized the sovereignty of the American nation, and ironed out many pressing details in the aftermath of the conflict.

Among the major points of contention was the fate of Canada as well as the logistical disarray of cleaning up after almost a decade of war. For the Americans a great concern was the Canadian province; Benjamin Franklin believed that its continued colonial status would be a cause of eventual hostility in the years to come. The British scoffed at the idea and pushed toward their own self-preservation in the form of defining fixed borders with their new North American neighbors. In the end it was decided that the Great Lakes and St. Lawrence River would perpetually divide the United States from the Quebec colony, and both powers would retain unrestricted access to the Mississippi River. While neither nation knew it at the time, they would conduct a geopolitical "cold war" for the next three decades until hostilities commenced again in 1812.

On the same day that Britain came to terms with the American separatists they also concluded peace with their old enemies of France and Spain. In separate agreements the British Empire ceded both East and West Florida to the Spanish along with the coveted Mediterranean island of Minorca. In return for these immense concessions Britain saw the recently captured Montserrat, Bahamas, and Grenada returned to their control. It was a crushing loss, and it did not take into account the agreements still looming with France. Despite the fact that France only received the African colony of Senegal and the Caribbean island of Tobago from Great Britain, they scored an economic acquisition of major proportions by gaining guaranteed fishing rights off the coast of Newfoundland for years to come.

While the year 1783 represented a monumental shift in the diplomatic history of Europe and set in motion the creation of a new nation that would ultimately dominate as a world superpower, the conclusion of the War of the American Revolution left many with uncertain futures. Thousands of the Loyalists who stood firmly against the contrasting political vision of their Patriot foes now became refugees; in time Parliament would accommodate their woes by relocating them mercifully to the distant corners of the still growing empire. But not all of those who battled the rebel Americans were so lucky; the majority were abandoned and left to sift through the rubble. The native peoples who sided with the Crown saw their previous lives destroyed. Their traditions and political divisions were dissolved and thousands, left with seemingly no other option, swore to continue the wars of their fathers against the encroachment of the new United States. As for the Germans shuttled into the New World, they were faced with almost no ambiguity . . . just waiting. By the year 1783 most of these soldiers were paroled from their prisoner of war status to New York, where they toiled for months. While they were not certain where they would next be deployed they understood that their service was the most valuable commodity that their leaders possessed, and in time they would be back in Germany to await their fate.

Captain Johann Ewald was held as a prisoner of war after his capture at the siege of Yorktown in 1781 until he was paroled to New York. While living in the colonies he continued to study his American enemy, and his reputation grew so much that General Henry Knox offered him a personal tour of the facilities at West Point. After seven years in North America the captain returned to his home of Hesse-Cassel to little acclaim, and was immediately assigned to command a new Jäger company in the von Dittfurth regiment. As a true student in the art of war Ewald used his many experiences in the American colonies to complete his masterwork entitled *Essay on Partisan Warfare* that would be the standard in Germany for more than a century.

Although he was personally commended by Landgrave Frederick II on numerous occasions, his royal equity disappeared when the longtime ruler died in October 1785. Upon the ascension of his son William IX, nephew of George III of England, Ewald was passed over for a promotion and reassigned to Hesse-Hanau with orders to strengthen the state's light infantry. Slighted after a lifetime of service, the embittered captain abandoned his birth nation and joined the armies of Denmark in 1790. For the next twelve years Ewald served his new adopted home faithfully until he was promoted to general in 1802. With his coveted rank in hand Ewald served Denmark in the Napoleonic Wars during his twenty-two-year post-American career. In 1812 General Ewald was honored with the prestigious Grand Cross of the Order of Dannebrog by Danish King Frederick and soon retired. In June of the following year he died of natural causes at the age of sixty-nine.[1]

After a brief stint in the Cuban capital of Havana Chaplain Philipp Waldeck and his 3rd Regiment were paroled to New York with thousands of other Germans until the end of the war. After the peace was signed in 1783 his regiment was one the first to return to Waldeck later that year. After returning to his German homeland Philipp immediately took on the duties of pastor for the small German village of Affoldern, no doubt as a result of his ministry in Pensacola. During his first months after his North American sojourn the chaplain began to edit the notes of his experiences for publication in the newspaper *Waldeckisches Intelligenz-Blatt* to the delight of hundreds of readers.

As his celebrity grew, so did his desire to see his old comrades from the 3rd Regiment who were stationed some eighteen miles away at the city of Mengeringhausen. In late winter 1784 the chaplain decided on a short trip to reunite with his old friends in celebration of his thirty-fourth birthday, and they were elated to see him. Following a long night of drinking and merrymaking Philipp developed a fever and in a cruel twist of fate died suddenly, nine days later, on March 20, 1784. His former regiment mourned the loss of their dear pastor by burying him in the village of his death with the full honors of war.[2]

THE BARONESS VON RIEDESEL AND HER FAMILY LARGELY MISSED THE hardships of their captured army following the Battle of Saratoga. Living in their quaint townhome in Boston, she and her husband waited patiently while the details of their status as prisoners were ironed out between the two belligerents. By 1778 the American Continental Congress had agreed that "the Convention army," as General John Burgoyne's forces came to be known, were to be transported back to England under the pretense that they would not serve again for the duration of the war. Parliament, however, failed to accept these terms as they refused to recognize the American rebel government, and the army in Boston grew resigned to their uncertain fate. As inefficient as it was, the dispute was largely over allocation of funds; if Burgoyne's army were to be considered "prisoners" then it befell the Americans to provide them food and supplies. Sensing an opportunity to burden his already cash-poor enemies, General Howe officially refused to give supplies to the captured troops and placed the full financial responsibility on the Continental Congress.

With winter approaching the decision was made to relocate the Convention army south to warmer climates, and in November 1778 the Riedesel family made their way to Charlottesville, Virginia. While the majority of the imprisoned army remained scattered in roughly hewn cabins and tents, the baron and his wife rented a home from the state's governor, Thomas Jefferson, and the two families became close friends. For the duration of their two-year stay in the Old Dominion Frederika lived the life of a wealthy elitist and even went so far as to construct additional outbuildings on the property they rented. Finally in late 1779 the still captive Baron von Riedesel received word that he was being paroled and reported to New York. Once in the city Frederika and her husband welcomed a fourth baby girl into the world and subsequently named her "America." Upon hearing the news Thomas Jefferson personally sent his regards.

In October 1780, after a year in New York, the baron learned that he and his family would be released from their less-than-restrictive bondage in a direct prisoner exchange. The baron would be swapped for the American General Benjamin Lincoln, who was fresh off of his surrender at Charleston, South Carolina; in early 1781 the Riedesels then moved freely to Canada where they remained until 1783. During this time Frederika gave birth to a fifth daughter and named her "Canada," but the baby unfortunately died after only five months of life. During their stay in the Quebec the baroness took on an almost legendary status as the colony's premiere socialite, and offered a traditional German Christmas celebration that, by all accounts, saw the first Christmas tree ever illuminated in North American history.

The baroness and her newly extended family returned to Germany in 1783 and were given a royal reception by Duke Karl Wilhelm Ferdinand; they would go on to have a sixth child, a son, in 1785. Frederika and Friedrich lived out their years in Wolfenbüttel as comfortable German nobles, and after growing wealthy and charmingly corpulent the baroness died a grandmother in 1808 at the age of sixty-two. Her extraordinary journals still remain as one of the most valuable primary sources available to historians of the time period more than two hundred years later.[3]

AT ANY GIVEN POINT BETWEEN 1776 AND 1783, THE BRITISH ARMY had approximately twenty thousand German troops fighting in North America. Although only eighteen thousand came over in the initial offering of their respective princes, by the end of the conflict nearly thirty thousand soldiers from the Holy Roman Empire battled against the American rebellion. Throughout the struggle reinforcements were sent to replace those that were lost either to injury or captivity, and after spending a veritable fortune the Crown had virtually nothing to show for its efforts. The American rebellion began as a regional New England phenomenon that quickly spread through the entire northeast; its eventual movement into the south-

ern colonies was in many ways a worst-case scenario for Great
Britain. By the year 1781 the hostilities that grew out of debates
over taxation, representation, protection, and sovereignty had spi-
raled into a full-scale war on a global scale. For the average Briton
the popular depiction of the enemy was not the American rebel, but
the French or Spanish king who was inflicting the most damage at
the time.

That is not to say that the revolt in North America was inconsequential; it was by far the single most destructive and costly blow
that the British Empire would ever receive. It was however a spark
that ignited a blaze that had been in lying in wait on the European
geopolitical stage for decades. When viewed strictly from the modern American perspective the revolution is often represented as a
"David vs. Goliath" struggle pitting a ragtag army of freedom fighters against the world's reigning imperial power; this gross simplifi-
cation makes for a stirring rendition, but little else. In truth there
was nothing simple about the American Revolution, although it is
often viewed through the lens of Minuteman against Redcoat.
When the members of the Continental Congress affixed their sig-
natures to the Declaration of Independence they were not merely
changing the fate of North America, but quite literally altering the
course of history for the entire Western world.

The presence of those thirty thousand soldiers from the Holy
Roman Empire reveals immediately just how global the war really
was, and its aftermath puts the transformative power of the spirit of
1776 on full display. In the wake of the battles of Saratoga,
Pensacola, and Yorktown the fates of the Germans who participated were directly intertwined with their British comrades; an
American musket killed a Hessian just the same as a Briton. In the
aftermath of the war this held true as well: prisoner-of-war status
was applied equally to both. After the smoke had cleared, however,
the German auxiliaries were once again on their own. How separate
their trajectory was from that of their British counterparts is striking. At the end of the war approximately seventeen thousand
Germans returned to Europe, a startling 56 percent. While their
respective princes may have celebrated these figures due to the fact
that they would be handsomely reimbursed for each man lost, not
all were killed in the fighting. Numbers reveal that roughly 7,500
German soldiers were killed during the rebellion: 1,200 from combat and 6,300 from accident or disease. But most impressive of all
were the nearly 5,000 men who, according to imperial records, were

unaccounted for—they remained in North America. Early on in the proceeding regarding whether German armies should have been employed by the Crown, members of Parliament speculated that many of the auxiliaries would simply desert, and following the war that was precisely what occurred. Despite the ideological divides and political differences between Old World and New, approximately one out of every six German soldiers sent to reduce the American colonies chose to remain behind to live under the promises of republican government—no longer Hessians, but Americans.

# NOTES

**PREFACE**

1 Atwood, *The Hessians*, 60.

**PROLOGUE**

1 Middlekauf, *The Glorious Cause*, 266–267.
2 Wilhelmy, *Soldiers for Sale*, 33.
3 Ibid., 34-35.
4 Krebs, *A Generous and Merciful Enemy*, 20.
5 Lowell, *The Hessians*, chap. 2.
6 Ibid., chap. 2.
7 Wilhelmy, *Soldiers for Sale*, 44.
8 Ibid., 44.
9 Motion by Lord North, that the Treaties be referred to the Committee of Supplies Page v6: 277, Thursday, February 29, 1776.
10 Lowell, *The Hessians*, chap. 3.
11 Motion by Lord North, that the Treaties be referred to the Committee of Supplies, Page v6: 277, Thursday, February 29, 1776.
12 Lowell, *The Hessians*, chap. 3.
13 Motion by Lord North, that the Treaties be referred to the Committee of Supplies Page v6: 277, Thursday, February 29, 1776.

**I: JOHANN EWALD**

1 McCullough, *1776*, 135.
2 Ewald, *Diary*, 7.
3 Ibid., 10.
4 Ibid., 11.
5 Atwood, *The Hessians*, 74.
6 Ewald, *Diary*, 12.
7 Ibid., 13.
8 Ibid.
9 Middlekauff, *The Glorious Cause*, 359.
10 Ewald, *Diary*, 15.
11 Atwood, *The Hessians*, 79.
12 Ewald, *Diary*, 24.
13 Ibid., 25.
14 Ibid.
15 Lengel, *General George Washington*, 185.

16 Fischer, *Washington's Crossing*, 199.
17 Ewald, *Diary*, 38.
18 Ibid., 39.
19 Ibid., 44.
20 Ibid., 49.
21 Ketchum, *The Winter Soldiers*, 291.
22 Ewald, *Diary*, 49.
23 Ibid., 87.
24 Ibid., 89.
25 Ibid., 91.
26 Ibid., 92.
27 Middlekauff, *The Glorious Cause*, 400.
28 Ibid., 96.
29 Lowell, *The Hessians and the Other German Auxiliaries of Great Britain*, 204.
30 Ibid., 205.
31 Ewald, *Diary*, 98.
32 Ibid., 99.
33 *Appleton's Cyclopedia of American Biography*, 1900.
34 Ewald, *Diary*, 109.
35 Ibid., 110.
36 Ibid., 120.
37 Ibid., 119.
38 Ibid., 123.
39 Ibid., 126.
40 Ibid., 127.
41 Atwood, *The Hessians*, 158.
42 Ewald, *Diary*.
43 Ibid., 128.
44 Ibid.
45 Ibid., 130.
46 Middlekauff, *The Glorious Cause*, 430.
47 Ewald, *Diary*, 136.
48 Ibid., 145.
49 Ewald, *Journal*, 157.
50 Ibid., xxv.
51 Ibid., 160.
52 Ibid., 161.
53 Johnston, "The Storming of Stony Point on the Hudson," 1900, 45.
54 Ewald, *Diary*, 161.
55 Ibid., 163.
56 Ibid., 166.
57 Ibid., 167.
58 *Harper's Popular Cyclopedia of American History*, vol. 2, 1355.
59 Ibid., 172.
60 Morrill, *Southern Campaigns of the American Revolution*, 64.
61 Ewald, *Diary*, 174.
62 Ibid., 179.
63 Atwood, *The Hessians*, 134.
64 Middlekauff, *The Glorious Cause*, 444.

65 Ewald, *Diary*, 196.
66 Ibid., 197.
67 Walter Edgar, "The American Revolution in the South: A Story Seldom Told," George Rogers Clark Lecture, Society of the Cincinnati, 2012.
68 Ewald, *Diary*, 198.
69 Ibid., 199.
70 Ibid., 203.
71 Ibid.
72 Middlekauff, *The Glorious Cause*, 447.
73 Ewald, *Diary*, 209.
74 Ibid., 214.
75 Ibid., 217.
76 Ibid., 230.
77 Ibid., 235.
78 Ibid., 236.
79 Middlekauf, 455.
80 Ewald, *Diary*, 239.
81 Ibid., 259.
82 Ibid., 260.
83 Ibid., 261.
84 Ibid., 267.
85 Ibid., 269.
86 Ibid., 268.
87 Ibid., 296.
88 Ibid., 289.
89 Ibid., 291.
90 Ibid., 296.
91 Ibid.
92 Ibid., 302.
93 Ibid., 305.
94 Ibid., 336.
95 Ibid.
96 Ibid., 341.

## II: FREDERIKA CHARLOTTE LOUISE VON MASSOW

1 Gen. Riedesel to Mrs. Riedesel, Feb. 22, 1776, 148–149.
2 Stone, *Diary of Baroness*, 183.
3 Stone, *Diary of Baroness*, 38.
4 Brown, *Baroness von Riedesel and the American Revolution*, 4.
5 Ibid., 5.
6 Ibid., 6.
7 Ibid., 7.
8 Gen. Riedesel to Mrs. Riedesel, April 24, 22, 1776, as quoted in Brown, *Baroness von Riedesel and the American Revolution*, 169.
9 Brown, *Baroness von Riedesel and the American Revolution*, 10.
10 Mrs. Riedesel to Mother, May 3, 1776 as quoted in Brown, *Baroness von Riedesel and the American Revolution*, 170.
11 Stone, *Diary of Baroness*, 46.
12 Brown, *Baroness von Riedesel and the American Revolution*, 12.

13 Ibid.
14 Stone, *Diary of Baroness*, 48.
15 Ibid.
16 Gen. Riedesel to Mrs. Riedesel, June 28, 1776, as quoted in Brown, *Baroness von Riedesel and the American Revolution*, 176.
17 Brown, *Baroness von Riedesel and the American Revolution*, 15.
18 Ibid., 16.
19 Mrs. Riedesel to Gen. Riedesel, September 19, 1776, as quoted in Brown, *Baroness von Riedesel and the American Revolution*, 187.
20 Brown, *Baroness von Riedesel and the American Revolution*, 18.
21 Ibid.
22 Ibid., 23.
23 Stone, *Diary of Baroness*, 59.
24 A. Brown, *Beside Old Hearth-Stones*, 168.
25 Stone, *Diary of Baroness*, 60.
26 Brown, *Baroness von Riedesel and the American Revolution*, 24–25.
27 Ibid., 27.
28 Ibid.
29 Stone, *Diary of Baroness*, 70.
30 Ibid.
31 Brown, *Baroness von Riedesel and the American Revolution*, 28.
32 Ibid., 29.
33 Ibid.
34 Stone, *Diary of Baroness*, 73.
35 Ibid.
36 Brown, *Baroness von Riedesel and the American Revolution*, 30.
37 Desjardins, *Through a Howling Wilderness*, 5.
38 Stone, *Diary of Baroness*, 73.
39 Brown, *Baroness von Riedesel and the American Revolution*, 32.
40 Gen. Riedesel to wife, June 1, 1776, as quoted in Brown, *Baroness von Riedesel and the American Revolution*, 173.
41 Gen. Riedesel to wife, June 8, 1776, as quoted in Brown, *Baroness von Riedesel and the American Revolution*, 174.
42 Stanley, *Canada Invaded 1775–1776*, 132–133.
43 Gen. Riedesel to wife, April 6, 1776, as quoted in Brown, *Baroness von Riedesel and the American Revolution*, 167.
44 Brown, *Baroness von Riedesel and the American Revolution*, 32.
45 Stone, *Diary of Baroness*, 77.
46 Gen. Riedesel to wife, June 13, 1777, as quoted in Brown, *Baroness von Riedesel and the American Revolution*, 173.
47 Brown, *Baroness von Riedesel and the American Revolution*, 35.
48 Stone, *Diary of Baroness*, 82–83.
49 Ibid.
50 Chartrand, *French Fortresses in North America*, 30–31.
51 Brown, *Baroness von Riedesel and the American Revolution*, 36.
52 *Dictionary of Canadian Biography*, vol. 4, 1979.
53 Brown, *Baroness von Riedesel and the American Revolution*, 37.
54 Chartrand, *French Fortresses in North America*, 30–31.
55 Brown, *Baroness von Riedesel and the American Revolution*, 37.

56 Stone, *Diary of Baroness*, 84.
57 Ibid.
58 Ibid.
59 Ibid.
60 Ibid.
61 Ibid., 85.
62 Ibid., 87.
63 Ibid.
64 Logusz, *With Musket and Tomahawk*, vol. 1., 43.
65 Stone, *Diary of Baroness*, 89.
66 Brown, *Baroness von Riedesel and the American Revolution*, 43.
67 Ibid., 44.
68 Ibid., 45.
69 Ibid., 44.
70 Ibid., 48.
71 Ibid., 47.
72 Logusz, *With Musket and Tomahawk*, 237.
73 Brown, *Baroness von Riedesel and the American Revolution*, 49.
74 Ibid., 49.
75 Ibid., 50.
76 Logusz, *With Musket and Tomahawk*, 256.
77 Brown, *Baroness von Riedesel and the American Revolution*, 50.
78 Ibid., 51.
79 Ibid.
80 Ibid., 52.
81 Ibid.
82 Ibid., 53.
83 Brown, *Baroness von Riedesel and the American Revolution*, 53.
84 Ibid., 54.
85 Logusz, *With Musket and Tomahawk*, 285–286.
86 Brown, *Baroness von Riedesel and the American Revolution*, 54.
87 Ibid., 55.
88 Ibid.
89 Ibid., 57.
90 Ibid., 58.
91 Stone, *Diary of Baroness*, 128.
92 Logusz, *With Musket and Tomahawk*, 289.
93 Stone, *Diary of Baroness*, 130.
94 Brown, *Baroness von Riedesel and the American Revolution*, 61.
95 Stone, *Diary of Baroness*, 129.
96 Brown, *Baroness von Riedesel and the American Revolution*, 59.
97 Stone, *Diary of Baroness*, 130.
98 Ibid., 131.
99 Logusz, *With Musket and Tomahawk*, 304.
100 Stone, *Diary of Baroness*, 140.
101 Ibid., 142.
102 Ibid.

III: PHILIPP WALDECK

1 Bruce Burgoyne, *Eighteenth Century America: A Hessian Report on the People, the Land, the War as Noted in the Diary of Chaplain Philipp Waldeck (1776–1780)* (hereafter Waldeck Diary), 92.
2 Burgoyne, *The 3rd Waldeck Regiment*, 3.
3 Starr, *Tories, Dons and Rebels*, 130.
4 Waldeck Diary, 89.
5 Ibid., 90.
6 Ibid.
7 Ibid., 91.
8 Ibid., 92.
9 Ibid., 94.
10 Ibid.
11 Ibid., 95.
12 Ibid., 96.
13 Ibid., 98.
14 Ibid., 100.
15 Ibid., 104.
16 Ibid.
17 Ibid., 102.
18 Starr, *Tories, Dons, and Rebels*, 131.
19 Waldeck, Diary 112.
20 Ibid., 111.
21 Ibid., 114.
22 Ibid., 118.
23 Ibid., 120.
24 Ibid., 124–125.
25 Ibid., 123.
26 Ibid.
27 Ibid., 125.
28 Ibid.
29 Starr, *Tories, Dons, and Rebels*, 1.
30 Raab, *Spain, Britain, and the American Revolution*, 15.
31 Ibid., 35.
32 Starr, *Tories, Dons, and Rebels*, 4.
33 Ibid., 7.
34 Raab, *Spain, Britain, and the American Revolution*, 33.
35 Ibid., 39.
36 Ford, *Journals of the Continental Congress*, 1:101–3.
37 Ibid., 2:54.
38 Dartmouth to Chester, July 5, 1775. Starr, *Spain, Britain, and the American Revolution*, 47.
39 Raab, *Spain, Britain, and the American Revolution*, 131.
40 Waldeck Diary, 126.
41 Campbell to Clinton, Feb. 10, 1779, Starr, *Tories, Dons, and Rebels*, 133.
42 Ibid.
43 Campbell to Clinton, March 10, 1779, Starr, *Tories, Dons, and Rebels*, 13.
44 Campbell to Germain, March 22, 1779, Starr, *Tories, Dons, and Rebels*, 138.

45 Waldeck Diary, 127.
46 Ibid.
47 Ibid., 181.
48 Ibid., 132.
49 Germain to Cornwallis Sept. 23, 1779, Starr, *Tories, Dons, and Rebels*, 144.
50 Starr, *Tories, Dons, and Rebels*, 148.
51 Ibid., 151.
52 Learned, *Philipp Waldeck's Diary of the American Revolution*, 128.
53 Waldeck Diary, 133–134.
54 Starr, *Tories, Dons, and Rebels*, 156.
55 Waldeck Diary, 136.
56 Waldeck Diary, 138.
57 Gálvez to Navarro, Oct. 16, 1779, Starr, *Tories, Dons, and Rebels*, 165.
58 Waldeck Diary, 141.
59 Starr, *Tories, Dons, and Rebels*, 168.
60 Waldeck Diary, 153.
61 Waldeck Diary, 154.
62 Starr, *Tories, Dons, and Rebels*, 185
63 Waldeck Diary, 130.
64 Starr, *Tories, Dons, and Rebels*, 177.
65 Ibid., 183.
66 Raab, *Spain, Britain, and the American Revolution in Florida*, 136.
67 Starr, *Tories, Dons, and Rebels*, 176.
68 Ibid., 195.
69 Benjamin Baynton to Peter Baynton, Pensacola, 2 February 1781. Pennsylvania State Archives, MG 19, Sequestered Baynton, Wharton and Morgan Papers, 1725-1827, Part III, Baynton Family Papers, 1770-1827, Correspondence of Benjamin Baynton, 1777–1785.
70 Holmes, *German Troops in Alabama*, 8-9 (Burgoyne 268).
71 Campbell to Germain, Jan. 11, 1781. Starr, *Tories, Dons, and Rebels*, 183.
72 Waldeck Diary, 172.
73 Starr, *Tories, Dons, and Rebels*, 195.
74 Ibid., 195.
75 Savas, *A Guide to the Battles of the American Revolution*, 301.
76 Ibid., 302.
77 Starr, *Tories, Dons, and Rebels*, 207.
78 Savas, *A Guide to the Battles of the American Revolution*, 302–303.
79 Ibid., 303.

EPILOGUE

1 Ewald, *Journal*, xxx.
2 Burgoyne, *Waldeck Diary*, xi.
3 Brown, *Baroness von Riedesel and the American Revolution*, xxxv–xl.

# BIBLIOGRAPHY

Allen, Thomas B. *Tories: Fighting for the King in America's First Civil War*. New York: Harper, 2010.

Atwood, Rodney. *The Hessians: Mercenaries from Hessen-Kassel in the American Revolution*. Cambridge: Cambridge University Press, 1980.

Berleth, Richard J. *Bloody Mohawk: the French and Indian War and American Revolution on New York's Frontier*. Delmar, N.Y.: Black Dome Press, 2010.

Brown, Abram English. *Beside Old Hearth-Stones*. Boston: Lee and Shepard, 1897.

Brown, Marvin L. *Baroness von Riedesel and the American Revolution: Journal and Correspondence of a Tour of Duty, 1776–1783*. Chapel Hill: University of North Carolina Press, 1965.

Burgoyne, Bruce. *Defeat, Disaster, and Dedication*. Westminster: Heritage Books, 1997.

——. *Diaries of Two Ansbach Jaegers*. Westminster: Heritage Books, 1997.

——. *Diary of Lieutenant von Bardeleben and Other von Donop Regiment Documents*. Westminster: Heritage Books, 1998.

——. *Eighteenth Century America: A Hessian Report on the People, the Land, the War as Noted in the Diary of Chaplain Philipp Waldeck (1776–1780)*. Westminster: Heritage Books, 1999.

——. *Enemy Views: The American Revolutionary War as Recorded by the Hessian Participants*. Westminster: Heritage Books, 1997.

——. *Georg Pausch's Journal and Reports of the Campaign in America*. Westminster: Heritage Books, 1996.

——. *Hesse-Cassel Mirbach Regiment in the American Revolution*. Westminster: Heritage Books, 1998.

——. *Hessian Diary of the American Revolution*. Norman: University of Oklahoma Press, 1990.

——. *Hessian Officer's Diary of the American Revolution*. Westminster: Heritage Books, 1994.

———. *The 3rd Waldeck Regiment in the American Revolution.*
Westminster: Heritage Books, 1999.

———. *Waldeck Soldiers of the American Revolutionary War.*
Westminster: Heritage Books, 1991.

Chartrand, René. *The Forts of New France in Northeast America
1600–1763.* Oxford: Osprey, 2008.

———. *French Fortresses in North America 1535–1763: Quebec,
Montreal, Louisbourg, and New Orleans.* Oxford: Osprey, 2005.

Cruikshank, Ernest. *The Story of Butler's Rangers and the Settlement of
Niagara.* Welland: Tribune Printing House, 1893.

Crytzer, Brady J. *Fort Pitt: A Frontier History.* Charleston: History
Press, 2012.

———. *Major Washington's Pittsburgh and the Mission to Fort LeBoeuf.*
Charleston: History Press, 2011.

Dawdy, Shannon Lee. *Building the Devil's Empire: French Colonial New
Orleans.* Chicago: University of Chicago Press, 2008.

Desjardin, Thomas A. *Through a Howling Wilderness: Benedict Arnold's
March to Quebec, 1775.* New York: St. Martin's Griffin, 2006.

Dixon, David D. "A High Wind Rising: George Washington, Fort
Necessity, and the Ohio Country Indians." *Pennsylvania History* 74:
33-51.

———. *Never Come to Peace Again: Pontiac's Uprising and the Fate of
the British Empire in North America.* Norman: University of
Oklahoma Press, 2005.

Doblin, Helga. *The American Revolution, Garrison Life in French
Canada and New York: Journal of an Officer in the Prinz Friedrich
Regiment, 1776–1783.* Westport: Greenwood Press, 1993.

Dowd, Gregory A. *A Spirited Resistance: The North American Indian
Struggle for Unity, 1745–1815.* Baltimore: Johns Hopkins University
Press, 1993.

Dunn, Richard S. *Sugar and Slaves: The Rise of the Planter Class in the
English West Indies, 1624–1713.* Chapel Hill: University of North
Carolina Press, 1972.

Eccles, W. J. *The Canadian Frontier, 1534–1760.* New York: Holt,
Rinehart and Winston, 1969.

Ewald, Johann. *Diary of the American War.* New Haven: Yale
University Press, 1979.

———. *Treatise on Partisan Warfare.* Westport: Greenwood Press,
1991.

Fischer, David H. *Washington's Crossing.* Oxford: Oxford University
Press, 2006.

Graymont, Barbara. *The Iroquois in the American Revolution.* Syracuse:
Syracuse University Press, 1972.

Halpenny, Francess G and Jean Hamelin. *Dictionary of Canadian Biography;* Volume IV, 1771 to 1800. University of Toronto Press, 1979.

Hibbert, Christopher. *George III*. New York: Basic Books, 1998.

Holmes, Jack. "German Troops in Alabama During the American Revolution: The Battle of January 7, 1781." *Alabama Historical Quarterly* 38 (Spring 1976).

Ingrao, Charles. *The Hessian Mercenary State: Ideas, Institutions, and Reform under Frederick II 1760-1785*. Cambridge: Cambridge University Press, 1987.

James, Lawrence. *The Rise and Fall of the British Empire*. New York: St. Martin's, 1994.

Jasanoff, Maya. *Liberty's Exiles: American Loyalists in the Revolutionary World*. New York: Alfred A. Knopf, 2011.

Johnston, Henry P. *The Storming of Stony Point on the Hudson*. New York: James T. White and Co., 1900.

Ketchum, Richard M. *The Winter Soldiers: The Battles for Trenton and Princeton*. New York: Holt, 1999.

Krebs, Daniel. *A Generous and Merciful Enemy: Life for German Prisoners of War During the American Revolution*. Norman: University of Oklahoma Press, 2013.

Lengel, Edward. *General George Washington*. New York: Random House, 2005.

Logusz, Michael O. *With Musket and Tomahawk Volume I: The Saratoga Campaign and the Wilderness War of 1777*. Havertown, PA: Casemate, 2009.

———. *With Musket and Tomahawk Volume II: The Mohawk River Valley Campaign in the Wilderness War of 1777*. Havertown, PA: Casemate, 2012.

Lossing, Benson. *Harper's Popular Cyclopedia of United States History*. Vol. 2. New York: Harper and Brothers, 1882.

Lowell, Edward J. *The Hessians and the Other German Auxiliaries of Great Britain in the Revolutionary War*. New York: Harper and Brothers, 1884.

Lunt, James D. *John Burgoyne of Saratoga*. London: Macdonald and Jane's, 1976.

McCullough, David G. *1776*. New York: Simon and Schuster, 2005.

Middlekauff, Robert. *The Glorious Cause: The American Revolution, 1763–1789*. Oxford: Oxford University Press, 2005.

Morrill, Dan. *Southern Campaigns of the American Revolution*. Mt. Pleasant: Nautical and Aviation Co., 1993.

Morton, Desmond. *A Short History of Canada*. Edmonton: Hurtig, 1983.

Nickerson, Hoffman. *The Turning Point of the Revolution, or Burgoyne in America*. Cambridge: Riverside Press, 1928.

Parker, Matthew. *The Sugar Barons: Family, Corruption, Empire, and War in the West Indies*. New York: Walker, 2011.

Raab, James W. *Spain, Britain, and the American Revolution, 1763–1783*. Jefferson: McFarland, 2008.

Reuter, Claus. *Brunswick Troops in North America 1776–1783; Index of all Soldiers who Remained in North America*. Westminster: Heritage Books, 1999.

Savas, Theodore P. and J. David Dameron. *A Guide to the Battles of the American Revolution*. New York: Savas Beatie, 2006.

Shannon, Timothy. *Iroquois Diplomacy on the Early American Frontier*. New York: Penguin, 2008.

Silver, Peter. *Our Savage Neighbors: How Indian War Transformed Early America*. New York: W.W. Norton, 2009.

Stanley, George. *Canada Invaded 1775–1776*. Toronto: Hakkert, 1973.

Starr, J. Barton. *Tories, Dons, and Rebels: The American Revolution in West Florida*. Gainesville: University of Florida Press, 1976.

Stone, William L. *Letters and Journals Relating to the American Revolution and the Capture of the German Troops at Sarataga by Mrs. General Riedesel*. Albany: Joel Munsell, 1867.

Taylor, Peter K. *Indentured to Liberty: Peasant Life and the Hessian Military State, 1688–1815*. Ithaca: Cornell University Press, 1994.

Tharp, Louise Hall. *The Baroness and the General*. New York: Little, Brown, 1962.

Tonsetic, Robert L. *Special Operations During the American Revolution*. Havertown, PA: Casemate, 2013.

Von Eelking, Max. *German Allied Troops in the North American War of Independence, 1776–1783*. Westminster: Heritage Books, 1987.

Wilhemy, Jean-Pierre. *Soldiers for Sale: German "Mercenaries" with the British in Canada during the American Revolution (1776–83)*. Montreal: Baraka Books, 2009.

Williams, Glenn F. *Year of the Hangman: George Washington's Campaign Against the Iroquois*. Yardley: Westholme, 2005.

Wilson, James Grant. *Appleton's Cyclopedia of American Biography*, ed. John Fisk, 1900. s.v. "Donop, Carl Emil Kurt von."

# ACKNOWLEDGMENTS

THIS BOOK WAS AN AMBITIOUS PROJECT THAT REQUIRED A GREAT DEAL OF support from many people. I would like to thank my family and friends for their patience as I completed this project, with special consideration to Jane Miller and my wife Jennifer for their helpful critiques. I would like to thank my numerous colleagues for providing the opportunity to join the ongoing conversation of American Revolutionary War studies, and to Ronald E. Moore for joining me in investigating the battlefields and sites in this book. I would like to acknowledge my publisher Bruce H. Franklin, as well as the staff at Westholme Publishing, for their efforts to prepare the manuscript for publication.

# INDEX